Made in Court

SUPREME COURT DECISIONS
THAT SHAPED CANADA

Made in Court
SUPREME COURT DECISIONS
THAT SHAPED CANADA

Richard W.Pound

Fitzhenry & Whiteside

Published in Canada by Fitzhenry & Whiteside, 195 Allstate Parkway, Markham, Ontario L3R 4T8
Published in the United States by Fitzhenry & Whiteside, 311 Washington Street, Brighton, Massachusetts 02135

10 9 8 7 6 5 4 3 2 1

Fitzhenry & Whiteside acknowledges with thanks the Canada Council for the Arts, and the Ontario Arts Council for their support of our publishing program. We acknowledge the financial support of the Government of Canada through the Canada Book Fund (CBF) for our publishing activities.

Library and Archives Canada Cataloguing in Publication
ISBN 978-1-55455-347-1
Cataloguing data available from Library and Archives Canada

Publisher Cataloging-in-Publication Data (U.S.)
ISBN 978-1-55455-347-1
Data available on file

Cover design by Tanya Montini
Text design by Daniel Choi
Printed in Canada

Contents

Acknowledgments   10

Introduction   12

Reconciling Prevention of Terrorism with Fair Process
Minister of Citizenship and Immigration v. Mohamed Harkat [2014] S.C.C. 37   23

Ignoring Racism
Quong-Wing v. The King [1914] 49 S.C.R.   29

Fumbling the Discrimination Ball
Christie v. The York Corporation [1940] S.C.R. 139   34

Interference with Freedom of Religion
Chaput v. Romain [1955] S.C.R. 834   39

Sunday Shopping: Sin or Constitutional Right?
R. v. Big M Drug Mart Ltd. [1985] 1 S.C.R. 295   44

Reasonable and Justifiable Limits on Charter Rights
R. v. Oakes [1986] 1 S.C.R. 103   50

Charter Decriminalizes Abortion
R. v. Morgentaler [1988] 1 S.C.R. 30   54

Even if You Agree, Your Charter Rights Can Be Infringed
Syndicat Northcrest v. Amselem [2004] 2 S.C.R. 551   60

Religious Freedom Includes the Right to Wear a Kirpan
Multani v. Commission Scolaire Marguerite-Bourgeoys [2006] 1 S.C.R. 256   67

The Niqab – Identifying the Inherent Difficulties
R. v. N.S. [2012] 3 S.C.R. 726   72

The Right to Die: Beginning a Legal Debate
Rodriguez v. British Columbia [1993] 3 S.C.R. 519   78

Discrimination Based on Sexual Orientation
Vriend v. Alberta [1998] 1 S.C.R. 493   84

Judicial Deference to Specially Created Tribunals
C.U.P.E. v. N.B. Liquor Corporation [1979] 2 S.C.R. 227   90

Administrative Procedures: Procedural Fairness and
Reasonable Apprehension of Bias
Baker v. Canada (Minister of Citizenship and Immigration) [1999] 2 S.C.R. 817   96

Can Courts Follow-up on their Own Rulings?
Doucet-Boudreau v. Nova Scotia (Minister of Education) [2003] 3 S.C.R. 3   102

Health Service Waiting Times: Violation of Charter Rights?
Chaoulli v. Quebec (Attorney General) and Canada (Attorney General)
[2005] 1 S.C.R. 791   108

Judicial Review and the Meaning of "Reasonable"
Dunsmuir v. New Brunswick [2008] 1 S.C.R. 190   114

Arbitrary Closing of Public Drug-Injection Sites
Canada v. PHS Community Services Society [2011] 3 S.C.R. 134   119

Fighting for Language Rights
Attorney General of Quebec v. Blaikie et al. [1979] 2 S.C.R. 1016   124

Can Pregnant Women Be Forced to Undergo Medical Treatment?
Winnipeg Child and Family Services (Northwest Area) v. D.F.G. [1997] 3 S.C.R. 925   129

Mandatory Drug Testing in Dangerous Workplaces: Allowed or Not Allowed?
CEPU v. Irving Pulp & Paper, Limited [2013] S.C.C. 34   135

An Early Look at Nuisance
Drysdale v. Dugas [1896] 26 S.C.R. 20   141

Responsibility for Damages Caused by Things Under One's Care
Shawinigan Carbide Co. v. Doucet [1909] 42 S.C.R. 281   145

Abuse of Power by Elected Officials
Roncarelli v. Duplessis [1959] S.C.R. 121   149

A Prosecutor Must Never "Win" or "Lose"
Boucher v. The Queen [1955] S.C.R. 16   154

Obscenity: Going to Bat for the Lady Chat
Brody, Dansky, Rubin v. The Queen [1962] S.C.R. 681   159

Rape: Mistake of Fact as a Defence?
Pappajohn v. The Queen [1980] S.C.R. 120   165

The Battered-Wife Defence
R. v. Lavallée [1990] 1 S.C.R. 852   171

Hate Propaganda: Does Prosecution Violate the Accused's Charter Rights?
Regina v. Keegstra [1990] 3 S.C.R. 697   176

Death Penalty: No Extradition
United States v. Burns [2001] 1 S.C.R. 283   182

Juries Decide the Facts: the Judge Determines the Law
R. v. Latimer [2001] 1 S.C.R. 3   187

DNA Evidence: Balancing Identification of the Guilty with
Exoneration of the Innocent
R. v. S.A.B. [2003] 2 S.C.R. 678   193

Division of Legislative Powers: the Canadian Constitutional Obsession
Citizens' and The Queen Insurance Cos. v. Parsons [1879-80] 4 S.C.R. 215   199

Trade and Commerce: Escaping from the Privy
Council Bondage
Canadian Industrial Gas & Oil Ltd. v. Saskatchewan [1978] 2 S.C.R. 545   204

Trade and Commerce: Unravelling the Privy Council's Gordian Knot
General Motors of Canada Ltd. v. City National Leasing [1989] 1 S.C.R. 641   209

Is a Woman a "Person"?
Henrietta Edwards et al. v. Attorney General of Canada
[1928] S.C.R. 276; [1930] A.C. 124   215

Marital Breakdown: Wives Without Rights
Murdoch v. Murdoch [1975] 1 S.C.R. 423   220

De Facto Spouses: Some Have No Rights
Quebec (Attorney General) v. A [2013] S. C. C. 5   226

Damages for Abuse of Rights by Bank
Houle v. National Bank of Canada [1990] 3 S.C.R. 122   232

Discrimination against Common-Law Spouses
Miron v. Trudel [1995] 2 S.C.R. 418   238

Damages for Breach of Fiduciary Responsibility to Indian Band
Guerin v. The Queen [1984] 2 S.C.R. 335   244

Aboriginal Property Rights: What Do They Mean?
Delgamuukw v. British Columbia [1997] 3 S.C.R. 1010   249

Aboriginal Land Claims: Where Ancient Rights Trump Current Might
Tsilhqot'in Nation v. British Columbia [2014] S.C.C. 44   254

Aboriginal Treaties: the "Word of the White Man"
Attorney General of Quebec v. Sioui [1990] 1 S.C.R. 1025   261

Unconstitutional Restriction on Band Voting Rights
Corbière v. Canada (Minister of Indian and Northern Affairs) [1999] 2 S.C.R. 203   269

Aboriginal Treaties: the "Honour of the Crown"
Regina v. Marshall [1999] 3 S.C.R. 456   275

Métis: Not Part-Time Indians
Blais v. The Queen [2003] 2 S.C.R. 236   281

A Bargaining Chip for Aboriginal Negotiations
Manitoba Métis Federation Inc. v. Canada (Attorney General) [2013] S.C.C. 14   286

Provincial Involvement in Federal Treaties
Reference re Minimum Wages Act [1936] S.C.R. 461; [1937] A.C. 326
(decided 28 January 1937)   293

Regulation of Firearms: Federal or Provincial Responsibility?
Reference re Firearms Act [2000] 1 S.C.R. 783   298

Changing from Denominational to Linguistic Basis of School Organization
Reference re Education Act (Quebec) [1993] 2 S.C.R. 511   304

War-Time Reality: Acting in the Interests of the Nation
Reference re Validity of Regulations in Relation to Chemicals [1943] S.C.R. 1   309

Fooling with the Senate: Law as Opposed to Politics
Reference re Authority of Parliament in Relation to the Upper House
[1980] S.C.R. 54   315

Patriation of Constitution: No Need to Consult the Provinces
Reference re Resolution to Amend the Constitution [1981] 1 S.C.R. 753   321

Judges Cannot Negotiate their Salaries
Reference re Remuneration of Judges; Reference re Independence and Impartiality of Judges [1997] 3 S.C.R. 3   326

Quebec Secession: Legal Treatment of a Political Issue
Secession of Quebec [1998] 2 S.C.R. 217   332

Prostitution: A Dangerous Profession Made More Dangerous
Attorney General of Canada v. Bedford, Lebovitch and Scott [2013] S.C.R. 72   339

Index   346

ACKNOWLEDGMENTS

A part from the obvious enjoyment of reading and commenting on many judgments of the Supreme Court of Canada, one of the most gratifying aspects of the experience in putting the Work together was the enthusiastic assistance afforded me by many scholars, jurists, lawyers and others having an interest in how the nation has been shaped. All have seemed to welcome the concept of a book written for a lay audience and have been more than generous in their suggestions regarding cases to be included.

Limitations regarding the size of the book have prevented me from being able to deal with many fascinating decisions of the Court. It is always difficult to determine whether the choices have identified the most important cases and it would have been fun to do a vertical analysis of several cases in one or more specific areas, which would not have been suitable for a review of decisions across a broad spectrum of subject matter, designed to show the many aspects of Canadian society on which the Court has had a significant impact.

I have kept careful note of all the suggestions and time will tell whether there might someday be a companion volume. The responsibility for the final selection of decisions was, however, mine and I accept that there are undoubtedly some "gems" not dealt with and that may be viewed by some as even more important than those included here.

In particular, I want to thank those who have been so helpful. My angst about possible omissions in this list is even greater than that regarding case selection, so my fingers are crossed!

Kirsten Anker, G. Blaine Baker, Serge Blais, Hon. Thomas Cromwell, Michel Décary, Nathalie Des Rosiers, Isabelle Dupuis, Evan Fox-Decent, Fabien Gélinas, Colin K. Irving, Richard Janda, Pierre-Gabriel Jobin, Daniel Jutras, Hon. Nicholas J. Kasirer, Alana Klein, Hoi Kong, David Lametti, Robert Leckey, Armand de Mestral, Hon. Richard Scott, Stephen A. Scott, Richard J. Shadley, Colleen Sheppard, Lionel Smith, Daniel Turp, David Weinstock.

Introduction

We live in a world increasingly informed by sound bites, as if we exist only in the present, have the attention spans of fruit flies, are unburdened with any sense of past, and entertain little appreciation of the impact of the present on the future. Many of the so-called facts with which we are bombarded are, in reality, little more than uninformed opinions masquerading as authoritative statements, often advanced by those having a particular social or political agenda, who may well possess only a nodding acquaintance with the truth. In an era of information overload that shows no hint of abatement, one of the greatest challenges facing society is that of separating the proverbial wheat from the chaff; most do not have the methodological experience, the intellectual discipline, nor even the inclination to do so.

If you have gotten this far, you may be an exception.

The purpose of this work (yes, there still are real books) is to try to illustrate, with reference to selected decisions, how our society today, and perhaps tomorrow, has been shaped by judges, in this case by judges of the Supreme Court of Canada. They are nine in number, appointed by the federal government, now with some minimal oversight by a parliamentary committee, and hold office until they reach the age of seventy-five, unless they choose to retire sooner. The Supreme Court of Canada now consists, as a result of constitutional negotiations, of three judges appointed from Quebec, three from Ontario, and three from the rest of Canada. Most, but not all, judges have had some judicial experience before they come to the Supreme Court of Canada. There is no legal requirement for such prior judicial experience, but a previous track record of judgments rendered may provide some pre-appointment indications of the calibre of their legal reasoning and perhaps of their approach to some of the important issues likely to find their way to the nation's highest court. The recent tendency (although not the rule) has been to look among judges of the provincial courts of appeal for such appointments.

There was a legal challenge to a very recent appointment of a "Quebec" judge, who was sitting as a supernumerary (i.e., semi-retired) on the bench of the Federal Court of Appeal at the time of his appointment. According to the Constitution, the judges on the Supreme Court of Canada from Quebec must be appointed from among the judges of either the Quebec Court of Appeal or the Quebec Superior Court, or directly from the Quebec Bar. The appointee fitted into none of these requirements; once a person is appointed as a judge, he or she is no longer a member of the Bar and he was not on the bench of either of the specified Quebec courts. The Supreme Court of Canada ruled that the judge was not constitutionally qualified to be appointed and nullified the purported appointment, restoring him to the Federal Court of Appeal.

Canada has been generally fortunate to have attracted intelligent and conscientious individuals to sit on the Court, judges who try their best to wrestle with the many and various matters that come before them. While it is always reassuring to have unanimous decisions from the Court, many of the issues are subtle enough that there can be disagreement as to the appropriate outcome and split decisions are relatively common. Intellectual differences between judges in the Supreme Court of Canada are not, however, nearly as sharp and personally directed as occurs in decisions of the Supreme Court of the United States, where judges occasionally make clear, in highly personal terms, their disdain for an opposing view, much of which may reflect an ideological, rather than legal, perspective.

Until 1982, more than a century after the Court was established, no woman had been appointed to the bench of the Supreme Court of Canada. Since that time, following the appointment of the first female judge of the Court, Bertha Wilson (Ontario), several have been named: Claire L'Heureux-Dubé (Quebec), Beverly McLachlin, the current Chief Justice of Canada (British Columbia), Louise Arbour (Ontario), Louise Charron (Ontario), Marie Deschamps (Quebec), Rosalie Abella (Ontario) and Andromache Karakatsanis (Ontario). To date, no Aboriginal or visible-minority judges have been appointed to the Court, although several such appointments have been made to other courts and it will be, presumably, only a matter of time before qualified judges from these communities will reach the Supreme Court of Canada.

Starting in 1949, the end of the judicial road in Canada has been the Supreme Court of Canada. Until that time, litigants unsatisfied with a decision of the Supreme Court of Canada had the opportunity to appeal to the United Kingdom's highest court dealing with Commonwealth appeals, the Judicial Committee of the Privy Council. Extraordinarily enough for a country as sophisticated and socially developed as Canada, it was not until after the Second World War that Canadian courts became the final authority on Canadian legal disputes. We seemed to have been quite content to leave international matters in the hands of the British government, perhaps proving Lord Durham to have been correct in his assessment that granting responsible government in local matters would enhance, not diminish, the connection between the former colonies and the mother country.

That said, however, there could not have been serious doubt that many of the Privy Council decisions in constitutional matters did little to clarify and much to confuse that constitutional landscape and threw much judicial cold water on the development of the country. Frederick Vaughan, commenting on this background in *Viscount Haldane, The Wicked Step-father of the Canadian Constitution*, said:

> The desire for full self-government, for full nation status, became so strong throughout Canada, however, that termination of appeals became an object too difficult, politically, to resist. After the elimination of appeals in criminal cases—made easy by the rarity with which the Judicial Committee granted leave to appeal and after several earlier attempts to do so had failed—it became only a matter of time before the termination of appeals in other cases would be achieved. The initial parliamentary move to end appeals came in 1947. Stuart Garson, the minister of justice, asserted in his remarks on the second reading of the bill in 1948 that termination of appeal to the Judicial Committee would remove 'one of the two badges of colonialism.'
>
> Ironically, it was an opinion of the Judicial Committee itself that had provided the final impetus towards termination of appeals. The Great Depression presented both the federal and provincial levels of government with unprec-

edented challenges. The provinces sought the financial assistance of the federal government and Parliament to lift them out of the dreadful political and social morass caused by extensive economic collapse. Unemployment soared with the widespread failure of business. The absence of social agencies by which to assist the hungry and hundreds of thousands of unemployed made the provincial governments turn to the federal government for assistance. The federal government and Parliament began to listen. In January 1935 Prime Minister Bennett acknowledged that 'the old order' had gone and in its stead he promised a 'New Deal' for Canadians, one that would see government enter into the economic life of the nation and come to the relief of the hungry and unemployed. Little did he know at the time that the Judicial Committee, armed with volumes of past judgments, would negate his efforts to bring the economy out of the doldrums. And nothing stood in the way more formidably than the judgments of Viscount Haldane, especially his determination of the criminal law power of Parliament and his narrow rulings on the federal government's authority over trade and commerce.

John T. Saywell cannot resist referring to Haldane's 'bizarre *dicta* which had strangled the federal power over criminal law and trade and commerce.' Haldane's judgments, he says, were 'constitutional absurdities.' Although expressed many years after the fact, these sentiments dominated the discourse of Canadian constitutional experts at the time and resulted in the call for termination of appeals to the Judicial Committee. It was clear that the opposition of Watson and Haldane, deeply entrenched in the record, stood squarely in the way of Parliament's—and the Supreme Court's—efforts to come to the relief of the provinces. The Watson–Haldane legacy was a huge barrier preventing Parliament's use of the 'Peace, Order and Good Government' clause in matters that did not constitute a 'national emergency' and forbade federal authority to grant relief in economic matters under provincial areas of jurisdiction, a doctrine that the Supreme Court of Canada reinforced in the Anti-Inflation reference case years later in 1976.

The demands on the two levels of government in Canada during the Great Depression showed the constitutional jurisprudence of the Judicial Committee to be a tangled nightmare which prevented the country from responding to the needs of its people and their governments. Despite the momentary setback to the pressure for termination of appeals caused by the *Edwards* de-

cision [the "Persons" case], Prime Minister Louis St. Laurent served notice
that his Liberal government would begin the steps to eliminate appeals to the
Judicial Committee.

A bill was introduced in 1947, debated in 1948, and received royal assent and came into force in 1949. A reference case had confirmed the right of Parliament to terminate such appeals. The provinces were not consulted, even though the provincial governments had the right of direct appeals to the Privy Council and could, in that manner, circumvent appeals to the Supreme Court of Canada.

Since its establishment in 1875, the Court has evolved in outlook and approach as the legal order (in Canada and in the world at large) has expanded from a relatively restricted field of activity, marked by a distinct *laissez-faire* approach to non-constitutional and non-criminal matters, to one which affects almost every element of today's society. What was originally a fairly narrow range of judicial consideration of legislative competence in the federal system established by the *British North America Act, 1867* (finally imported into Canada from the United Kingdom as the *Constitution Act, 1982*), plus some criminal cases and the occasional private-law matter, now extends to almost every conceivable aspect of current life. The initial approach of the Court tended to be very conservative and it would be difficult to wax enthusiastic about the general literary quality of its decisions. The broadened range of modern subject matter and a willingness on the part of the Court to write with a pedagogical view of providing guidance for lower courts (as opposed to simply disposing of the particular piece of litigation before the Court) has allowed the writing to become far more flexible and literary—as well as lengthy. The Court has come to regard itself as much a court of judicial policy as a court of appeal which corrects errors in the decisions of lower courts.

For the most part, the Court picks the cases it wishes to hear on the basis of its view of their importance, the nature of the legal issues involved, and the potential impact on Canadian society. These cases range from constitutional to criminal to administrative to Aboriginal to interpretations of the *Canadian Charter of Rights and Freedoms*, and to various aspects of civil and private law. On occasion, questions are referred to the Court by the federal government (known as References) for advisory legal opinions on certain important questions or legislation, usually of a constitutional nature.

One of the most demanding current tasks facing the Court is the need to give practical meaning to the *Canadian Charter of Rights and Freedoms*, adopted as part of the constitutional patriation initiative in 1982. The *Charter* reflected the desire of the Trudeau government of the day to replace the Diefenbaker government's *Bill of Rights* adopted in 1960 with a much grander set of rules, constituting the bedrock of the Canadian Constitution, although it fumbled the moral football by permitting a "notwithstanding" clause to be included, an appeasement measure for the provinces, allowing them, in effect, to opt out of the application of the *Charter*. The *Charter* was expressed in terms of general principles, with few, if any, specific guidelines indicating what Parliament may have intended. As a practical matter, Parliament basically punted the interpretation of all issues to the courts and, eventually, to the Supreme Court of Canada, as the highest court in the land.

Although there is a statutory basis underlying each *Charter* decision (i.e., the *Charter* itself) it is the courts that have had to struggle to clothe the statutory skeleton with practical and structural coherence. Their efforts to do so have, on occasion, led to complaints about so-called judicial activism, as if that were some odious, albeit undefined, crime. The implication is that the courts are somehow usurping the legislative powers of the institution that stuck them with the problem in the first place. Bear in mind as well that litigation is essentially confrontational in nature and that at least one of the parties will always be unsatisfied with a particular outcome. Who better to blame than the judges who rendered the decision? In fairness, however, every judicial outcome is the result of independent judges trying their best to discharge their duties of office. Judges do not control the legislative process, nor, in most cases, the content of the pieces of litigation with which they must deal.

The Court, while somewhat removed from the general societal fray, is not insensitive to the activism complaints directed at it. In the *Vriend* appeal [see page 47], one of the judges made a point of commenting on the general relationship between the courts and the legislatures in the *Charter* era.

Much was made in argument before us about the inadvisability of the Court interfering with or otherwise meddling in what is regarded as the proper role of the legislature, which in this case was to decide whether or not sexual orientation would be added to Alberta's human rights legislation. Indeed, it seems like hardly a day goes by without some comment or criticism to the effect that under the *Charter* courts are wrongfully usurping the role of the legislatures. I believe this allegation misunderstands what took place and what was intended when our country adopted the *Charter* in 1981–82.

When the *Charter* was introduced, Canada went, in the words of former Chief Justice Brian Dickson, from a system of Parliamentary supremacy to a constitutional supremacy. … Simply put, each Canadian was given individual rights and freedoms which no government of legislature could take away. However, as rights and freedoms are not absolute, governments and legislatures could justify the qualification or infringement of these constitutional rights under s. 1 as I previously discussed. Inevitably, disputes over the meaning of the rights and their justification would have to be settled, and here the role of the judiciary enters to resolve these disputes. Many countries have assigned the important role of judicial review to their supreme or constitutional courts … .

We should recall that it was the deliberate choice of our provincial and federal legislatures in adopting the *Charter* to assign an interpretive role to the courts and to command them under s. 52 [of the *Constitution Act, 1982*] to declare unconstitutional legislation invalid.

However, giving the courts the power and the commandment to invalidate legislation where necessary has not eliminated the debate over the "legitimacy" of taking such action. As eloquently put by A. M. Bickel in his outstanding work *The Least Dangerous Branch: The Supreme Court of Canada at the Bar of Politics* (2nd ed. 1986), "it thwarts the will of the representatives of the … people." … So judicial review, it is alleged, is illegitimate because it is anti-democratic in that unelected officials (judges) are overruling elected representatives (legislators). …

To respond, it should be emphasized again that in our *Charter's* introduction and the consequential remedial role of the courts were the choices of the Canadian people through their elected representatives as part of a redefinition of our democracy. Our constitutional design was refashioned to state that henceforth the legislators and executive must perform their roles in conformity with the newly conferred constitutional rights and freedoms. That the courts were the trustees of these rights insofar as disputes arose concerning their interpretation was a necessary part of this new design.

So courts in their trustee or arbiter role must perforce scrutinize the work of the legislature and executive not in the name of the courts, but in the interests of the new social contract that was democratically chosen. All of this is implied in the power given to the courts under s. 24 of the *Charter* and s. 52 of the *Constitution Act, 1982.*

Because the courts are independent from the executive and legislature, litigants and citizens generally can rely on the courts to make reasoned and principled decisions according to the dictates of the constitution even though specific decisions may not be universally acclaimed. In carrying out their duties, courts are not to second-guess legislatures and the executives; they are not to make value judgments on what they regard as the proper policy choice; that is for the other branches. Rather, the courts are to uphold the Constitution and have been expressly invited to perform that role by the Constitution itself. But respect by the courts for the legislature and executive role is as important as ensuring that the other branches respect each other's role and the role of the courts.

This mutual respect is in some ways expressed in the provisions of our constitution as shown by the wording of certain of the constitutional rights themselves. For example, s. 7 of the *Charter* speaks of no denial of the rights therein except in accordance with the principles of fundamental justice, which includes the process of law and legislative action. Section 1 and the jurisprudence under it are also important to ensure respect for legislative action and the collective or societal interests represented by legislation. In addition, as will be discussed below, in fashioning a remedy with regard to a *Charter* violation, a court must be mindful of the role of the legislature. Moreover, s. 33, the notwithstanding clause, establishes that the final word in our constitutional structure is in fact left to the legislature and not the courts. ...

As I view the matter, the *Charter* has given rise to a more dynamic interaction among the branches of governance. This interaction has been aptly described as a "dialogue" by some. ... In reviewing legislative enactments and executive decisions to ensure constitutional validity, the courts speak to the legislative and executive branch. As has been pointed out, most of the legislation held not to pass constitutional muster has been followed by new legislation designed to accomplish similar objectives. ... By doing this, the legislature responds to the courts; hence the dialogue among the branches.

To my mind, a great value of judicial review and this dialogue among the branches is that each of the branches is somewhat accountable to the other. The work of the legislature is reviewed by the courts and the work of the courts in its decisions can be reacted to by the legislature in the passing of new legislation (or even overarching laws under s. 33 of the *Charter*). This dialogue between and accountability of each of the branches have the effect of enhancing the democratic process, not denying it.

From the fruits of the Court's labours have come decisions with which we may not be familiar, but which have nevertheless defined the nature of our country, shaped the way we live and interact, protected our basic rights, and provided for a rule of law, rather than governance by decree or administrative whim. As a result of living in a society governed by the rule of law, legislative and administrative decisions that do not comply with the law can be challenged before the courts and the ability of the legislatures and the executive to act arbitrarily can be curtailed.

One of my main concerns when setting out to produce this work was how to limit the number of cases to be considered. My goal was to settle on approximately fifty important cases, while recognizing that all decisions of the Court are important in their own way. Where possible, I have tried to identify the seminal cases, where significant principles were established. Subsequent cases often polish or tweak the original decision to extend it into somewhat different circumstances, but the real importance remains in the original decision. The Court has an occasional tendency to refer to more recent expressions of principles established many years ago and to give the impression that the restatements are the source of the applicable principle. There were many intelligent judges in earlier years.

I also wanted to canvass a number of different areas of law, even knowing that a focus on constitutional law in a federal confederation could easily fill an entire volume. In addition, I had to accept the risk of disapproval, not only of my treatment of the selected cases, but also of the choice of cases—the complaint of "How could you not have picked such-and-such a case?" To mitigate against what will likely be an inevitable criticism, I sought guidance from members of the McGill Faculty of Law, other law faculties, senior lawyers, and others, to give me their top ten cases from various fields and I am most grateful to them for their valuable assistance. The final selection was mine, so they must be absolved from all blame for any shortcomings in the matter of choice.

An additional objective was to produce a useful survey for the consumption of interested members of the public who are not themselves lawyers, as well as younger members of our community, but to avoid it becoming a hernia-producing tome or several volumes. So, I have done three things in particular. First, despite the all-but-irresistible predilection of lawyers to have more footnotes and references than text, I have deliberately refrained from interrupting the flow with such extraneous material. I have given the reference to and citation of each decision, so that if the brief discussion of any case stimulates a desire on the part of the reader to examine the full text of any judgment, it can easily be found. Second, although it is occasionally tempting simply to paraphrase material from the judgments (and I have done some of that), I thought it would be important for readers to get some sense of the approach of judges to different subject matters and to the language they use in the course of deciding cases. I have, therefore, included several extracts from their reasons for judgment. Again, to minimize potentially distractive clutter, I have not identified particular pages for the quotations, but anything quoted has been taken directly from the reasons for judgment in the case under discussion.

And, finally, I have tried to avoid decisions involving legal niceties that may appeal to lawyers and the legal profession, but which are likely over-technical and will be of no particular interest to a general reader. There are many cases decided by the Court that fall into this category and their absence in this work is not intended to be dismissive of the important contributions they have made to the development of Canadian law.

You will also discover that the courts are able (and willing) to say things that politicians are seemingly unable or unwilling to say, especially in cases involving Aboriginal rights, where political treatment of Aboriginals by governments has been less than transparent, often patronizing, and sometimes illegal.

Observers may, on occasion, speculate regarding the real audience to which judgments of the Court are directed. Because of the policy nature of many of its pronouncements, the actual parties to the litigation sometimes seem to be merely incidental stage props in comparison with, for example, policymakers, legislators, media, and academics.

Another fascinating aspect of Supreme Court of Canada judgments, almost always worth studying, is the dissents. Where the Court may be split on an issue, the decision reached by majority is presumed to be a correct statement of the law at the time the decision is rendered. Those in dissent were unable to convince a majority of their judicial colleagues to adopt their conclusions and hence are regarded as the losers (at least in a mathematical sense) in the decision. Quite often, however, today's dissent can become tomorrow's law as society and legal thinking evolve, or it can influence legislation to adapt the substantive law when a decision that may be correct in law is not seen as responsive to a particular societal need. Legislators can step in to change the law, provided they have the legislative competence to do so and provided they do not breach the *Charter* in so doing. I have included references to particularly important dissents.

The work of the Court will continue. New decisions will be rendered each year, at the rate of between five and ten per month, many having significant impacts on the Canada of tomorrow, as those commented upon here have already had on our current society. I hope that the nascent interest which has brought the reader to the point of examining the selected decisions for this work will evolve into a broader interest in following decisions of the Court on a current basis.

It will be well worth the watch. After all, you, as citizens of Canada will be observing the evolution of our Canadian society and the constant reinforcement of that vital element of a truly democratic society, namely the rule of law.

Reconciling Prevention of Terrorism with Fair Process

Minister of Citizenship and Immigration v. Mohamed Harkat
[2014] S.C.C. 37

The threat of terrorism has, regrettably, become an increasing part of daily life, especially in the post-September 11, 2001 era. Almost every country in the world has adopted measures to try to combat the threat, and Canada is no exception. It has adopted the *Immigration and Refugee Protection Act* (IRPA), a portion of which permits the removal of non-citizens who live in Canada (whether as permanent residents or foreign nationals) on various grounds, which include connection with terrorist activities.

Procedurally, the responsible government ministers decide whether the evidence against a non-citizen indicates reasonable grounds on which to declare the person "inadmissible" to Canada and to issue a removal order. If they reach such a conclusion, a certificate of inadmissibility (sometimes referred to as a "security certificate") is issued. The security certificate is then referred to the Federal Court, which reviews it. If the Court finds the security certificate to be reasonable, the non-citizen named in the certificate (referred to in the judgment as the "named person") becomes subject to a removal order.

Mohamed Harkat, a non-citizen, was alleged to have come to Canada for purposes of engaging in terrorism. He had been detained, or required to live under strict conditions for more than a decade. The legal difficulties in his case began as a result of provisions of the IRPA that prevented Harkat from examining some of the evidence and information raised against him, on the grounds that public disclosure of it would harm national security.

This led to a constitutional challenge against the IRPA scheme, principally on the basis that the constitutional guarantee (in the *Canadian Charter of Rights and Freedoms*) of Harkat's life, liberty and security of the person had been infringed. It was argued that the statutory scheme of the IRPA deprived Harkat of a fair opportunity to defend himself against the allegations made by the ministers, especially since he was not permitted to see the entire record and could not personally participate in all the hearings. The Court had to decide, therefore, how far the principle of full disclosure in an open court could be restricted in order to address the threat posed by non-citizens who may be involved with terrorism.

The statutory scheme applicable to Harkat reflected amendments made to an earlier version of the IRPA that the Supreme Court had declared unconstitutional in the case of Charkaoui in 2007. There, the legislation was held to have infringed the *Charter* protections because the Federal Court judge was precluded from making a decision based on all the facts and the relevant law, since the IRPA did not provide for representation of the named person in the closed portion of the proceedings and there was no provision to ensure full disclosure (or a substitute for full disclosure) of the government's case against the named person. The government's response to the decision was to amend the scheme to provide for special advocates to protect the interests of the named person in closed hearings, after full disclosure of the entire record. Such a process had been used in other countries and was seen as responsive to the criticism of the previous process. While perhaps not perfect, this was a major step forward, especially when combined with the statutory duty of the judge to ensure that a fair process occurred.

Any named person must be given summaries of the information and evidence so that he can be reasonably informed regarding the case to be met. The judge must be satisfied that nothing in those summaries would be injurious to national security or endanger the safety of any person if disclosed. The judge is also required to appoint one or more special advocates to protect the interests of the named person in closed hearings. Such hearings are held *in camera* and *ex parte*, to enable the government to present information and evidence which could be injurious to national security, or which might endanger the safety of a person, out of the public view.

> Special advocates are security-cleared lawyers whose role is to protect the interests of the named person and "to make up so far as possible for the [named person's] own exclusion from the evidentiary process": ... During the closed hearings, they perform the functions that the named person's counsel (the "public counsel") performs in the open hearings. They do so by challenging the Minister's claims that information or evidence should not be disclosed, and by testing the relevance, reliability, and sufficiency of the secret evidence: ... They are the active participants in the closed hearings. They may make submissions and cross-examine witnesses who appear in those hearings: ... The IRPA scheme also provides that the special advocates may "exercise, with the judge's authorization, any other powers that are necessary to protect the interests" of the named person:...

The judge is expected to demonstrate a reasonable degree of skepticism (recognizing that government officials may be prone to exaggeration of the need for confidentiality in matters of national security) and to ensure that the overall process is fair. Fair does not mean perfect. The Court noted that there is some "give and take" inherent in fashioning a process that accommodates national security concerns. As it relates to the judge,

> First, the designated judge is intended to play a gatekeeper role. The judge is vested with broad discretion and must ensure not only that the record supports the reasonableness of the ministers' finding of inadmissibility, but also that the overall process is fair. ... Indeed, the IRPA scheme expressly requires the judge to take into account "considerations of fairness and natural justice" when conducting the proceedings. ... The designated judge must take an interventionist approach, while stopping short of assuming an inquisitorial role.

> Second, participation of the special advocates in closed hearings is intended to be a substantial substitute for personal participation by the named person in those hearings. With respect to the confidential portion of the case against

the named person, the special advocates must be in a position to act as vigorously and effectively as the named person himself would act in a public proceeding.

The special advocate portion of the IRPA scheme had been added to bring it within the *Charter* requirements. The Court was satisfied with the resultant outcome and concluded that the constitutionality concerns had been sufficiently addressed by Parliament.

In ordinary criminal matters, there is generally full disclosure of the government's case against the accused and all evidence is given in open court. Matters are, however, somewhat different in national security cases, both as to the stringency of the normal rules of evidence and the disclosure of the source of the evidence.

The usual rules of evidence do not apply to the proceedings. Instead, "the judge may receive into evidence anything that, in the judge's opinion, is reliable and appropriate, even if it is inadmissible in a court of law, and may base a decision on that evidence."

On the other hand, the Court stated that the requirement that the named person be "reasonably informed" of the Minister's case should be read as a recognition that the named person must receive "an incompressible minimum amount of disclosure." That will, of course, vary in accordance with the particular circumstances of each named person.

In criminal matters generally, there is what is called an informer's privilege, pursuant to which police are not required to disclose the identity of their informants. In national security matters, disclosure of the source of information and even, to some degree, the information itself could be very problematic. A majority of the Court was not willing, on its own initiative, to extend the informer privilege to persons providing evidence in such security matters. The two minority judges (who agreed with all the other elements of the decision) thought the privilege should extend to informers. They noted that when national security matters and investigations were previously in the hands of the RCMP, the usual informer privilege applied and, even though such work is now done by CSIS, the principles were the same, so there was no reason why it should not continue to apply. Both the majority and the minority were clearly speaking to the legislators, to find a "fix" for the problem, since if informers cannot be assured that their identities will not be disclosed, they will be reluctant or unwilling to come forward with what might be vital information affecting national security.

Each case has its own peculiarities. In Harkat's file, some original evidence of intercepted communications had been destroyed, under the terms of a general policy regarding retention of evidence, a policy having no particular connection with Harkat. The Court found that such destruction had infringed his rights, although not sufficiently to have resulted in an unfair process. Summaries of the documents had been retained and were sufficient to disclose the nature of the evidence. Similarly, the ministers had been requested by the special advocates to make efforts to obtain updated information that might shed light on the case affecting Harkat. They had made an effort, but the information received was not as definitive as the special advocates might have wished. The ministers' efforts to make the inquiries were regarded by the Court as sufficient in the circumstances to fulfill their obligations. It was not for the ministers to judge what may be provided by third parties in response to their inquiries.

Should a trial judge's decision on inadmissibility (or admissibility) of a named person be appealed, the appellate courts will show deference to the findings of the trial judge, unless there has been a palpable and overriding error. In the Harkat case,

> After consideration of evidence tendered in both public and closed hearings, [the trial judge] came to the conclusion that the certificate declaring Mr. Harkat inadmissible to Canada was reasonable: ... He made adverse findings of credibility against Mr. Harkat and found that the evidence provided reasonable grounds to believe that Mr, Harkat had been involved with terrorist organizations. He held that Mr. Harkat's behaviour and lies were consistent with the theory that he had come to Canada as a "sleeper" agent for terrorist organizations.

The Court concluded that Harkat benefitted from a fair process and that the trial judge did not err when he refused to exclude summaries of intercepted conversations nor when he refused to allow cross-examination of human sources by the special advocates. He did not commit a palpable or overriding error in concluding that the record before him provided reasonable grounds to conclude that Harkat was inadmissible to Canada on security grounds.

Perhaps the key element in the IRPA scheme is the obvious confidence of Parliament in the ability of judges to make certain that the process as a whole is fair and that appropriate evidence, whether within the standard rules of admissible evidence or the lesser standard in national security matters, is considered. As proof of such confidence, once a security certificate is issued, Parliament requires that the Federal Court make a determination as to whether or not the ministers have made a reasonable decision. If the judge determines that the certificate is not reasonable, the certificate will be quashed. This is not a mere rubber stamp process. Although operational decisions may be made by government departments and ministers, the ultimate determinations that may affect the lives and rights of named persons are made by independent judges, who must balance constitutional principles with the national security interests of the country.

Ignoring Racism

Quong-Wing v. The King [1914] 49 S.C.R.

Not every decision of the Supreme Court of Canada is a home run of wise and elegant reasoning. From time to time, the Court gets it wrong, and wrong even on moral or ethical grounds. In 1914, on appeal from the Supreme Court of Saskatchewan, it heard the case of Quong-Wing and rendered a judgment less than two weeks later. The judgment of the majority of the Court was clearly racist in nature.

Quong-Wing was the owner of a restaurant in Moose Jaw, where he employed two waitresses. Quong-Wing was Chinese, having been born in China of Chinese parents, but had become a naturalized British subject (the then-current description of a citizen). The two waitresses were white women.

A Saskatchewan statute provided:

1. No person shall employ in any capacity any white woman or girl or permit any white woman or girl to reside or lodge in or to work in or save as a bona fide customer in a public apartment thereof only, to frequent, any restaurant, laundry or other place of business or amusement owned, kept or managed by any Chinaman.

2. Any employer guilty of any contravention or violation of this Act, shall, upon summary conviction be liable to a penalty not exceeding $100 and, in default of payment, to imprisonment for a term not exceeding two months.

He was convicted and the conviction was upheld by the Supreme Court of Saskatchewan.

Before the Supreme Court of Canada, he argued that the aim of the Saskatchewan statute was to deprive him and Chinese generally, whether naturalized or not, of the rights ordinarily enjoyed by others living in Saskatchewan and that the subject matter of the Act was within the exclusive legislative authority of the federal Parliament.

The Chief Justice took less than a page to dispose of the appeal. He stated:

> In terms the section purports merely to regulate places of business and re-sorts owned and managed by Chinese, independent of nationality, in the interest of the morals of women and girls in Saskatchewan. There are many factory Acts passed by provincial legislatures to fix the age of employment and to provide for proper accommodation for workmen and the convenience of the sexes which are intended not only to safeguard the bodily health, but also the morals of Canadian workers, and I fail to understand the difference in principle between that legislation and this.

> It is also undoubted that the legislatures authorize the making by municipal-ities of disciplinary and police regulations to prevent disorders on Sundays and at night, and in that connection to compel tavern and saloon keepers to close their drinking places at certain hours. Why should those legislatures not have power to enact that women and girls should not be employed in certain industries or in certain places or by a certain class of people? This legislation may affect the civil rights of Chinamen, but it is primarily directed to the pro-tection of children and girls.

> The Chinaman is not deprived of the right to employ others, but the class-es from which he may select his employees are limited. In certain factories women or children under a certain age are not permitted to work at all, and, in others, they may not be employed except subject to certain restrictions in the interest of the employee's bodily and moral welfare. The difference be-tween the restrictions imposed on all Canadians by such legislation and those resulting from the Act in question is one of degree, not of kind.

Three of the other four judges who heard the appeal agreed with the outcome. Only one judge dissented.

There was a certain amount of judicial "distancing" from the racist nature of the legislation by the other members of the majority, who determined that the matter before the Court was not related to the policy or justice of the statute, but simply the legislative power of the province to enact it. There could be little question that it seriously affected the civil rights of Chinese in Saskatchewan, whether aliens or naturalized British subjects.

The federal legislative power to deal with "naturalization and aliens," said the majority, did not touch on the consequences of naturalization or being an alien. This enabled the majority to justify not having to follow earlier cases, such as Union Colliery Company of British Columbia v. Bryce, in which the Privy Council had struck down provincial legislation that was directed at Chinese in British Columbia and that prevented them from working in coal mines. The regulations were later described by the Privy Council as not really being directed at regulation of coal mines, but were devised to deprive Chinese (whether naturalized or not) "of the ordinary rights of the inhabitants of British Columbia and, in effect, to prohibit their continued residence in that province, since it prohibited their earning their living in that province." This was held to interfere with the federal power regarding naturalization and aliens. Not long after Union Colliery, the Privy Council modified its approach in the case of Cunningham v. Tomey Homma to note that the language of the section did not deal with the consequences of either naturalization or alienage. This approach led to the following statement in the majority's comments in Quong-Wing's appeal:

> The legislation under review does not, in this view, trespass upon the exclusive power of the Dominion legislature. It does deal with the subject-matter of "property and civil rights" within the province, exclusively assigned to the provincial legislatures, and so dealing cannot be held ultra vires, however harshly it may bear upon Chinamen, naturalized or not, residing in the province. There is no inherent right in any class of the community to employ women and children which the legislature may not modify or take away altogether.

> There is nothing in the "British North America Act" which says that such legislation may not be class legislation. Once it is decided that the subject-

matter of the employment of white women is within the exclusive powers of the provincial legislature and does not infringe upon any of the enumerated subject-matters assigned to the Dominion, then such provincial powers are plenary.

What objects or motives may have controlled or induced the passage of the legislation in question I do not know. Once I find its subject-matter is not within the power of the Dominion Parliament and is within that of the provincial legislature, I cannot enquire into its policy or justice or into the motives which prompted its passage.

There was clearly no doubt in the mind of any of the judges that the prohibition was racial. Indeed, it would have been remarkable had a serious challenge to such characterization been attempted. Although the Saskatchewan statute referred, in its title, to female labour, it dealt only with white women and its evident purpose was to curtail or restrict the rights of Chinese.

The lone dissenting judge approached the matter by pointing out that the *Naturalization Act* had been in force since long before the creation of the province of Saskatchewan, and, in addition to allowing aliens to acquire and hold real and personal property, this Act provided:

An alien to whom a certificate of naturalization is granted shall, within Canada, be entitled to all political and other rights, powers and privileges, and be subject to all obligations to which a natural-born British subject is entitled or subject within Canada, with this qualification, that he shall not, when within the limits of the foreign state of which he was a subject previously to obtaining his certificate of naturalization, be deemed to be a British subject unless he has ceased to be a subject of that state in pursuance of the laws thereof, or in pursuance of a treaty or convention to that effect.

The dissenting judge pointed out that no one had a right to become naturalized. There was a residence requirement and the need to become known to those who could vouch for good character. Unless a person had fulfilled these conditions, he or she could not become naturalized. Quong-Wing, having become a British subject under the Act, had been certified to be a man of good character and enjoyed the assurance of equal treatment with other British subjects. The legislature should not violate that assurance provided by the Naturalization Act.

> It may well be argued that the highly prized gifts of equal freedom and equal opportunity before the law, are so characteristic of the tendency of British modes of thinking and acting in relation thereto, that they are not to be impaired by the whims of a legislature, and that equality taken away unless and until forfeited for causes which civilized men recognize as valid.

> For example, is it competent for a legislature to create a system of slavery and, above all, such a system as applied to naturalized British subjects? This legislation is but a piece of the product of the mode of thought that begot and maintained slavery, not so long ago fiercely claimed to be a laudable system of governing those incapable of governing themselves.

This is a much closer approximation to the judicial approach which would be taken by the courts today. The approach would also be significantly tempered by the existence of the *Charter of Rights and Freedoms*, as well as any analogous provincial charters. As a practical matter, it is unlikely that any legislature, whether federal or provincial, would seriously entertain the introduction of such a statute in the face of both the Charter protections and of an increasing respect for minority rights, as well as public concerns about profiling.

But, there it was, as a judgment of Canada's highest court, and its place in history is that the eventual adoption of the *Charter of Rights and Freedoms* made certain that it would become a relic of an earlier and less enlightened era.

Fumbling the Discrimination Ball

Christie v. The York Corporation [1940] S.C.R. 139

Just because the Supreme Court of Canada has (or may have had, prior to abolition of appeals to the British Privy Council) the last word in a particular piece of litigation, does not necessarily mean that it is (or was) right.

On Saturday, July 11, 1936, Fred Christie, a black man, accompanied by two friends, one of whom was white, entered the tavern operated by the defendant company and seated themselves at a table. Christie had come from Jamaica and had resided in Quebec for more than twenty years. He was living in Verdun at the time, now part of Montreal. He had a good position as a private chauffeur and was a season box subscriber to hockey matches played at the Montreal Forum, the building in which the York Tavern operated. Christie placed fifty cents on the table and ordered three beers. He was informed by the waiter that he was unable to serve them. When pressed for a reason, the waiter said those were the instructions that he had received. Christie then spoke to the bartender on the same issue, receiving a similar reply. The assistant manager of the tavern then informed him that, according to the regulations of the establishment, it was forbidden to serve "coloured people." Christie left the premises, called the police, and when the police arrived, he repeated the request, which resulted in the same response, whereupon he and his friends left the tavern. There had been no altercation of any sort, nor disturbance caused.

Christie then filed an action in the Quebec Superior Court claiming damages for pain and suffering and humiliation in the presence of a number of people present in the tavern. On March 24, 1937, the Superior Court allowed his action. On May 31, 1938, the Quebec Court of Appeal (then Court of Queen's Bench, Appeal Side) reversed that decision, with one dissenting judgment. Special leave to appeal to the Supreme Court of Canada was granted on February 7, 1939. The case was argued on May 10, 1939, and judgment was rendered on December 9 of the same year, dismissing Christie's appeal.

The majority of the Court exhibited very little sympathy for Christie. Indeed, it seemed rather critical of the conduct of someone who had just been told that he would not be served in a public tavern for the sole reason that he was black.

> The respondent [York Corporation] alleged that in giving such instructions to its employees and in so refusing to serve the appellant it was well within its rights; that its business is a private enterprise for gain; and that, in acting as it did, the respondent was merely protecting its business interests.

> It appears from the evidence that, in refusing to sell beer to the appellant, the respondent's employees did so quietly, politely and without causing any scene or commotion whatever. If any notice was attracted to the appellant on the occasion in question, it arose out of the fact that the appellant persisted in demanding beer after he had been so refused and went to the length of calling the police, which was entirely unwarranted by the circumstances.

It started from the general principle of the law of Quebec that there was complete freedom of commerce. Any merchant was free to deal as he might choose with any member of the public. The issue was not one of motive or the reason for deciding to deal or not to deal—the freedom was complete. The only restriction to the general principle was said to be the existence of a specific law, or, in the carrying out of the principle, "the adoption of a rule contrary to good morals and public order." Discrimination solely on the basis of colour did not seem to cross the minds of the majority as being contrary to good morals and public order.

In part, this was in reliance of previous cases, several involving blacks, in which the freedom of choice by the operator of the business clearly trumped issues such as the colour of the customer, and the greater good morals and public order was easily held to be more important. One of the cases relied upon and approved had been an earlier Quebec case in which, solely because of his colour, the plaintiff had been denied a seat in the orchestra, because the management had decided that no person belonging to that race would be admitted to the orchestra seats. The court had decided that the management of a theatre was entitled to impose restrictions and make rules of that character. It was likened, incredibly enough, to having rules that required evening wear in the theatre. The rule in question, it said, may be arbitrary, but it was neither illegal nor prohibited. The Court also found that the law was similar to that in Ontario.

One of the arguments raised on behalf of Christie was that because a license was required in order to operate a tavern, the business was either a monopoly or a privileged enterprise. The majority brushed this aside by stating that the license was mainly for the purpose of raising revenue and, to a certain extent, to allow the government to control the industry. It failed to note statutory language in the governing legislation that referred to the "privilege conferred by the permit." The requirement to possess a license did not, however, (it said) prevent the operation of the tavern from being a private enterprise to be managed within the discretion of the proprietor.

The dissenting judge in the Court of Appeal had concluded that the conduct of the York Tavern toward Christie was contrary to good morals and public order. He thought that under the Quebec legislation governing the sale of liquor, the tavern was not entitled to the complete freedom of commerce embraced by the majority and that there was a duty arising from the quasi monopolistic right that triggered a corresponding duty to sell to the public, other than those cases prohibited by the statute. He would have affirmed the trial judgment.

As in the Court of Appeal, there was a single dissenting judge in the Court, who framed this issue in this manner:

> The sole question in this appeal then is whether the respondent [York], having been given under the statute the special privilege of selling beer in the glass to the public, has the right to pick and choose those of the public to

whom he would sell. In this case the refusal was on the ground of the colour of the person. It might well have been on account of the racial antecedents or the religious faith of the person. The statute itself has definitely laid down ... certain classes of persons to whom a licensee must not sell. The question is, Has the licensee the right to set up his own particular code, or is he bound, as the custodian of a government permit to sell to the public, to sell to anyone who is ready to pay the regular price? Disorderly conduct on the premises of course does not enter into our discussion because there is no suggestion of that in this case.

He reviewed the cases relied upon by the majority, which he clearly did not find to be persuasive. Concluding, he expressed himself as follows:

The question is one of difficulty, as the divergence of judicial opinion in the courts below indicates. My own view is that having regard to the special legislation in Quebec establishing complete control of the sale of beer in the province and particularly the statutory provision which prohibits anyone of the public from buying beer in the glass from anyone but a person granted the special privilege of selling the same, a holder of such a permit from the government to sell beer in the glass to the public has not the right of an ordinary trader to pick and choose those to whom he will sell.

In the changed and changing social and economic conditions, different principles must necessarily be applied to the new conditions. It is not a question of creating a new principle but of applying a different but existing principle of the law. The doctrine that any merchant is free to deal with the public as he chooses had a very different place in the older economy and still applies in the case of an ordinary merchant, but when the State enters the field and takes exclusive control of the sale to the public of such a commodity as liquor, then the old doctrine of the freedom of the merchant to do as he likes has in my view no application to a person to whom the State has given a special privilege to sell to the public.

If there is to be exclusion on the ground of colour or of religious faith or on any other ground not already specifically provided for by statute, it is for the legislature itself, in my view, to impose such prohibitions under the exclusive system of governmental control of the sale of liquor to the public which it has seen fit to enact.

In this case, neither the Quebec Court of Appeal nor the Supreme Court of Canada was able to take the principled step of declaring a blatant discrimination contrary to law. By the time the Court rendered its decision, the Second World War had begun, and, as a practical matter, appeals to the Privy Council were on indefinite hold, so we will never know what the Privy Council might have ruled had the case gone to it.

Interference with Freedom of Religion

Chaput v. Romain [1955] S.C.R. 834

For a province so deeply obsessed with the freedom and right to practice its traditional Roman Catholic religion in the context of a heavily Protestant country and continent, Quebec has had an equivocal record in relation to freedom of others to practice their own religions. In the middle of the last century, one religious group in particular, the Jehovah's Witnesses, attracted unwelcome official Quebec government interference.

Esymier Chaput was a Jehovah's Witness. Edmond Romain was one of three uniformed Quebec Provincial Police (now Surété du Québec) officers acting on the instructions of their superiors. Romain and his colleagues were instructed to break up a religious meeting or service conducted by a minister of the Jehovah's Witnesses at Chaput's house on September 4, 1949, and to seize any pamphlets they found there. The existence of the meeting was public knowledge, as was its purpose. The meeting, consisting of thirty or forty people, was orderly in all respects.

The officers arrived at Chaput's house and requested entry. They had no warrant for the purpose. They were allowed to enter the house and found the meeting underway. Nothing of a seditious nature was said or done during the service. After a matter of a couple of minutes, the police officers announced that they were there to break up the meeting. The presiding minister stated that he needed a further twenty minutes to finish his sermon. The police refused to grant the additional time.

The minister asked if he were under arrest, to which the officers replied that he was not.

The minister then said that, so long as he was not under arrest, he proposed to finish his service, whereupon he was taken by the arms and escorted to the police car and driven to a nearby ferry, where he was put on board. The minister's Bible was taken from him. Chaput's Bible, some pamphlets, hymn books, and the collection box were also seized by the police. The meeting was broken up and the participants left peacefully. No arrests were ever made. No charges were ever laid and the seized items were never returned.

Chaput took action for damages and the value of the articles seized against the three police officers. His actions were dismissed by the Quebec Superior Court and by what is now called the Quebec Court of Appeal. The Supreme Court of Canada, unanimously, allowed the appeal against those decisions. Differences between the judges related mainly to the paths through procedural defenses and the nature of the damages that could be claimed for the unlawful actions of the police officers. This was a case that predated the *Charter* and the *Canadian Bill of Rights*. There was clearly no legal entitlement to break up the meeting and several of the judges considered that such an action might also be criminal in nature.

Two provisions of the *Criminal Code* in force on the date the meeting was broken up provided:

199. Every one is guilty of an indictable offence and liable to two years' imprisonment who, by threats of force, unlawfully obstructs or prevents, or endeavours to obstruct or prevent, any clergyman or other minister in or from celebrating divine service, or otherwise officiating in any church, chapel, meeting-house, school-house or other place for divine worship, or in or from the performance of his duty in the lawful burial of the dead in any churchyard or other burial place.

200. Every one is guilty of an indictable offence and liable to two years imprisonment who strikes or offers any violence to, or arrests upon any civil process or under the pretense of executing any civil process, any clergyman or other minister who is engaged in or, to the knowledge of the offender, is about to engage in, any of the rites or duties in the last preceding section mentioned,

or who, to the knowledge of the offender, is going to perform the same, or returning from the performance thereof.

The police officers, despite acting on the orders of their superiors, could not hide behind that shield. They were personally responsible for their unlawful actions, although efforts were made to suggest that if they were acting in good faith, they should be protected by some form of privilege. This was unavailable in the face of a statute that specifically prohibited the very actions that occurred, namely, breaking up a religious service.

Two judges had no doubt that Chaput had suffered serious damage as a result of the highly reprehensible action by the police officers. He had the indisputable right to have the meeting in his home and to invite the minister, in that capacity, to conduct the religious service. The judges made the point that in our country there is no state religion, that no one was obliged to adhere to a particular faith, that all religions were on an equal footing and that all Catholics, Protestants, Jews, and adherents of different religious denominations had complete liberty to think as they wished. The conscience of each person was a personal matter and not the business of anyone else. It would be morally indefensible to think that a majority could impose its religious views on a minority. Likewise, it would be unthinkable that it would impose its views on a minority while at the same time insisting on its own rights in other provinces. In the present case, all that had happened was the exposure of religious views, undoubtedly contrary to those of the majority of the citizens of the area, but the opinions of the minority had the right to the same respect as those of the majority.

Others said that the moment the police officers became aware of the facts and the nature of the meeting and knew that the "total circumstances were innocent," their only duty was "to do nothing in the way of interfering with the owner, the meeting or the other persons attending it." There was, they said, "not a semblance of fact to call for any adverse or preventive action. What they did was not in execution of a public duty but in carrying out an illegal instruction."

It is therefore clear, in my opinion, that not only was there a total absence of authority for the acts of the [police officers] here complained of, but such conduct was specifically prohibited by law. It is therefore impossible for the [police officers] to bring themselves within the provisions of the statute. Accordingly, the [police officers] were not entitled to notice [before they could be sued] under the statute, and it has no application.

The appellant [Chaput] suffered an invasion of his home and his right of freedom of worship was publicly and peremptorily interfered with. In addition to that, his property was seized and kept. He was humiliated in his own home and before a considerable number of people.

Another statement concluded:

That these views as to the nature of the religious beliefs and practices of Jehovah's Witnesses [that they were seditious, odious and shameful] were generally entertained in the neighbourhood means, of necessity, that when, in this small community and the surrounding country, it was learned that police officers had entered the appellant's house, prevented the carrying on of a religious service, dispersed those assembled and ejected the Minister who had been conducting the service, it would be generally understood that the appellant had been carrying on activities of a criminal nature and, with others, participated in the commission of the offence of sedition. The fact that a so-called "raid" had been made, that books and pamphlets had been seized and the meeting in the appellant's home broken up, also received wide publicity by being reported in both an Ottawa and a Pembroke newspaper.

The appellant, as a resident of the Province of Quebec, was entitled to the privileges enjoyed by all of His Majesty's subjects in that province under the provisions of [a pre-Confederation statute dating from 1851] by which it is declared:

That the free exercise and enjoyment of Religious Profession and Worship, without discrimination or preference, so as the same be not made an excuse for acts of licentiousness, or a justification of practices inconsistent with the peace and safety of the Province [i.e., the then united Province of Canada, established in 1841], is by the constitution and laws of this Province allowed to all Her Majesty's subjects within the same.

The flagrant violation of that right by the [police officers] was a grievous wrong to the appellant and the damages sustained were undoubtedly greatly aggravated by the matters which I have above referred to. The offence was committed at the Village of Chapleau on September 4, 1949, and from that time until the trial of the action on April 25, 1952, the appellant suffered from the false imputation that he had been engaged in committing the criminal offence of sedition at the time referred to. The appellant's right to maintain his good name and to enjoy the privileges conferred upon him by the Statute of 1851 are absolute and very precious rights and he is entitled to recover substantial general damages.

The Court was willing to posit at this stage a complete freedom-of-religion principle, even without any statutory basis for such a statement.

Within four years of the decision in this case, the powerful Premier of Quebec, Maurice Duplessis, would be held personally responsible for damages caused by an unlawful order he gave to cancel a liquor permit held by Frank Roncarelli, a Jehovah's Witness [see page 149]. This case was, in some respects, a precursor to that decision, which was specifically based on abuse of political power.

Sunday Shopping: Sin or Constitutional Right?

R. v. Big M Drug Mart Ltd. [1985] 1 S.C.R. 295

This is a case that took the Court more than a year to decide. It arose from a charge in Calgary, Alberta, that Big M Drug Mart Ltd. was unlawfully carrying on the sale of goods on a Sunday, contrary to the *Lord's Day Act*. Police officers attended the premises, open to the public, and witnessed several transactions, including the sale of groceries, plastic cups, and a bicycle lock. As a result, charges were laid for violation of the statute. Big M was acquitted at trial and the Court of Appeal dismissed the Crown's appeal. The appeal to the Supreme Court of Canada was framed as a constitutional appeal—did the *Lord's Day Act* (especially s. 4) infringe the right to freedom of conscience and religion guaranteed by the *Charter*, and if it did so, were the infringements justified by s. 1 of the *Charter*, and had the *Charter* provisions been enacted pursuant to the criminal-law power contained in the *Constitution Act, 1867*? The province's appeal was dismissed.

Section 4 contained the basic prohibition:

4. It is not lawful for any person on the Lord's Day, except as provided herein, or in any provincial Act or law in force on or after the 1st day of March 1907, to sell or offer for sale or purchase any goods, chattels, or other personal property, or any real estate, or to carry on or transact any business of his ordinary calling, or in connection with such calling, or for gain to do, or employ any other person to do, on that day, any work, business, or labour.

Violating the *Act* was a punishable offence.

The new element in this usual equation was the advent of the Canadian *Charter of Rights and Freedoms*, enacted in 1982. Section 2 of the *Charter* guarantees, among other things, that everyone has fundamental freedom of conscience and religion.

Big M's first hurdle was to establish that a corporation had *Charter* rights. Canada's Supreme Court had no difficulty with this issue. Section 24(1) of the *Charter* "sets out a remedy for individuals (whether real persons or artificial ones such as corporations) whose rights under the *Charter* have been infringed." It reads, "Anyone whose rights or freedoms, as guaranteed by this Charter, have been infringed or denied may apply to a court of competent jurisdiction to obtain such remedy as the court considers appropriate in the circumstances." That, of course, was not the only recourse in the face of unconstitutional legislation. Should a challenge be based on the unconstitutionality of the legislation, recourse to s. 24 of the *Charter* is unnecessary and the effect on a challenging party is irrelevant. No one, the Court held, can be convicted of an offence under an unconstitutional law, so any accused can defend a criminal charge by arguing that the law under which the charge is brought is constitutionally invalid.

> The argument that the respondent [Big M], by reason of being a corporation, is incapable of holding religious belief and therefore incapable of claiming rights under s. 2(a) of the *Charter*, confuses the nature of this appeal. A law which infringes religious freedom, is by that reason alone, inconsistent with s. 2(a) of the *Charter* and it matters not whether the accused is a Christian, Jew, Muslim, Hindu, Buddhist, atheist, agnostic or whether an individual or a corporation. It is the nature of the law, not the status of the accused that is in issue.

Based on an extensive historical review of the legislation and previously decided cases, the Court concluded that a finding that the *Lord's Day Act* had a secular purpose (giving everyone a day off, on a day that "happened" to be the Christian Sabbath) was simply not possible. "Its religious purpose, in compelling sabbatical observance, has been long-established and consistently maintained by the courts of this country." The Crown argued that the religious purpose of the *Act* was not what mattered, but, instead, only its effects, when considering its constitutionality.

> I cannot agree. In my view, both purpose and effect are relevant in determining constitutionality, either an unconstitutional purpose or an unconstitutional effect can invalidate legislation. All legislation is animated by an object the legislature intends to achieve. This object is realized through the impact provided by the operation and application of the legislation. Purpose and effect respectively, in the sense of the legislation's object and its ultimate impact, are clearly linked, if not indivisible. Intended and actual results have often been looked to for guidance in assessing the legislation's object and thus, its validity.

> Moreover, consideration of the object of legislation is vital if rights are to be fully protected. The assessment by the courts of legislative purpose focuses scrutiny upon the aims and objectives of the legislature and assures they are consonant with the guarantees enshrined in the *Charter*. The declaration that certain objects lie outside the legislature's power checks governmental action at the first stage of unconstitutional conduct. Further, it will provide more ready and more vigorous protection of constitutional rights by obviating the individual litigant's need to prove effects violative of *Charter* rights. It will also allow courts to dispose of cases where the object is clearly improper, without inquiring into the legislation's actual impact.

If the acknowledged purpose of the legislation was the compulsion of sabbatical observance, and if that purpose offended freedom of religion, it was then unnecessary to consider the actual impact of Sunday closing on religious freedom. Apart from this general observation, the Court found it difficult to conceive of legislation with an unconstitutional purpose whose effects themselves would not also be unconstitutional.

> In short, I agree with the respondent [Big M] that the legislation's purpose is the initial test of constitutionality and its effects are to be considered when the law under consideration has passed or, at least, has purportedly passed the purpose test. If the legislation fails the purpose test, there is no need to consider further its effects, since it has already been demonstrated to be in-

valid. Thus, if a law with a valid purpose interferes by its impact, with rights or freedoms, a litigant could still argue the effects of the legislation as a means to defeat its applicability and possibly its validity. In short, the effects test will only be necessary to defeat legislation with a valid purpose; effects can never be relied upon to save legislation with an invalid purpose.

The Court also rejected an argument that it should recognize that the purpose of legislation might shift or be transformed over time by changing social conditions, essentially a variation of the "effects" submissions made by the Crown. The practical difficulties of accepting such an argument were that no legislation would be safe from a revised judicial assessment of purpose, which would create uncertainty, encourage re-litigation of the same issues and provide courts with a means to arrive at results other than those dictated by legal considerations. If the argument were accepted it could, in addition, end the doctrine of *stare decisis*, a principle by which courts proceed incrementally, on the basis of decided cases, and the presumption that purpose is a function of the intent of those who drafted and enacted legislation, at the time of adoption of the legislation, and not of any shifting variable.

Turning to the broader considerations of what is meant by freedom of religion, the Court dealt preliminarily with a free society, and then the notion of freedom generally.

A truly free society is one which can accommodate a wide variety of beliefs, diversity of tastes and pursuits, customs and codes of conduct. A free society is one which aims at equality with respect to the enjoyment of fundamental freedoms and I say this without any reliance upon s. 15 of the *Charter*. Freedom must surely be founded in respect for the inherent dignity and the inviolable rights of the human person. The essence of the concept of freedom of religion is the right to entertain such religious beliefs as a person chooses, the right to declare religious beliefs openly and without fear of hindrance or reprisal, and the right to manifest religious belief by worship and practice or by teaching and dissemination. But the concept means more than that.

Freedom can primarily be characterized by the absence of coercion or constraint. If a person is compelled by the state or the will of another to a course of action or inaction which he would not otherwise have chosen, he is not acting of his own volition and he cannot be said to be truly free. One of the major purposes of the *Charter* is to protect, within reason, from compulsion or restraint. Coercion includes not only such blatant forms of compulsion as direct commands to act or refrain from acting on pain of sanction, coercion includes indirect forms of control which determine or limit alternative courses of conduct available to others. Freedom in a broad sense embraces both the absence of coercion and constraint, and the right to manifest beliefs and practices. Freedom means that, subject to such limitations as are necessary to protect public safety, order, health, or morals or the fundamental rights and freedoms of others, no one is to be forced to act in a way contrary to his beliefs or his conscience.

To the extent that the *Lord's Day Act* binds everyone to a sectarian Christian ideal, it is a form of coercion inimical to all non-Christians and the spirit of the *Charter*. The Court agreed that to accept that Parliament retains the right to compel universal observance of the day of rest preferred by one religion is not consistent with the preservation and enhancement of the multicultural heritage of Canadians and was contrary to the provisions of the *Charter*, section 27 of which reads: "This Charter shall be interpreted in a manner consistent with the preservation and enhancement of the multicultural heritage of Canadians."

The Court rejected an argument that what was protected in relation to religious freedom had already been recognized in the 1960 Diefenbaker *Bill of Rights*, on the basis that the rights so recognized were those existing at the time it was adopted and notwithstanding the *Lord's Day Act*. The *Charter* does not simply recognize and declare existing rights at the time of its enactment; its language is imperative and sets a standard for testing both existing and future legislation. Its interpretation is to be guided by its purpose—the interests it was meant to protect.

In my view this [purposive] analysis is to be undertaken, and the purpose of the right or freedom in question is to be sought by reference to the character and the larger objects of the *Charter* itself, to the language chosen to articulate the specific right or freedom, to the historical origins of the concepts enshrined, and where applicable, to the meaning and purpose of the other specific rights and freedoms with which it is associated within the text of the *Charter*. The interpretation should be ... a generous rather than a legalistic one, aimed at fulfilling the purpose of the guarantee and securing for individuals the full benefit of the *Charter's* protection. At the same time it is important not to overshoot the actual purpose of the right or freedom in question, but to recall that the *Charter* was not enacted in a vacuum, and must therefore ... be placed in its proper linguistic, philosophic and historical contexts.

As one of the early *Charter* cases on the general principles of the rights and freedoms protected, this case sets out both the analytical framework and the purposive nature of any judicial inquiry to be undertaken. It also attempts to try to capture the nature of what constitutes a free society and what freedom within such a society may mean. *R. v. Big M Drug Mart Ltd.* has become a bedrock case for subsequent examination of *Charter* principles, not unlike the *Oakes* analysis, which was rendered the following year [see page 50].

Reasonable and Justifiable Limits on Charter Rights

R. v. Oakes [1986] 1 S.C.R. 103

David Edwin Oakes was found in possession of a minor amount of narcotics that he said was for his personal use. He was charged with unlawful possession for purposes of trafficking. The *Narcotic Control Act* contained a provision that if an accused was proved to be in possession of narcotics, unless he was able to show otherwise, he was presumed to be in possession for purposes of trafficking. The lower courts had held the *Narcotic Control Act* provision to be unconstitutional. A constitutional question was framed as to whether what was referred to as the "reverse onus" on the accused violated his right under section 11(d) of the *Charter* to be presumed innocent until proven guilty according to law in a fair and public hearing by an independent and impartial tribunal.

Section 1 of the *Charter* provides: "The *Canadian Charter of Rights and Freedoms* guarantees the rights and freedoms set out in it subject only to such reasonable limits prescribed by law as can be demonstrably justified in a free and democratic society."

The Court embarked on a systematic analysis of the impact of the reverse onus on the right to be presumed innocent and the obligation of the State to prove all of the elements of the offence with which the accused is charged. This included an examination of the purpose of the constitutional protection, namely the interests it was meant to protect.

The presumption of innocence is a hallowed principle lying at the very heart of criminal law. Although protected expressly in s. 11(d) of the *Charter*, the presumption of innocence is referable and integral to the general protection of life, liberty and security contained in s. 7 of the *Charter*. ... The presumption of innocence protects the fundamental liberty and human dignity of any and every person accused by the State of criminal conduct. An individual charged with a criminal offence faces grave social and personal consequences, including potential loss of physical liberty, subjection to social stigma and ostracism from the community, as well as other social, psychological and economic harms. In light of the gravity of these consequences, the presumption of innocence is crucial. It ensures that until the State proves an accused's guilt beyond all reasonable doubt, he or she is innocent. This is essential in a society committed to fairness and social justice. The presumption of innocence confirms our faith in humankind; it reflects our belief that individuals are decent and law-abiding members of the community until proven otherwise.

Its review included examination of similar concepts as well as a reverse onus, beginning with the 1960 *Canadian Bill of Rights*, which contained substantially similar language to that adopted in the *Charter*, then moved on to earlier *Charter* cases (in which six appellate courts had already declared the provision to be unconstitutional), United States jurisprudence, and the *European Convention on Human Rights* jurisprudence. The Court then concluded that requiring Oakes to prove he was not guilty denied his right to be presumed innocent, which was radically and fundamentally inconsistent with the societal values of human dignity and liberty espoused by Canada and was directly contrary to the presumption of innocence enshrined in the *Charter*.

This conclusion, however, only got Oakes partway home. The next issue was whether the unconstitutional provision was a reasonable and demonstrably justified limit pursuant to section 1 of the *Charter*. The Court explained one of the basic aspects of the interpretation of section 1:

A second contextual element of interpretation of s. 1 is provided by the words "free and democratic society." Inclusion of these words as the final standard of justification for limits on rights and freedoms refers the Court to the very purpose for which the Charter was originally entrenched in the Constitution:

Canadian society is to be free and democratic. The Court must be guided by the values and principles essential to a free and democratic society which I believe embody, to name but a few, respect for the inherent dignity of the human person, commitment to social justice and equality, accommodation of a wide variety of beliefs, respect for cultural and group identity, and faith in social and political institutions, which enhance the participation of individuals and groups in society. The underlying values and principles of a free and democratic society are the genesis of the rights and freedoms guaranteed by the Charter and the ultimate standard against which a limit on a right or freedom must be shown, despite its effect, to be reasonable and demonstrably justified.

That analysis begins with the acknowledgement that the provision violates constitutional rights and freedoms. Those rights and freedoms are not absolute, but the bar is set quite high if they are to be overridden, both as acknowledged violations of rights or freedoms and as governed by the fundamental principles of a free and democratic society. The onus is, of course, on the party seeking to justify the limitation. "The presumption is that the rights and freedoms enumerated are guaranteed unless the party invoking s. 1 can bring itself within the exceptional criteria which justify their being limited."

To establish that a limit is reasonable and demonstrably justified in a free and democratic society, two central criteria must be satisfied. First, the objective which the measures responsible for a limit on a Charter right or freedom are designed to serve, must be "of sufficient importance to warrant overriding a constitutionally protected right or freedom." ... The standard must be high in order to ensure that objectives which are trivial or discordant with the principles integral to a free and democratic society do not gain s. 1 protection. It is necessary, at a minimum, that an objective relate to concerns which are pressing and substantial in a free and democratic society before it can be characterized as sufficiently important.

Second, once a sufficiently significant objective is recognized, then the party invoking s. 1 must show that the means chosen are reasonable and demonstrably justified. This involves "a form of proportionality test." ... Although the nature of the proportionality test will vary depending on the circumstances, in each case courts will be required to balance the interests of society with those of individuals and groups. There are, in my view, three important components of a proportionality test. First, the measures adopted must be carefully designed to achieve the objective in question. They must not be arbitrary, unfair or based on irrational considerations. In short, they must be rationally connected to the objective. Second, the means, even if rationally connected to the objective in this first sense, should impair "as little as possible" the right or freedom in question. ... Third, there must be a proportionality between the effects of the measures which are responsible for limiting the Charter right or freedom, and the objective which has been identified as of "sufficient importance."

The first stage of the inquiry was satisfied. The Court acknowledged that the objective of protecting society against drug-trafficking was sufficiently important to allow overriding a constitutionally protected right or freedom in certain cases. The next stage was to consider the means chosen by Parliament to achieve that objective.

The means must be reasonable and demonstrably justified in a free and democratic society. As outlined above, this proportionality test should begin with a consideration of the rationality of the provision: is the reverse onus clause ... rationally related to the objective of curbing drug trafficking? At a minimum, this requires that [the provision] be internally rational; there must be a rational connection between the basic fact of possession and the presumed fact of possession for the purpose of trafficking. Otherwise, the reverse onus could give rise to unjustified and erroneous convictions for drug trafficking of persons guilty only of possession of narcotics.

The Court found that the provision did not survive the rational-connection test. Possession of a small or negligible quantity of narcotics did not support the inference of trafficking and it would be irrational to infer that trafficking was intended based on such a small quantity.

This is a landmark decision of the Court and it has been cited in the constitutional courts of many countries as a model of the systematic analysis of proportionality when it is proposed that certain guaranteed rights should be overridden in pursuit even of important social or governmental objectives.

Charter Decriminalizes Abortion

R. v. Morgentaler [1988] 1 S.C.R. 30

There was very little middle ground regarding Dr. Henry Morgentaler. He was reviled by some and admired by many more, especially women, because of his willingness to perform abortions. Abortions were essentially criminalized under the provisions of the *Criminal Code*, with the result that many dangerous and unwanted pregnancies came to term because women were denied access to relatively safe abortions. Morgentaler's view was that such decisions should be matters between the woman and her physician. Over the years, he was charged on several occasions and the Crown had great difficulty in obtaining convictions, since juries did not agree with the law and were often content to ignore it. However, more than a decade prior to this decision, the Supreme Court of Canada had upheld a conviction and Morgentaler was sentenced to prison.

Once released from prison, Morgentaler continued his crusade and was once again charged and convicted. His appeal on this occasion reached the Supreme Court of Canada in early October 1986, where it was given four days of argument in front of a seven-judge panel, presided over by the same Chief Justice who had upheld the previous conviction. It took the Court a full sixteen months to render its decision, but this time an acquittal was ordered by the majority of the Court. What accounted for the different outcome? It was the *Canadian Charter of Rights and Freedoms*, adopted as part of the Canadian Constitution in

1982. The key *Charter* provision was section 7, which guarantees "the right to life, liberty and the security of the person and the right not to be deprived thereof except in accordance with the principles of fundamental justice."

Framing the issue properly was important for the Court, which had no desire to become involved in the pros and cons of the abortion debate.

> During argument before this Court, counsel for the Crown emphasized repeatedly that it is not the role of the judiciary in Canada to evaluate the wisdom of legislation enacted by our democratically elected representatives, or to second-guess difficult policy choices that confront all governments. In [*Morgentaler 1975*] I stressed that the Court "had not been called upon to decide, or even enter, the loud and continuous public debate on abortion." Eleven years later, the controversy persists, and it remains true that this Court cannot presume to resolve all of the competing claims advanced in vigorous and healthy public debate. Courts and legislatures in other democratic societies have reached completely contradictory decisions when asked to weigh the competing values relevant to the abortion question. ...

> But since 1975, and the first *Morgentaler* decision, the Court has been given added responsibilities. I stated in *Morgentaler (1975)*, ... that:

> The values we must accept for the purposes of this appeal are those expressed by Parliament which holds the view that the desire of a woman to be relieved of her pregnancy is not, of itself, justification for performing an abortion.

> Although no doubt it is still fair to say that courts are not the appropriate forum for articulating complex and controversial programmes of public policy, Canadian courts are now charged with the crucial obligation of ensuring that the legislative initiatives pursued by our Parliament and legislatures conform to the democratic values expressed in the *Canadian Charter of Rights and Freedoms*. ... "the task of the Court in this case is not to solve nor seek to solve what may be called the abortion issue, but simply to measure the content of s. 251 [of the *Criminal Code*] against the *Charter*. It is in this latter sense that the current *Morgentaler* appeal differs from the one we heard a decade ago.

In the earlier case, the Court had considered the mechanism contained in the *Criminal Code* of having to apply to the therapeutic abortion committee of an accredited or approved hospital, which would (if a majority of the committee agreed) issue a certificate stating that continuation of a pregnancy would be likely to endanger the pregnant woman's life or health. Once such certificate was given to a qualified medical practitioner (not a member of the committee), the practitioner was permitted to perform an abortion and both the practitioner and the woman were freed from any criminal liability. Part of what led to the eventual decision of the Court was the uncertainty of outcome and the delay involved in working through the therapeutic abortion committees, both as to the mental stress involved and the fact that the risk of mortality increased with every passing day. In addition to this, almost 60 percent of the hospitals in Canada did not qualify and many that did had governing boards that refused to establish therapeutic abortion committees, or that had committees but recommended no abortions, or that imposed quotas.

The Court also declined to become embroiled in any question of foetal rights.

> The appellants [Morgentaler] contended that the sole purpose of s. 251 of the *Criminal Code* is to protect the life and health of pregnant women. The respondent Crown submitted that s. 251 seeks not only to protect the life and health of pregnant women, but also the interests of the foetus. On the other hand, the Crown conceded that the Court is not called upon in this appeal to evaluate any claim to "foetal rights" or to assess the meaning of "the right to life." I expressly refrain from so doing. In my view, it is unnecessary for the purpose of deciding this appeal to evaluate or assess "foetal rights" as an independent constitutional value. Nor are we required to measure the full extent of the state's interest in establishing criteria unrelated to the pregnant woman's own priorities and aspirations. What we must do is evaluate the particular balance struck by Parliament in s. 251, as it relates to the priorities and aspirations of pregnant women and the government's interests in the protection of the foetus.

Parliament had made it clear that the life or health of pregnant women was paramount, since abortion was permitted if the certificate could be obtained. The object was not to provide unrestricted access to abortion, but to restrict it to cases in which continuation of the pregnancy would likely be injurious to the life or health of the woman concerned. One judge turned the question around and concluded that the provision was really designed to protect the foetus, since the precursor to an abortion was a reliable, independent, and medically sound opinion, all this to protect the state interest in the foetus.

Turning to the proportionality analysis, that of whether the statutory solution was appropriate:

> I am equally convinced, however, that the means chosen to advance the legislative objectives of s. 251 do not satisfy any of the three elements of the proportionality component of *R. v. Oakes* [see page 50]. The evidence has led me to conclude that the infringement of the security of the person of pregnant women caused by s. 251 is not accomplished in accordance with the principles of fundamental justice. It has been demonstrated that the procedures and administrative structures created by s. 251 are often arbitrary and unfair. The procedures established to implement the policy of s. 251 impair s. 7 rights far more than is necessary because they hold out an illusory defence to many women who would *prima facie* qualify under the exculpatory provisions of s. 251(4). In other words, many women whom Parliament professes not to wish to subject to criminal liability will nevertheless be forced by the practical unavailability of the supposed defence to risk liability or to suffer harm such as a traumatic late abortion caused by the delay inherent in the s. 251 system. Finally, the effects of the limitation upon the s. 7 rights of many pregnant women are out of proportion to the objective sought to be achieved. Indeed, to the extent that s. 251(4) is designed to protect the life and health of women, the procedures it establishes may actually defeat that objective. The administrative structures of s. 251(4) are so cumbersome that women whose health is endangered by pregnancy may not be able to gain a therapeutic abortion, at least without great trauma, expense and inconvenience.

> I conclude, therefore, that the cumbersome structure of subs. (4) not only unduly subordinates the s. 7 rights of pregnant women but may also defeat the value Parliament itself has established as paramount, namely, the life and health of the pregnant woman. As I have noted, counsel for the Crown did contend that one purpose of the procedures required by subs. (4) is to protect

the interests of the foetus. State protection of foetal interests may well be deserving of constitutional recognition under s. 1. Still, there can be no escape from the fact that Parliament has failed to establish either a standard or procedure whereby any such interests might prevail over those of the woman in a fair and non-arbitrary fashion.

The only female judge on the panel had a much more visceral approach to the issue. She saw the heart of the matter to be whether, as a constitutional matter, a pregnant woman can be compelled by law to carry the foetus to term—a basis on which Parliament had proceeded and had made it a criminal offence, punishable by imprisonment, for the woman or her physician to terminate the pregnancy without observing the procedural requirements of the *Criminal Code*. The other four judges making up the majority (she was the fifth) had found that the requirements did not comply with fundamental justice in the procedural sense. She thought the fundamental question should first be dealt with: if a pregnant woman could not be compelled, as a constitutional matter, to carry a foetus to term against her will, a review of the procedural requirements by which she may be compelled to do so seemed pointless.

It seems to me, therefore, that to commence the analysis with the premise that the s. 7 right encompasses only a right to physical and psychological security and to fail to deal with the right to liberty in the context of "life, liberty and the security of the person" begs the central issue in the case. If either the right to liberty or the right to security of the person or a combination of both confers on the pregnant woman the right to decide for herself (with the guidance of her physician) whether or not to have an abortion, then we have to examine the legislative scheme not only from the point of view of fundamental justice in the procedural sense but in the substantive sense as well. I think, therefore, that we must answer the question: what is meant by the right to liberty in the context of the abortion issue? Does it … give the pregnant woman control over decisions affecting her own body? If not, does her right to security of the person give her such control?

She concluded that the right to liberty contained in s. 7 guarantees women a degree of personal autonomy over important decisions affecting their private lives, which extended to a decision to terminate a pregnancy. This is not just a medical decision, but a profound social and ethical one as well. She expressed the issue in powerful and compelling terms. The legislative scheme asserted that the woman's capacity to reproduce was not to be subject to her own control, but to that of the state. She is treated as a means to an end that she does not desire, but cannot control. As the passive recipient of a decision made by others as to whether her body is to be used to nurture a new life, what could comport less with human dignity and respect? How could a woman in this position have any sense of security with respect to her person?

This was a particularly important decision, not only for the de-criminalization of abortion, but also as a demonstration of how the Charter has become a constitutional bulwark. Under the pre-*Charter* legislation, the same individual—Morgentaler—had been imprisoned for precisely the same conduct.

Even if You Agree, Your Charter Rights Can Be Infringed

Syndicat Northcrest v. Amselem   [2004] 2 S.C.R. 551

The appellants in this appeal were Orthodox Jews. Each was the divided co-owner of residential units in Place Northcrest, luxury buildings in a very upscale complex in Montreal, called Le Sanctuaire. In September 1996, Moase Amselem set up a *succah*, a small enclosed temporary hut or booth, traditionally made of wood or other materials such as fastened canvas and open to the heavens, on the balcony outside his apartment. Jews are commanded to "dwell" temporarily in a succah during the festival of Succot, a nine-day festival commemorating the forty-nine-year period during which the Children of Israel wandered in the desert, living in temporary shelters. After he set up his succah, Amselem was requested by the syndicate of co-ownership to remove it on the basis that it was in violation of the Sanctuaire's by-laws as stated in the declaration of co-ownership, which prohibited decorations, alterations, and constructions on the balconies without the permission of the syndicate. For reasons that were not explained, the courts appear to have accepted the somewhat preposterous submission that none of the appellants had read the declaration of co-ownership, signed by each of them, prior to purchasing or occupying their individual units. There was no suggestion that the particular provisions in the declaration of co-ownership had been drafted with Orthodox Jews in mind, or for any other targeted reason.

The next year, Amselem (pursuant to the regulations in the declaration of co-ownership) requested permission to set up a succah on his balcony. Permission was refused, on the basis of the restrictions in the declaration, but as a matter of accommodation, the syndicate proposed to allow Amselem and other Orthodox Jews in the building to set up a communal succah in the gardens of Le Sanctuaire. Although Amselem had been inclined to accept the compromise, the offer was eventually refused and the request for individual succahs on the balconies was repeated. This was refused in turn by the syndicate. The appellants proceeded, notwithstanding this refusal, to set up the individual succahs. The syndicate responded by seeking permanent injunctions prohibiting the setting up of succahs and the demolition of them, if necessary. That application was granted by the Superior Court in June 1998 and affirmed by the Quebec Court of Appeal in 2002. Leave to appeal to the Supreme Court of Canada was granted and, in a five to four decision, that Court allowed the appeal in June 2004.

The issue, as framed by the majority, was in the context of freedom of religion.

> In my view, the key issues before us are: (1) whether the clauses in the by-laws of the declaration of co-ownership which contained a general prohibition against decorations or constructions on one's balcony, infringe the appellants' freedom of religion protested under the Quebec *Charter* (2), if so, whether the refusal by the respondent to permit the setting up of a succah is justified by its reliance on the co-owners' rights to enjoy property under s. 6 of the Quebec *Charter* and their rights of personal security under s. 1 thereof; and (3) whether the appellants waived their rights to freedom of religion by signing the declaration of co-ownership.

This prompted a lengthy consideration of what is meant by *freedom of religion*, including what is meant by religion, since the *Charter* protections apply only to freedom of religion.

> Defined broadly, religion typically involves a particular and comprehensive system of faith and worship. Religion also tends to involve the belief in a divine, superhuman or controlling power. In essence, religion is about freely and deeply held personal convictions or beliefs connected to an individual's

spiritual faith and integrally linked to one's self-definition and spiritual fulfil-
ment, the practices of which allow individuals to foster a connection with the
divine or with the subject or object of that spiritual faith.

In general, everyone is entitled to hold and manifest whatever beliefs the conscience dictates, provided that any manifestations do not injure others or their parallel rights. The matter is one of individual belief and not necessarily in conformity with either official religious dogma or the position of religious officials. While courts are not to be (and should not be) called upon to rule on religious practices, they are qualified to determine the sincerity of an individual's belief, as a matter of fact, where such sincerity may be in issue. Once the religious freedom has been established, courts must then decide whether there has been enough interference to constitute an infringement of that freedom (under one or other of the *Charters)*, that such infringement is one that is more than trivial or insubstantial.

The majority concluded that the appellants' rights to freedom of religion had been significantly impaired, while the rights of the other co-owners had been impacted, at best, to a minimal degree and, therefore, could not be construed as validly limiting the exercise of the appellants' religious freedom. The approach was that the right was impinged by the declaration of co-ownership (which all the appellants had signed) and that "extreme distress" would be incurred as a result of the restrictions (a view not shared by the trial judge, the Quebec Court of Appeal, or the dissenting members of the Supreme Court). There was an essentially dismissive treatment of the objectives of the declaration of co-ownership and the right of peaceful enjoyment of the property and personal security as simply economic and aesthetic in nature, that could easily survive the nine-day inconvenience of the erection of the succahs. The majority said there was not sufficient evidence regarding the impairment of the value of the units and referred to such claim as unsubstantiated.

In a multiethnic and multicultural country such as ours, which accentuates
and advertises its modern record of respecting cultural diversity and human
rights and of promoting tolerance of religious and ethnic minorities "and is
in many ways an example thereof for other societies," the argument of the re-

spondent that nominal, minimally intruded-upon aesthetic interests should outweigh the appellants' religious freedom is unacceptable. Indeed, mutual tolerance is one of the cornerstones of all democratic societies. Living in a community that attempts to maximize human rights invariably requires openness and recognition of the rights of others. In this regard, I must point out, with respect, that labelling an individual's steadfast adherence to his or her religious beliefs "intransigence," as [one of the judges of the Court of Appeal] asserted ... does not further an enlightened resolution of the dispute before us.

It then concluded that there had been no waiver of the freedom of religion by the appellants as having signed the unread declaration of co-ownership and concluded that they should be entitled to erect the succahs, so long as they allowed room for a passageway in the event of an emergency and conformed "as much as possible" with the general aesthetics of the property.

The remaining four judges of the Court were equally adamant, but came to a completely different result. They focused on the terms of the declaration of co-ownership signed by the appellants, the flexibility within the religion regarding the convenience and comfort of the practitioners, the accommodation demonstrated by the syndicate in providing alternative facilities on the property, the approval of the Canadian Jewish Congress acknowledging the efforts of the syndicate to assist in compliance and the initial acceptance of Amselem. In addition, the infringement, if any, did not rise from a statute, but in a contract freely signed by the appellants when they purchased a co-owned property. There was little difference between the majority and minority as to the meaning of freedom of religion and the sincerity required to establish the religious practices involved, at the level of the individual claiming the right.

The divergence began with the distinction between the context of the possible infringement (public law or private arrangements), the manner of exercising the particular rights, possible differences between the Canadian and Quebec *Charter*s, the possible infringements of the rights of others in the course of exercising the individual right and the need to reconcile the various interests involved. The sincerity issue was not in doubt and the appellants had established the necessary level of sincerity.

> The evidence shows that the appellants sincerely believed that they were under an obligation to eat their meals and celebrate Succot in a succah. Although it would be preferable to do so in their own succah whenever possible, there are numerous circumstances, such as the ones noted by the trial judge, in which using another person's succah would appear to be justified. Based on the evidence that was adduced and accepted by the trial judge, I accept that the appellants sincerely believe that, whenever possible, it would be preferable for them to erect their own succahs; however it would not be a divergence from their religious precept to accept another solution, so long as the fundamental obligation of eating their meals in a succah was discharged. I therefore cannot accept that the appellants sincerely believe, based on the precepts of their religion that they are relying on, that they are under an obligation to erect their *own* [It was underlined in the judgment.]succahs on their balconies, patios or porches. Rather, it is their practice of eating or celebrating Succot in a succah that is protected by the guarantee of freedom of religion set out in s.3 of the Quebec *Charter*. The declaration of co-ownership does not hinder this practice, as it does not bar the appellants from celebrating Succot in a succah, whether at the homes of friends or family or even in a communal succah, as proposed by the respondent. Consequently, the prohibition against erecting their own succahs does not infringe the purpose of the appellants' right to freedom of religion. Any inconvenience resulting from the prohibition against erecting individual succahs is not sufficient to elevate the preference to the status of a mandatory religious practice.

As to the conflict between the particular religious rights and the rights of the other property owners, the trial judge had concluded that the restrictions were justified, particularly as to their personal security, since the balconies were routes to be used in cases of emergency and could have been blocked by the succahs.

> Finally it should be noted that all the co-owners have an interest in maintaining harmony in the co-owned property and an undivided right therein, especially with respect to a common portion reserved for restricted use in which, by contract, they have a collective right of ownership. Reconciliation cannot amount to a simple request made to the co-owners to renounce their rights in

the common portion consisting of the balconies. Co-owners have the right to expect contracts to be respected; this expectation is also consistent with the general interest of the citizens of Quebec.

The right of co-ownership was to be exercised in harmony with the rights of all the other co-owners, which was not a repudiation of the freedom of religion. Instead, it was a matter of facilitating the exercise of the rights in a manner that took the rights of others and their general well-being into account. This led to the conclusion that since the right to freedom of religion could not be exercised in harmony with the rights and freedoms of others, the infringement of the appellants' rights was legitimate. Even though the declaration of co-ownership prohibited building succahs on the balconies, it did not violate the freedom of religion.

The fourth dissenting judge wrote separate reasons. He placed much more emphasis on the private contract voluntarily made among the parties.

> There is a vast difference, it seems to me, between using freedom of religion as a shield against interference with religious freedoms by the State and as a sword against co-contractors in a private building. It was for the appellants, not the other co-owners, to determine in advance of their unit purchase what the appellants' particular religious beliefs required. They had a choice of buildings in which to invest. They undertook by contract to the owners of *this* building even if (as is apparently the case) they accepted the rules without reading them. They thereafter rejected the accommodation offered by their co-owners of a communal succah in the garden because it did not fully satisfy their religious views although the accommodation was not, as will be seen, inconsistent even with Mr. Moase Amselem's sense of religious obligation in the circumstance where a personal succah is simply not available.

There was no state action involved. None of the co-ownership restrictions had a religious purpose and were not aimed at persons of the Jewish faith. Given the importance attached to construction of a succah on a communally owned balcony, the other co-owners could reasonably have expected the appellants to have satisfied their concerns prior to purchasing. Persons not taking the trouble to read the rules should not have greater rights under the contract than the diligent and conscientious purchasers who do. The appellants' religious beliefs did not preclude recourse to a communal succah when a personal one was not available.

> The point in this case is that the appellants themselves were in the best position to determine their religious requirements and must be taken to have done so when entering into the co-ownership agreement in the first place. They cannot afterwards *reasonably* insist on their preferred solution at the expense of the countervailing rights of their co-owners.

The two sides of the Court were, therefore, sharply divided and each was quite articulate in the reasons for which it concluded, one way or the other.

Cases like this demonstrate the broad ranges of approach to different and often difficult matters that find their way to court, as well as the need for appellate courts to base their decisions in the appropriate conduct in respect of matters that, in judicial theory at least, are best left for the trial judge to decide. The majority seems to have ignored many important findings of fact by the trial judge (who had heard and weighed the evidence) that did not fit comfortably with the direction in which it perceived the desired solution to lie. Such conduct has the potential to upset a long-standing practice and to create far more uncertainty than is warranted in a sophisticated judicial process.

Religious Freedom Includes the Right to Wear a Kirpan

Multani v. Commission Scolaire Marguerite-Bourgeoys
[2006] 1 S.C.R. 256

The appellant and his twelve-year-old son were orthodox Sikhs. The son had been baptized and his religion required him to wear a kirpan at all times, including when he attended school. A kirpan is a religious object that resembles a dagger; it must be made of metal and not some other material. One day, in the schoolyard, the son accidentally dropped the kirpan, which he had been wearing under his clothes. This led to a letter from the legal counsel of the school board to the son authorizing him to wear his kirpan, provided that he complied with certain conditions to ensure that it was sealed inside his clothing. Both parents and son agreed to such arrangement, which had been offered as a "reasonable accommodation."

This would likely have ended the matter, but for a decision of the school's governing board not to ratify the agreement. The basis for the refusal was that wearing a kirpan at the school violated the school's code of conduct, properly approved by the governing board, which prohibited the carrying of weapons and dangerous objects. The family requested a review board to reconsider the decision. The review board issued a unanimous recommendation to the school board (CSMB— the respondent in the appeal) to uphold the decision. It also said that a symbolic kirpan in another form, perhaps a pendant, made of a material rendering it harmless, would be acceptable.

The father, on his own behalf and as tutor to his son, applied for an order from the Quebec Superior Court declaring that the CSMB decision was of no force and effect, that the son had the right to wear the kirpan at school, provided that it was sealed and sewn up in his clothing. He argued that this would represent a reasonable accommodation to reconcile the freedom of religion and right to equality guaranteed in both the Quebec and Canadian *Charters*. The motion was granted, but the decision was reversed by the Quebec Court of Appeal, leading to the appeal to the Supreme Court of Canada.

Although the Court unanimously reversed the Appeal Court's decision, there were different paths to the eventual conclusion. Two thought that the matter could, and should, be dealt with using administrative-law principles, as had the Quebec Court of Appeal (despite having reached the opposite conclusion), while the principal majority judges considered that the key was the constitutional nature of the rights involved and that reduction of those essential values to mere administrative-law principles was not appropriate. The complaint had been based entirely on the constitutional freedoms and it was the constitutionality of the CSMB decision that was in issue, thus requiring a constitutional analysis.

Dealing with the allegation that freedom of religion has been infringed, the individual has the burden of demonstrating a sincere belief that a particular practice or belief is required by the religion. The religious belief is to be asserted in good faith and may not be capricious, fictitious or an artifice. A court that is assessing the sincerity of that belief takes into account, among other things, the credibility of the person asserting the belief as well as the consistency of that belief with the person's other current religious practices.

None of the parties contested the sincerity of the son's religious belief, nor his genuine belief that he would not be compliant with the requirements of that religion were he to wear a plastic or wooden kirpan. The interference with those beliefs was not insignificant, since, forced to choose between leaving the kirpan at home and leaving the public school system, the son had decided to follow his religious convictions and had changed to a private school, thus the prohibition had deprived him of the right to attend a public school. Looking at the limit resulting from the prohibition, the onus shifted to the CSMB to show that the infringement was reasonable and could be justified in a free and democratic society, under s. 1 of the *Charter*. There are two requirements for this: the legislative objective being pursued must be sufficiently important to warrant limiting a constitutional right, and the means chosen by the state authority must be proportional to that objective.

As to the first, the objective of safety of students and staff was conceded to be laudable—the first stage of the test was satisfied. CSMB had also submitted considerable evidence from various stakeholders in the educational community demonstrating the importance of safety in schools and the upsurge in problems relating to weapons and violence in schools. The appropriate level of safety was held to be reasonable safety, not absolute safety, and the objective of ensuring such a level was a pressing and substantial objective. The CSMB decision had a rational connection with the objective of ensuring that level of safety.

The next consideration was whether the religious rights were impaired more than minimally (which need not be the least intrusive solution). The legislator, or decision-maker in this case, is given some leeway, so that the decision to establish an absolute prohibition regarding wearing a kirpan had to fall "within a range of reasonable alternatives."

> According to the CSMB, to allow the kirpan to be worn to school entails the risk that it could be used for violent purposes by the person wearing it or by another student who takes it away from him, that it could lead to a proliferation of weapons at the school, and that its presence could have a negative impact on the school environment. In support of this last point, the CSMB submits that the kirpan is a symbol of violence and that it sends a message that the use of force is the way to assert rights and resolve conflicts, in addition to undermining the perception of safety and compromising the spirit of fairness that should prevail in schools, in that its presence suggests the existence of a double standard.

There cannot be much doubt that, on the basis of the record, the CSMB was overcooking the argument. The son did not have behavioural problems and had never resorted to violence at school. There had been no suggestion that he would use his kirpan for violent purposes.

As for the risk of another student taking his kirpan away from him, it also seems to me to be quite low, especially if the kirpan is worn under conditions such as were imposed by ... the Superior Court. In the instant case, if the kirpan were worn in accordance with those conditions, any student wanting to take it away from Gurbaj Singh would first have to physically restrain him, then search through his clothes, remove the sheath from his guthra [undergarment], and try to unstitch or tear open the cloth enclosing the sheath in order to get to the kirpan. There is no question that a student who wanted to commit an act of violence could find another way to obtain a weapon, such as bringing one in from outside the school. Furthermore, there are many objects in schools that could be used to commit violent acts and that are much more easily obtained by students, such as scissors, pencils and baseball bats.

There had been no evidence of violence involving kirpans in Quebec schools. In fact, "... over the 100 years since Sikhs have been attending schools in Canada, not a single violent incident related to the presence of kirpans in schools has been reported." Nor did the evidence support the contention that other students would be forced to arm themselves in order to defend themselves.

The argument that the wearing of kirpans should be prohibited because the kirpan is a symbol of violence and because it sends a message that using force is necessary to assert rights and resolve conflict failed. Not only was that assertion contradicted by the evidence regarding the symbolic nature of the kirpan, it was also disrespectful to believers in the Sikh religion and did not take into account Canadian values based on multiculturalism. The conclusion was that CSMB had failed to demonstrate that it would be reasonable to conclude that an absolute prohibition against wearing a kirpan minimally impaired the son's rights.

A total prohibition against wearing a kirpan to school undermines the value of this religious symbol and sends students the message that some religious practices do not merit the same protection as others. On the other hand, accommodating Gurbaj Singh and allowing him to wear his kirpan under certain conditions demonstrates the importance that our society attaches to protecting freedom of religion and to showing respect for its minorities. The deleterious effects of a total prohibition thus outweigh its salutary effects.

Since Gurbaj Singh was no longer attending the school where the controversy began, the Court saw no point in restoring the judgment of the Superior Court (which had set out the conditions of wearing the kirpan at school), and simply declared the decision prohibiting the wearing of it to be null.

It was somewhat reassuring that the judges who preferred the administrative approach to the appeal nevertheless reached the same conclusion as the portion of the majority which considered the constitutional approach to be preferable. The eighth judge attempted to demonstrate that there was a range of flexibility in the approach to cases where one field of law (administrative) overlapped or intersected with another (constitutional)—it was not always clear, or settled in law, which would always be appropriate nor in what circumstances.

> The approaches followed to apply the *Canadian Charter* must be especially flexible when it comes to working out the relationship between administrative law and constitutional law. In verifying whether an administrative act is consistent with the fundamental normative order, recourse to administrative law principles remains initially appropriate for the purpose of determining whether the adopted measure is in conformity with the powers delegated by legislation to school authorities. If it is authorized by that delegation, the exercise of the discretion to adopt safety measures to protect the public and students must then be assessed in light of constitutional guarantees and the values they reflect.

This is a good example of how the Court keeps its attention focused on the broad principles embraced by the *Charter* and then works toward purposeful solutions that give meaning to the protections that are part of the Canadian Constitution. What appears in the media is often judgmental, but seldom focuses on the careful and principled analysis that led to the decision by the Court.

The Niqab – Identifying the Inherent Difficulties

R. v. N.S. [2012] 3 S.C.R. 726

The accused, the cousin and the uncle of N.S., were charged with having sexually assaulted her. N.S. was a Muslim and wished to testify during the preliminary inquiry, while wearing her niqab, a garment that covered all of her features except for her eyes. The accused sought an order from that court that she be obliged to remove her niqab while testifying. Her response was that her religious belief required her to wear a niqab in public where men might see her. She acknowledged that she had removed the niqab for purposes of the photograph on her driver's license (taken by a female photographer) and that she would, if required, remove it for security purposes at a border crossing. The judge who was conducting the preliminary inquiry concluded that her religious belief was "not that strong" and ordered her to remove the niqab. N.S. objected and the inquiry was adjourned while she applied to the Ontario Superior Court of Justice to quash the order and to allow her to testify while wearing the niqab.

This was a case that was certainly destined to reach the Supreme Court of Canada. In the Superior Court of Justice, the order of the judge conducting the preliminary inquiry was quashed and N.S. was held to be allowed to testify while wearing the niqab, if she asserted a sincere religious reason for doing so, but that the preliminary inquiry judge would have the option to exclude her evidence if the niqab were found to have prevented true cross-examination. This outcome satisfied neither N.S. nor the co-accused and the matter then went to the Ontario Court of Appeal. There the matter of a reconciliation between the religious beliefs of N.S. and the possible impingement of the fair trial rights was dealt with in some detail. If the court procedures could not be reconciled to accommodate the religious practices, then the fair-trial interest of the accused might require that N.S. be ordered to remove her niqab. That, in turn, would depend on whether her credibility was in issue, how much the niqab interfered with the assessment of credibility, whether the trial was a jury trial or a judge-alone trial, the nature of the evidence to be given (central/peripheral—controversial/uncontested), the nature of the defense offered, as well as other constitutional values and societal interests. The Court of Appeal returned the matter to the preliminary-inquiry judge, to be dealt with as directed. N.S. appealed to the Supreme Court of Canada.

The Court agreed with the assessment of the competing *Charter* rights, namely freedom of religion and fair-trial rights, which include the right to make full answer and defense.

> The first task ... is to determine whether ... allowing the witness to testify in a niqab is necessary to protect her freedom of religion. The second task is to determine whether requiring the witness to testify without the niqab is necessary in order to protect the fairness of the trial. This involves considering whether there are alternative measures for protecting trial fairness that would also allow the witness to exercise her religious practice. Finally, if there is a true conflict that cannot be avoided, it is necessary to assess the competing harms and determine whether the salutary effects of requiring the witness to remove the niqab (for example, reducing the risk of a wrongful conviction) outweigh the deleterious effects of doing so (for example, the harm from interfering with the witness' sincerely held religious belief)....

> Applying this framework involves answering four questions:

> 1. Would requiring the witness to remove the niqab while testifying interfere with her religious freedom?
> 2. Would permitting the witness to wear the niqab while testifying create a serious risk to trial fairness?

3. Is there a way to accommodate both rights and avoid the conflict between them?

4. If no accommodation is possible, do the salutary effects of requiring the witness to remove the niqab outweigh the deleterious effects of doing so?

The Court concluded that the preliminary-inquiry judge failed to conduct an adequate inquiry as to whether N.S. had a sincere religious belief regarding her refusal to remove the niqab. The question was whether she had a sincere belief, not necessarily the strength of the belief. Regarding the trial-fairness argument, there was no evidence before the Court connecting seeing a witness's face with effective cross-examination and accurate assessment of the witness's credibility. On the other hand (although this was not conclusive), there was a long tradition at common law, in the provisions of the *Criminal Code*, and in judicial pronouncements, that the ability to see a witness was an important feature of a fair trial.

As a rule, witnesses in criminal trials testify in open court, with their faces visible to counsel, judge, and jury. Nothing in the record before the Court tended to displace the long-standing assumptions of the common law in that regard. In addition, covering the face of a witness may well impede credibility assessment by the trier of fact—be it judge or jury. Thus, on the record, there was a strong connection between the ability to see the face of a witness and a fair trial, although that could be tempered depending on the evidence to be provided by the witness. If a niqab were to pose no serious risk to trial fairness, then a witness who, based on sincere religious belief wishes to wear it, may do so.

The question of how to reconcile the two rights is more difficult.

> When the matter returns to the preliminary inquiry judge, the parties should be able to place before the court evidence relating to possible options for accommodation of the potentially conflicting claims. This is the first step of the reconciliation process. The question is whether there is a reasonably available alternative that would conform to the witness's religious convictions while still preventing a serious risk to trial fairness. On the facts of this case, it may be that no accommodation is possible; excluding men from the courtroom would have implications for the open court principle, the right of the accused to be present at his trial, and potentially his right to counsel of his choice.

Testifying without the niqab via closed-circuit television or behind a one-way screen may not satisfy N.S.'s religious obligations. However, when this case is reheard, the preliminary inquiry judge must consider the possibility of accommodation based on the evidence presented by the parties.

Finally, as to the balancing of the salutary and deleterious effects of one choice over the other, the Court could do little more than provide some general guidelines. It rejected both of the extreme positions urged upon it by various parties and interveners, namely that a witness should always be permitted to wear a niqab while testifying in court, on the one hand, and, on the other, that she should never be allowed to do so. The whole consideration involves a proportionality inquiry, weighing the effect of insisting that a witness remove the niqab if she is to testify against the effect of permitting her to wear it on the stand.

Lower courts and trial judges were alerted to some of the applicable considerations. First was the possible damage to religious freedom:

In terms of the deleterious effects of requiring the witness to remove her niqab while testifying, the judge must look at the harm that would be done by limiting the sincerely held religious practice. Sincerity of belief is already established as the first step in determining whether the [*Charter*] s. 2(a) right is engaged; at this stage the task is to evaluate the impact of failing to protect that sincere belief in the particular context. It is difficult to measure the value of adherence to religious conviction, or the injury caused by being required to depart from it. The value of adherence does not depend on whether a religious practice is a voluntary expression of faith or a mandatory obligation under religious doctrine. ... However, certain considerations may be helpful. How important is the practice to the claimant? What is the degree of state interference with the religious practice? ... How does the actual situation in the courtroom "the people present and any measures that can be put in place to limit facial exposure" affect the harm to the claimant of limiting her religious practice? These are but some considerations that may be relevant to determining the impact of an order to remove the niqab on the witness's right to freedom of religion.

Then came some of the implications on requiring removal of the niqab:

The judge should also consider the broader societal harms of requiring a witness to remove the niqab in order to testify. N.S. and supporting interveners argue that if niqab-wearing women are required to remove the niqab while testifying against their sincere religious belief they will be reluctant to report offences and pursue their prosecution, or to otherwise participate in the justice system. The wrongs done to them will remain unredressed. They will effectively be denied justice. The perpetrators of crimes against them will go unpunished, immune from legal consequences. These considerations may be especially weighty in a sexual assault case such as this one. In recent decades the justice system, recognizing the seriousness of sexual assault and the extent to which it is under-reported, has vigorously pursued those who commit this crime. Laws have been changed to encourage women and children to come forward to testify. Myths that once stood in the way of conviction have been set aside.

The Court then reinforced the fundamental nature of a fair trial as an essential societal value:

Having considered the deleterious effects of requiring the witness to remove the niqab, the judge must consider the salutary effects of doing so. These include preventing harm to the fair trial interest of the accused and safeguarding the repute of the administration of justice. An important consideration will be the extent to which effective cross-examination and credibility assessment on this witness's testimony is central to the case. On an individual level, the cost of an unfair trial is severe. The right to a fair trial is a fundamental pillar without which the edifice of the rule of law would crumble. No less is at stake than an individual's "liberty," his right to live in freedom unless the state proves beyond a reasonable doubt that he committed a crime meriting imprisonment. This is of critical importance not only to the individual on trial, but to public confidence in the justice system.

These are not easy cases for the courts to decide. The onus placed on trial judges in circumstances of this nature is, to put it at its lowest, extremely difficult. It is, however, a measure of the openness of Canadian society and the existence of the *Charter* as part of the Canadian Constitution that such questions are given such earnest attention and that every possible effort is made to attempt to reconcile the competing societal interests.

This debate is far from concluded and we may yet see the Court dealing with future appeals in the same case. The longer it takes, the more likely that the accused will never get to trial on the charges.

The Right to Die: Beginning a Legal Debate

Rodriguez v. British Columbia   [1993] 3 S.C.R. 519

The facts in this case were not in dispute and were publicly well-known. Sue Rodriguez was a forty-two-year-old woman suffering from amyotrophic lateral sclerosis (ALS), generally referred to as Lou Gehrig's disease. Her life expectancy was between two and fourteen months, but her condition was rapidly deteriorating. Very soon she would lose the ability to swallow, speak, walk, and move her body without assistance. Thereafter she would lose the capacity to breathe without a respirator, eat without gastrotomy and would eventually be confined to a bed. She knew of her condition, the trajectory of the illness and the inevitability of how her life would end. Her wish was to control the circumstances, timing and manner of her death. She did not want to die so long as she still had the capacity to enjoy life, but by the time she was no longer able to enjoy life, she would be physically unable to terminate her life without assistance. She sought an order that would allow a qualified medical practitioner to set up technological means by which she might, by her own hand, at the time of her choosing, end her life.

The Supreme Court of British Columbia dismissed her application. She appealed to the B.C. Court of Appeal, where a divided court dismissed her appeal. She then obtained leave to appeal to the Supreme Court of Canada, which also dismissed her appeal by the narrowest of margins (five to four).

The majority framed the issues as follows:

I have read the reasons of the Chief Justice and those of McLachlin J. herein. The result of the reasons of my colleagues is that all persons who by reason of disability are unable to commit suicide have a right under the *Canadian Charter of Rights and Freedoms* to be free from government interference in procuring the assistance of others to take their life. They are entitled to a constitutional exemption from the operation of s. 241 of the *Criminal Code* … which prohibits the giving of assistance to commit suicide (hereinafter referred to as "assisted suicide"). The exemption would apply during the period that this Court's order would be suspended and thereafter Parliament could only replace the legislation subject to this right. I must respectfully disagree with the conclusion reached by my colleagues and with their reasons. In my view, nothing in the *Charter* mandates this result which raises the following serious concerns:

1. It recognizes a constitutional right to legally assisted suicide beyond that of any country in the western world, beyond any serious proposal for reform in the western world and beyond the claim made in this very case.
2. It fails to provide the safeguards which are required either under the Dutch guidelines or the recent proposals for reform in the states of Washington and California which were defeated by voters in those states principally because comparable and even more stringent safeguards were considered inadequate.
3. The conditions imposed are vague and in some respects unenforceable. While the proposals in California were criticized for failure to specify the type of physician who is authorized to assist and the Dutch guidelines specify the treating physician, the conditions imposed by my colleague do not require that the person assisting be a physician or impose any restriction in this regard. Since much of the medical profession is opposed to being involved in assisting suicide because it is antithetical to their role as healers of the sick, many doctors will refuse to assist, leaving open the potential for the growth of a macabre speciality in this area reminiscent of Dr. Kervorkian and his suicide machine.
4. To add to the uncertainty of the conditions, they are to serve merely as guidelines, leaving it to individual judges to decide upon application whether to grant or withhold the right to commit suicide. In the case of the appellant, the remedy proposed by the Chief Justice, concurred in by McLachlin J., would not require such an application. She alone is to decide that the conditions or guidelines

are complied with. Any judicial review of this decision would only occur if she were to commit suicide and a charge were laid against the person who assisted her. The reasons of McLachlin J. remove any requirement to monitor the choice made by the appellant to commit suicide so that the act might occur after the last expression of the desire to commit suicide is stale-dated.

I have concluded that the conclusion of my colleagues cannot be supported under the provisions of the *Charter*.

The analysis that followed was essentially mainstream, in the sense that the majority was reluctant to venture into changes in the effect of the criminal law, notwithstanding the impact of the *Charter*. To give effect to Rodriguez's application would have been to move uncertain yardsticks far beyond where they might be today. The history of the law regarding suicide and the assistance in committing suicide showed an overriding concern with the sanctity of life as a fundamental underpinning of societal values, including the protection of the weak, who might be vulnerable and unduly influenced. Although it was not possible to say that the *Criminal Code* provisions against assisted suicide did not infringe on the *Charter* right to security of the person, on balance they did not do so in a manner that offended fundamental principles of justice. It was also clear that suicide itself was not a crime (although historically it was held to have been one), but assisting in suicide remained criminal behaviour. Thus, Rodriguez, had she been able to commit suicide on her own, would not have committed a crime; it was her (anticipated) physical inability to act on her own that provided the particular feature of the appeal.

One of the dissenting judges expressed the conundrum as follows:

> This brings us to the critical issue in this case. Does the fact that the legal regime which regulates suicide denies to Sue Rodriguez the right to commit suicide because of her physical capacity, render the scheme arbitrary and hence in violation of s. 7? Under the scheme Parliament has set up, the physically able person is legally allowed to end his or her life; he or she cannot be criminally penalized for attempting or committing suicide. But the person who is physically unable to accomplish the act is not similarly allowed to end her life. This is the effect of s. 241(b) of the *Criminal Code*, which criminalizes the

act of assisting a person to commit suicide and which may render the person who desires to commit suicide a conspirator to that crime. Assuming without deciding that Parliament could criminalize all suicide, whether assisted or not, does the fact that suicide is not criminal make the criminalization of all assistance in suicide arbitrary?

... What is the difference between suicide and assisted suicide that justifies making the one lawful and the other a crime, that justifies allowing some this choice, while denying it to others?

The answer to this question depends on whether the denial to Sue Rodriguez of what is available to others can be justified. It is argued that the denial to Sue Rodriguez of the capacity to treat her body in a way available to the physically able is justified because to permit assisted suicide will open the doors, if not the floodgates, to the killing of disabled persons who may not truly consent to death. The argument is essentially this. There may be no reason on the facts of Sue Rodriguez's case for denying her the choice to end her life, a choice that those physically able have available to them. Nevertheless, she must be denied that choice because of the danger that other people may wrongfully abuse the power they have over the weak and ill, and may end the lives of those persons against their consent. Thus, Sue Rodriquez is asked to bear the burden of the chance that other people in other situations may act criminally to kill others or improperly sway them to suicide. She is asked to serve as a scapegoat.

Continuing, the judge noted that the principle of fundamental justice requires that each person, considered individually, be treated fairly by the law. The fear that abuse might arise if an individual is permitted that which she is wrongly denied was said to play no part at the initial stage of assessment. For Sue Rodriguez to be denied what was available to others merely because it was possible that other people, at some other time, might suffer not what she sought, but an act of killing without consent, did not accord with the principles of fundamental justice. There was, in addition, no absolute rule that causing or assisting in the death of another was criminally wrong (e.g., omissions that lead to death, failure to provide "necessities of life," killing in self-defence). In summary, the effect of the distinction between suicide and assisted suicide, one being criminal and the other not, was to prevent people like Rodriguez from exercising the autonomy over their bodies that was available to other people.

This case was another in which the often delicate balance between the roles of Parliament and the courts needed consideration. The courts are generally more sensitive on this issue than are the legislatures. There had been "strenuous" argument that it was the role of Parliament to deal with assisted suicide and that the courts should not get involved. In the B.C. Court of Appeal, each of the judges forming the majority in that court had said "it is my view in areas with public opinion at either extreme, and which involve basically philosophical and not legal considerations, it is proper that the matter be left in the hands of Parliament as historically has been the case," and "On the material available to us, we are in no position to assess the consensus in Canada with respect to assisted suicide ... I would leave to Parliament the responsibility of taking the pulse of the nation." This prompted the following observation:

> Were the task before me that of taking the pulse of the nation, I too should quail, although as a matter of constitutional obligation, a court faced with a *Charter* breach may not enjoy the luxury of choosing what it will and will not decide. I do not, however, see this as the task which faces the Court in this case. We were not asked to second guess Parliament's objective of criminalizing the assistance of suicide. Our task was the much more modest one of determining whether, given the legislative scheme regulating suicide which Parliament has put in place, the denial to Sue Rodriguez of the ability to end her life is arbitrary and hence amounts to a limit on her security of the person which does not comport with the principles of fundamental justice. Parliament has in fact chosen to legislate on suicide. It has set up a scheme which makes suicide lawful, but which makes assisted suicide criminal. The only question is whether Parliament, having chosen to act in this sensitive area touching the autonomy of people over their bodies, has done so in a way which is fundamentally fair to all. The focus is not on why Parliament has acted, but on the way it has acted.

The courts, indeed each of the three that heard the application by Rodriguez, denied her the relief that she sought. She did, however, in the end, resort to assisted suicide by lethal injection, notwithstanding those judgments. No charges were laid against whomever may have been involved.

It is all but certain that this case will not be the last to reach the Supreme Court of Canada dealing with the right to die.

In late 2013, a variation on the same theme arose in the case of *Cuthbertson v. Rasouli*, in which withdrawal by physicians of medical life support for someone in a persistent vegetative state and with no hope of recovery was not permitted when the spouse of the patient refused to give consent to such withdrawal. The matter was left to be determined by the Board established under the provincial *Health Care Consent Act*, which would have the duty to weigh the various considerations involved.

Lawyers aside, it was a case that demonstrates the utility of expressing one's wishes in such circumstances (e.g., no "heroic measures" or continuation of medical treatment in case of complete disability) well in advance of any crisis—the so-called "living will."

Discrimination Based on Sexual Orientation

Vriend v. Alberta [1998] 1 S.C.R. 493

When Alberta introduced the *Individual's Rights Protection Act*, the Minister responsible for the legislation stated:

> ... it is ... the commitment of this legislature that we regard The Individual's Rights Protection Act in primacy to any other legislative enactment. ... [We] have committed ourselves to suggest that Alberta is not the place for partial rights or half freedoms, but that Alberta hopefully will become the place where each and every man and woman will be able to stand on his (*sic*) own two feet and be recognized as an individual and not as a member of a particular class.

The statute prohibited discrimination in a number of areas of public life and established a Human Rights Commission to deal with complaints regarding discrimination. Over the years, additional grounds of discrimination were added, including some arising from the Canadian *Charter* and judicial interpretation of it. By 1990, the statute included the following grounds of prohibited discrimination: race, religious beliefs, colour, gender, physical disability, mental disability, age, ancestry, and place of origin. The list did not include sexual orientation. This was not an oversight. There had been many calls for its inclusion. The government had chosen not to respond to those calls.

Delwin Vriend was a laboratory coordinator at King's College in

Edmonton, having begun work in 1987, and he became a permanent and full-time employee in 1988. In the course of his employment, he received positive evaluations, salary increases, and promotions for his work performance. In February 1990, the president of the College inquired as to whether Vriend was homosexual. He acknowledged that he was. In January 1991, the College's board of governors adopted a position statement on homosexuality. Shortly thereafter, the College president requested Vriend's resignation. Vriend declined this invitation and, on January 28, 1991, the College terminated his employment, on the sole basis that he did not comply with the College's policy on homosexual practice. An appeal and application for reinstatement was refused.

His next step was to file a complaint in June 1991 with the Alberta Human Rights Commission based on his employer's discrimination on the grounds of sexual orientation. A month later, the Commission advised him that he could not file such a complaint under the statute because sexual orientation was not a protected ground. This led to filing a motion with the Alberta Court of Queen's Bench (the provincial superior court) for declaratory relief and a challenge to the constitutionality of several provisions of the statute on the basis that they contravened section 15(1) of the *Charter*. The trial judge agreed that the omission of protection against sexual orientation was an unjustified violation of the *Charter* and ordered that *sexual orientation* be read into the specific provisions of the statute as a prohibited ground of appeal. In a majority decision, the Court of Appeal allowed the government's appeal. The Supreme Court of Canada granted leave to appeal in 1997. The case was heard in November of that same year and the decision rendered in early April 1998.

One of the first questions the Court had to ask itself was whether there could be a *Charter* violation when the particular matter arose from a legislative omission. The *Charter*, in the context of this appeal, applies to the legislature and government of each province in respect of all matters within the authority of the legislature of each province. Alberta argued that section 15 of the *Charter* should not apply because the case concerned a legislative omission. This argument was rejected on the basis that the legislation was within the scope of the provincial legislative authority. A further argument was that the courts must defer to a decision of the legislature not to enact a particular provision and that *Charter* review should be restricted so that such decisions (not to enact) will not be challenged. The Court rejected the argument, partly on the "very problematic distinction it draws between legislative action and inaction," but also on the substantial alteration of the considerations of legislative deference in *Charter* analysis.

> It is suggested that this appeal represents a contest between the power of the democratically elected legislatures to pass the laws they see fit, and the power of the courts to disallow those laws, or to dictate that certain matters be included in those laws. To put the issue in this way is misleading and erroneous. Quite simply, it is not the courts which limit the legislatures. Rather, it is the Constitution, which must be interpreted by the courts, that limits the legislatures. This is necessarily true of all constitutional democracies. Citizens must have the right to challenge laws which they consider to be beyond the powers of the legislatures. When such a challenge is properly made, the courts must, pursuant to their constitutional duty, rule on the challenge. It is said, however, that this case is different because the challenge centres on the legislature's failure to extend the protection of a law to a particular group of people. This position assumes that it is only a positive act rather than an omission which may be scrutinized under the *Charter*. In my view … there is no legal basis for drawing such a distinction. In this as in other cases, the courts have a duty to determine whether the challenge is justified. It is not a question … of the courts imposing their view of "ideal" legislation, but rather of determining whether the challenged legislative act or omission is constitutional or not.

The Court was generally unsympathetic to the arguments submitted by the Alberta government, all the more so in the face of the government's considered and specific positive actions to make sure that the protective procedures of the Human Rights Commission were not available to persons discriminated against on the basis of sexual orientation.

The fundamental principle underlying the *Charter* and section 15 is that of equality.

> It is easy to say that everyone who is just like "us" is entitled to equality. Everyone finds it more difficult to say that those who are "different" from us in some way should have the same equality rights that we enjoy. Yet so soon as

we say any enumerated or analogous group is less deserving and unworthy of equal protection and benefit of the law all minorities and all of Canadian society are demeaned. It is so deceptively simple and so devastatingly injurious to say that those who are handicapped or of a different race, or religion, or colour or sexual orientation are less worthy. Yet, if any enumerated or analogous group is denied the equality provided by s. 15 then the equality of every other minority group is threatened. That equality is guaranteed by our constitution. If equality rights for minorities had been recognized, the all too frequent tragedies of history might have been avoided. It can never be forgotten that discrimination is the antithesis of equality and that it is the recognition of equality which will foster the dignity of every individual.

Working from this platform, the Court rejected Alberta's argument that no reference to sexual orientation created a "neutral silence," and that the provisions of the statute treated heterosexuals and homosexuals identically, so there could be no discrimination. It had been repeatedly decided that identical treatment will not always constitute equal treatment. The Court had already held in other cases that discrimination can arise from under-inclusive legislation. The "silence" in the legislation regarding sexual orientation was not "neutral." Homosexuals were treated differently from other disadvantaged groups and from heterosexuals. This included exclusion from government policy on discrimination and access to the established remedial process of a complaint to the Human Rights Commission.

The Alberta government failed to demonstrate that it had a reasonable basis to exclude sexual orientation from the legislation, thus giving homosexuals no protection, let alone equal protection, against discrimination on the basis of sexual orientation. There was, accordingly, no need for judicial deference to the decision of the legislature in those circumstances. Similarly, since Alberta had also failed to show any beneficial effect of the exclusion in the promotion and protection of human rights, there was no proportionality between achieving the legislative goal and the infringement of Vriend's equality rights, so it could not be justified as appropriate in a free and democratic society.

That left only the consideration of what was the best remedy for the Court to apply. The *Charter* inconsistency was the exclusion of sexual orientation from the protection granted by the Alberta statute. The possible remedies include striking down the legislation, severance of the offending sections, striking down, or severance with a temporary suspension of the declaration of invalidity, reading down, and reading provisions into the legislation. The Court eliminated reading down the statute, since the violation was the result of an omission. Because several sections had been challenged as a result of the appeal, severing them from the balance of the statute might effectively amount to striking down the entire statute. Two of the judges in the Court of Appeal had stated that the appropriate remedy would be to declare the relevant provisions unconstitutional and to suspend the declaration for a period of time to allow the legislature to address the matter. Vriend and the other appellants wanted the remedy to be reading in of sexual orientation into the provisions.

Reading in calls for a balancing of two principles: that of respect for the role of the legislature and of respect for the purposes of the *Charter*. "The purpose of reading in is to be as faithful as possible within the requirements of the Constitution to the scheme enacted by the Legislature." Since the avowed purpose of the statute was the "recognition and protection of the inherent dignity and inalienable rights of Albertans through the elimination of discriminatory practices," the Court concluded that reading in would "minimize interference with this clearly legitimate legislative purpose and thereby avoid excessive intrusion into the legislative sphere." Striking down the statute would risk depriving all Albertans of human-rights protection, which would unduly interfere with the enacted scheme. Respect for the purpose of the *Charter* was assured by its concern with the promotion of inherent dignity and inalienable rights. Expanding the list of prohibited grounds of discrimination would augment the scope of the Alberta statute's protections, which would be consistent with the purposes of the *Charter*, while striking down the statute would be antithetical to its purposes.

The Court took additional comfort from the fact that in 1993, Alberta had created a Human Rights Review Panel to conduct a public review of the statute and the Human Rights Commission. The Panel's report included a recommendation to include sexual orientation as a prohibited ground of discrimination in all areas covered by the statute. The government punted, stating that the recommendation would be dealt with through the current case. The Court considered that to be an express invitation to read sexual orientation into the statute in the event that it found the *Charter* to have been violated. Thus, the reading-in remedy was entirely consistent with the legislative intention.

One of the Alberta Court of Appeal judges had been particularly strident about reading in, stating: "Allowing judicial, and basically final, proclamation of legislative change ignores our adopted British parliamentary safeguards, historic in themselves, and which are the practical bulkheads that protect representative government. When unelected judges choose to legislate, parliamentary checks, balances and conventions are simply shelved." The Court's answer to this rhetoric was clear and concise:

> With respect, I do not agree. When a court remedies an unconstitutional statute by reading in provisions, no doubt this constrains the legislative process and therefore should not be done needlessly, but only after considered examination. However, in my view, the "parliamentary safeguards" remain. Governments are free to modify the amended legislation by passing exceptions and defences which they feel can be justified under s. 1 of the *Charter*. Thus, when a court reads in, this is not the end of the legislative process because the legislature can pass new legislation in response ... Moreover, the legislators can always turn to s. 33 of the *Charter*, the override provision, which in my view is the ultimate "parliamentary safeguard."

The impact of this decision on Canadian society cannot be overstated: discrimination on the basis of sexual orientation is unacceptable.

Judicial Deference to Specially Created Tribunals

C.U.P.E. v. N.B. Liquor Corporation   [1979] 2 S.C.R. 227

This was a unanimous decision of the full Court on the matter of the degree of deference to be shown by the courts where the legislature has assigned a particular subject matter to a specialized board or tribunal. In this case, involving public service labour relations in New Brunswick, the designated entity was the Public Service Labour Relations Board.

The background was a lawful strike by Local 963 of the Canadian Union of Public Employees against the New Brunswick Liquor Corporation (NBLC). *Lawful* in this context meant that the necessary conditions permitting the strike had been followed, so there was no issue of the strike being illegal. NBLC did not dispute the fact that, during the course of the strike, it was replacing the employees who were striking with management personnel, who were then doing work that was normally done by the striking employees. The union complained to the Board that such practice was contrary to the *Public Service Labour Relations Act (Act)*, which was denied by NBLC, which, in turn, filed its own complaint regarding the picketing tactics used by the union, alleging that they violated the *Act*. The complaints were heard by the Board at the same time.

The Board agreed with NBLC regarding the picketing activities of the union and made an order for it to cease and desist from its picketing practices. No appeal was taken from that portion of the decision. The

Board also agreed with the union regarding the use of management personnel by NBLC, which portion of the decision gave rise to appeals to the Supreme Court of New Brunswick, Appeals Division, and then to the Supreme Court of Canada.

The provision of the *Act* that applied read as follows:

> 102(3) Where subsection (1) and subsection (2) are complied with [they had been] employees may strike and during the continuance of the strike
> a. The employer shall not replace the striking employees or fill their position with any other employee, and
> b. No employee shall picket, parade or in any manner demonstrate in or near any place of business of the employer.

Both courts were clear that subsection 102(3)(a) was very badly drafted. The Court stated that, "It bristles with ambiguities." In the Appeals Division of the lower court, one of the judges had said, "Four possible interpretations immediately come to mind." Poorly worded statutes provide grist for the mill of lawyers and acid indigestion for those called upon to interpret them.

The Board's view, summarized by the Court, had been that:

> ... when the Legislature saw fit to grant the right to strike to public employees, it intended through the enactment of s. 102(3) to restrict the possibility of picket-line violence by prohibiting strikebreaking, on the one hand, and picketing, on the other. This apparent intention, the Board held, would be frustrated if the words "with any other employee" were to be interpreted as modifying "replace" as well as "fill their position," "for in that case there would be nothing to stop the Employer from replacing the strikers with anyone not coming within the definition of 'employee' in the *Public Service Labour Relations Act*. ... The result of such an interpretation would be that the strikers would have been deprived of their right to picket, but the employer would not have been deprived of the right to employ strikebreakers."

The Board recognized the reach of their decision:

> In coming to this conclusion we have been mindful of the fact that the result of our decision will force the Employer to close down some of

the operations which are now being carried on and that this may have far reaching effects. The Board ordered the employer to refrain from the use of management personnel to do work normally done by the members of the bargaining unit in any of the employer's places of business.

When the NBLC challenge reached the Appeals Division, things went a bit sideways, as they often do in the process of litigation, and the question was raised as to whether section 102(3) of the *Act* raised a jurisdictional issue for the Board—in other words, whether the Board had the power to consider the challenge in the first place. The question of what is, or is not, jurisdictional can be difficult to determine and the Court simply noted this, as well as observing that the courts should not brand matters which are not reasonably clearly jurisdictional in nature, as jurisdictional. It ultimately disagreed with the Appeals Division's conclusion that jurisdiction had been exceeded. The Board's jurisdiction was provided by section 19(1)(a) of the *Act*:

19(1) The Board shall examine and inquire into any complaint made to it that the employer, or any person acting on its behalf, or that an employee organization, or any person acting on its behalf, or any other person, has failed
(a) to observe any prohibition or to give effect to any provision contained in the *Act* or the regulations under this *Act*.

The Court had little difficulty in disposing of the Appeals Division concerns. The parties before the Board were an employer and a bargaining unit. The general subject matter of the dispute was "unquestionably" within the confines of the *Act*. The Board had been asked to determine whether certain activities by the employer and of the union were in violation of the provisions of section 102(3) of the *Act* and neither of the parties had taken objection on the basis of jurisdiction. It was, therefore, not possible to suggest that the Board did not have the jurisdiction to undertake an inquiry.

Key as well was that the *Act* also contained what is called a "privative" clause, to protect the decisions taken by the Board and made within its jurisdiction. In essence, privative clauses are intended to prevent or limit appeals from decisions taken, in this case, by the statutorily created body. The clause was contained in section 101:

101(1) Except as provided in this *Act*, every award, order, direction, decision, declaration, or ruling of the Board, ... is final and shall not be questioned or reviewed in any court.

101(2) No order shall be made or process entered, and no proceedings shall be taken in any court, ... to question, review, prohibit or restrain the Board ... in any of its ... proceedings.

Commenting on this language, the Court stated:

Section 101 constitutes a clear statutory direction on the part of the Legislature that public sector labour matters be promptly and finally decided by the Board. Privative clauses of this nature are typically found in labour relations legislation. The rationale for protection of a labour board's decisions within jurisdiction is straightforward and compelling. The labour board is a specialized tribunal which administers a comprehensive statute regulating labour relations. In the administration of that regime, a board is called upon not only to find facts and decide questions of law, but also to exercise its understanding of the body of jurisprudence that has developed around the collective bargaining system, as understood in Canada, and its labour relations sense acquired from accumulated experience in the area. The usual reasons for judicial restraint upon review of labour board decisions are only reinforced in a case such as one at the bar. Not only has the Legislature confided certain decisions to an administrative board, but to a separate and distinct Public Service Labour Relations Board. That Board is given broad powers—broader than those typically vested in a labour board—to supervise and administer the novel system of collective bargaining created by the *Public Service Labour Relations Act*. The *Act* calls for a delicate balance between the need to maintain public services, and the need to maintain collective bargaining. Considerable sensitivity and unique expertise on the part of Board members is all the more required if the twin purposes of the legislation are to be met. Nowhere is the application of those skills more evident than in the supervision of a lawful strike by public service employees under the *Act*.

The Court went on to note that the language of section 102(3) was unique to the New Brunswick legislation and not found in any other public-sector labour legislation in Canada, so that its interpretation was at the heart of the specialized jurisdiction confided to the Board. The implication of this was that even if the Board's decision might not be "correct," any such error would be protected from review by the privative clause in section 101.

The Court concluded that the Board's decision on the interpretation of section 102(3) was neither better nor worse than some of the interpretations offered by the Appeals Division and certainly could not be characterized as patently unreasonable.

The importance of section 102(3) can be highlighted by the difference between a public-sector strike and one in the private sector. In the private sector, in particular, the idealized version of a picket line is that it is simply informative. The real purpose, however, generally goes much further—it is to shut down the employer's business, or at the very least to make it as difficult as possible to maintain it, by dissuading groups and individuals from having anything to do with it. This may also extend to managerial personnel. On the other side of the confrontation, the employer attempts to maintain the business by using managerial personnel to do the strikers' work, hiring strikebreakers and maintaining lines of communication and access to incoming and outgoing services and products. These actions, in private-sector labour relations, are typically legal and are integral parts of the economic conflict. Section 102(3) provides a completely different dynamic for the public service. The striking employees are barred from picketing in or near any place of the employer's business and the employer is barred from replacing strikers or filling their positions with any other employee.

The standard of deference in the circumstances was very high, as it was clear that the legislative scheme was both unique and entrusted to the administration of the Board. It is not the role of the courts to substitute themselves for the legislatures. They will step in if such boards exceed the jurisdiction conferred upon them by the legislatures; the boards must be "correct" as to their capacity to make the decisions within the scope of the legislation, and they must act in good faith, on the basis of the evidence before them and not on any extraneous factors, but, thereafter, they are free to reach whatever decisions seem appropriate.

The importance of the case is the definitive statement by a unanimous Court that the courts should not lightly interfere with the legisla-

tive intention of governments, when such governments assign administrative responsibility to specialized tribunals.

Administrative Procedures: Procedural Fairness and Reasonable Apprehension of Bias

Baker v. Canada (Minister of Citizenship and Immigration)
[1999] 2 S.C.R. 817

Mavis Baker, a Jamaican citizen, entered Canada as a visitor in 1981. She remained here, without ever being granted permanent-resident status, supporting herself illegally as a live-in domestic worker for eleven years. During that time, she gave birth to four children, all of whom were Canadian citizens. Following the birth of her fourth child in 1992, Ms. Baker suffered post-partum psychosis and was diagnosed with paranoid schizophrenia. She applied for welfare. Two of her children were in the care of their natural father, and two were temporarily in foster care, but returned to Ms. Baker's care when her condition improved.

In December 1992, Ms. Baker was ordered deported. She had overstayed her visitor's visa, in addition to working in this country illegally. Normally, in order to be re-admitted to Canada, Ms. Baker would have had to apply for permanent resident status from outside the country. Instead she applied for an exemption from this requirement, based on a battery of humanitarian and compassionate considerations, including the fact that she was making progress with her illness, that she might become ill again if forced to return to Jamaica, that she was the sole caregiver for two of her children, that her two other children in the care of their natural father depended on her for emotional support and that she too would suffer emotional hardship if separated from them.

The answer to this application came in April 1994, in a letter from the immigration authorities advising Ms. Baker that there were insufficient humanitarian and compassionate grounds to warrant processing her application within Canada. No reasons for the decision were given. Upon request, Ms. Baker was provided with the notes an immigration officer had made on her case, which were subsequently forwarded to the author of her refusal letter. Ms. Baker appealed the decision. In May 1994, she was directed to report for removal from Canada in the following month, although her deportation was stayed until the outcome of the appeal. In 1995, the Federal Court – Trial Division rejected Ms. Baker's appeal, as did the Federal Court of Appeal in 1997. Ms. Baker was, however, granted leave to appeal to the Supreme Court of Canada.

The Court did not need to consider the *Charter* issues, since the matter could be resolved by reference to the principles of administrative law and statutory interpretation. The basic questions were whether the principles of procedural fairness had been violated and whether there was a reasonable apprehension of bias in the making of the decision. There were some collateral issues that did not bear on the concerns discussed in this summary.

There was no dispute between the parties that a duty of procedural fairness was owed in all human and compassionate decisions (referred to by the Court as H&C decisions)—the mere fact that such decisions were administrative and that they affect "the rights, privileges or interests" of the persons involved was sufficient to trigger application of the duty. The key, however, was to determine the applicable requirements flowing from that duty in particular circumstances.

Although the duty of fairness is flexible and variable, and depends on an appreciation of the particular statute and the rights affected, it is helpful to review the criteria that should be used in determining what procedural rights the duty of fairness requires in a given set of circumstances. I emphasize that underlying all these factors is the notion that the purpose of the participatory rights contained within the duty of procedural fairness is to ensure that administrative decisions are made using a fair and open procedure, appropriate to the decision being made and its statutory, institutional, and social context, with an opportunity for those affected by the decision to put forward their views and evidence fully and have them considered by the decision-maker.

Several issues were identified as examples. First, the closer the determinations to be made resembled judicial decision-making, the more the procedural protections would be required to approach the trial model. Second, greater procedural protections would likely apply when there was no appeal procedure contained within the applicable statute. Third, the greater the importance of the decision on the lives of those affected, the more stringent the procedural protections should be. Fourth, while legitimate expectations do not create substantive rights, nevertheless, they may affect the content of the duty of fairness, such as following the regular practices of the decision-makers. Fifth, important weight should be given to the choice of procedures made by the deciding agency and its institutional constraints.

The lack of an oral hearing prior to reaching the deportation decision did not violate the requirements of procedural fairness. Ms. Baker had had the opportunity to submit all of the written documentation necessary for consideration of her application and all of this information was in the possession of the decision-makers. More troublesome was the fact that no reasons were given for rejection of her application.

> In my opinion, it is now appropriate to recognize that, in certain circumstances, the duty of procedural fairness will require the provision of a written explanation for a decision. The strong arguments demonstrating the advantages of written reasons suggest that, in cases such as this where the decision has important significance for the individual, when there is a statutory right of appeal, or in other circumstances, some form of reasons should be required. This requirement has been developing in the common law elsewhere. The circumstances of the case at bar, [i.e., the present case] in my opinion, constitute one of the situations where reasons are necessary. The profound importance of an H&C decision to those affected ... militates in favour of a requirement that reasons be provided. It would be unfair for a person subject to a decision such as this one which is so critical to their [sic] future not to be told why the result was reached.

In this case, only the notes of the junior immigration officer were provided when Ms. Baker asked for reasons. No other reasons were proffered.

This set up the Court's consideration as to whether there was a reasonable apprehension of bias. Generally, the Court has held that the duty to act fairly is to act in a manner which does not give a reasonable apprehension of bias, a ruling which applies to all immigration officers playing a significant role in the making of decisions, whether they be subordinate in the process or be those who make the final decisions. This test for reasonable apprehension of bias has been expressed as:

> ... the apprehension of bias must be a reasonable one, held by reasonable and right minded persons, applying themselves to the question and obtaining thereon the required information. ... [T]hat test is "what would an informed person, viewing the matter realistically and practically—and having thought the matter through—conclude. Would he think it is more likely than not that [the decision-maker], whether consciously or unconsciously, would not decide fairly?

The Court concluded that a well-informed member of the community would perceive bias when reading the junior immigration officer's notes and conclude that he had failed to display an open mind, and that he had not weighed the circumstances of Baker's case free from stereotypes. Examples of his statements included:

HAS A TOTAL OF EIGHT CHILDREN

This case is a catastrophy [*sic*]. It is also an indictment of our "system" that the client came as a visitor in Aug. '81, was not ordered deported until Dec. '92 and in April '94 IS STILL HERE!

The PC [reference to Baker] is a paranoid schizophrenic and on welfare. She has no qualifications other than as a domestic. She has FOUR CHILDREN IN JAMAICA AND ANOTHER FOUR BORN HERE. She will, of course, be a tremendous strain on our social welfare systems for (probably) the rest of her life. There are no H&C factors other than her FOUR CANADIAN-BORN CHILDREN. Do we let her stay because of that? I am of the opinion that Canada can no longer afford this type of generosity. However, because of the circumstances involved, there is a potential for adverse publicity. I recommend refusal but you may wish to clear this with someone at Region.

There is a potential for violence—see charge of assault with a weapon.

The manner in which the notes were written, the linkage displayed between Baker's mental illness, her lack of training except as a domestic worker, the fact that she had several children, and the conclusion that she would be a strain on the social welfare system, were regarded by the Court as unfortunate. In addition, the immigration officer's conclusion drawn regarding Ms. Baker's health was contrary to the psychiatrist's letter-on-file, which had stated that, with treatment, she could remain well and return to being a productive member of society. Whether or not intended, the statements in the immigration assessment report gave the impression that the officer had been drawing conclusions based on his personal frustration with the "system," not on the evidence before him. There was, therefore, a reasonable apprehension of bias.

The finding of reasonable apprehension of bias was sufficient to dispose of the appeal in Baker's favour, but the Court went on to consider the proper approach to the review of discretionary decision-making. The concept of discretion is one that relates to decisions where the law does not provide for a specific outcome, or where a choice of options is available to a decision-maker, within a statutory framework. In general terms:

> Administrative law has traditionally approached the review of decisions classified as discretionary separately from those seen as involving the interpretation of law. The rule has been that decisions classified as discretionary may only be reviewed on limited grounds such as the bad faith of the decision-makers, the exercise of discretion for an improper purpose, and the use of irrelevant considerations. ... A general doctrine of "unreasonableness" has also sometimes been applied to discretionary decisions. ... In my opinion, these doctrines incorporate two central ideas—that discretionary decisions, like all other administrative decisions, must be made within the bounds of the jurisdiction conferred by the statute, but that considerable deference will be given to decision-makers by courts in reviewing the exercise of that discretion

and determining the scope of the decision-maker's jurisdiction. These doctrines recognize that it is the intention of a legislature, when using statutory language that confers broad choices on administrative agencies, that courts should not lightly interfere with such decisions, and should give considerable effect to decision-makers when reviewing the manner in which discretion was exercised. However, discretion must still be exercised in a manner that is within a reasonable interpretation of the margin of manoeuvre contemplated by the legislature, in accordance with the principles of the rule of law ... in line with general principles of administrative law governing the exercise of discretion, and consistent with the *Canadian Charter of Rights and Freedoms* ...

In such circumstances, the Court held that the standard of review should be reasonableness, giving some, but not complete, deference to the decision-maker. An unreasonable decision is one that "is not supported by reasons that can stand up to a somewhat probing examination." The failure to consider the interests of the children in Baker's case—in fact, the complete dismissal of their interests—was unreasonable, despite the deference that should be accorded the official's decision.

Although there were other important aspects to this decision, it clearly sets out principles of fairness, lack of bias, and reasonableness that must be applied by decision-makers, especially where decisions may have a profound impact on those persons affected by such rulings.

Can Courts Follow-up on their Own Rulings?

Doucet-Boudreau v. Nova Scotia (Minister of Education)
[2003] 3 S.C.R. 3

In this appeal, a sharply divided (five to four) Supreme Court decided that the courts have, in the case of *Charter* violations, broad scope to devise appropriate remedies and a power to enforce the judgments they have rendered. A strong minority was of the view that, once a court has rendered its decision, it has no further powers and, indeed, any subsequent involvement in the matter was both undesirable and unconstitutional, impinging on the implicit separation of powers between the legislative, executive, and judicial branches of a democratic society.

The background to the appeal was the effort on the part of francophone parents in Nova Scotia to force the Nova Scotia government to provide French-language facilities and programs at the secondary-school level. The government had advanced many explanations, unpersuasive to the parents, for its lack of action and the plaintiffs took action in the Nova Scotia courts on the basis of the *Charter*. The particular provisions were sections 23 and 24.

23.(1) Citizens of Canada

(a) whose first language learned and still understood is that of the English or French linguistic minority population of the province in which they reside, or

(b) who have received their primary school instruction in Canada in English or French and reside in a province where the language in which they received that instruction is the language of the English or French linguistic minority population of the province, have the right to have their children receive primary and secondary school instruction in that language in that province.

(2) Citizens of Canada of whom any child has received or is receiving primary or secondary school instruction in English or French in Canada, have the right to have all their children receive primary and secondary school instruction in the same language.

(3) The right of citizens of Canada under subsections (1) and (2) to have their children receive primary and secondary school instruction in the language of the English or French linguistic minority of a province

(a) applies wherever in the province the number of children of citizens who have such a right is sufficient to warrant the provision to them out of public funds of minority language instruction; and

(b) includes, where the number of those children so warrants, the right to have them receive that instruction in minority language educational facilities provided out of public funds.

24.(1) Anyone whose rights or freedoms, as guaranteed by this Charter, have been infringed or denied may apply to a court of competent jurisdiction to obtain such remedy as the court considers appropriate and just in the circumstances.

The trial judge had little difficulty in concluding that there had been a violation of the plaintiffs' *Charter* rights under section 23.

What gave rise to the subsequent appeals was the nature of the particular Order devised by the trial judge, who thought the real issue was not so much the existence and content of the section-23 rights as the date by which the programs and facilities would finally be made available, since the province had not afforded the constitutional rights sufficient priority, and the rate of assimilation of the francophone students had become serious. His Order concluded with the following:

...

6. The Respondents [the Nova Scotia government] shall use their best efforts to comply with this Order.

7. The Court shall retain jurisdiction to hear reports from the Respondents respecting the Respondents' compliance with this Order. The Respondents shall report to this Court on March 23, 2001 at 9:30 a.m., or on such other date as the Court may determine.

It was the judge's retention of jurisdiction that was considered problematic. The Nova Scotia Court of Appeal was split, but the majority held that, once he had rendered his decision, the trial judge had no further jurisdiction in the matter, and the *Charter* did not extend the court's jurisdiction to permit it to enforce its remedies.

In the Supreme Court of Canada, the majority reviewed the need for a generous and expansive, purposive, interpretation in *Charter* cases, as opposed to a narrow and technical approach, both as to the rights themselves and the related remedies.

Purposive interpretation means that remedies provisions must be interpreted in a way that provides "a full, effective and meaningful remedy for *Charter* violations" since "a right, no matter how expansive in theory, is only as meaningful as the remedy provided for its breach." ... A purposive approach to remedies in a *Charter* context gives modern vitality to the ancient maxim *ubi jus, ibi remedium*: where there is a right, there must be a remedy. More specifically, a purposive approach to remedies requires at least two things. First, the purpose of the right being protected must be promoted: courts must craft *responsive* remedies. Second, the purpose of the remedies provision must be promoted: courts must craft *effective* remedies.

The purpose of section 23 was clear: to preserve and promote the two official languages of Canada and their related cultures. It was also designed to correct past injustices. The numbers requirement left minority-language education rights particularly vulnerable to government delay or inaction. "If delay is tolerated, governments could potentially avoid the duties imposed upon them by s. 23 through their own failure to implement the rights vigilantly." The combination of the *Charter* right and timely compliance could require courts to "order affirmative remedies to guarantee that language rights are meaningfully, and therefore necessarily promptly protected."

The majority then moved on to consider the role of courts in the enforcement of the law.

> Canada has evolved into a country that is noted and admired for its adherence to the rule of law as a major feature of its democracy. But the rule of law can be shallow without proper mechanisms for its enforcement. In this respect, courts play an essential role since they are the central institutions to deal with legal disputes through the rendering of judgments and decisions. But courts have no physical or economic means to enforce their judgments. Ultimately, courts depend on both the executive and the citizenry to recognize and abide by their judgments.

> Fortunately, Canada has had a remarkable history of compliance with court decisions by private parties and by all institutions of government. That history of compliance has become a fundamentally cherished value of our constitutional democracy; we must never take it for granted but always be careful to respect and protect its importance, otherwise the seeds of tyranny can take root.

This led to reminders that the courts should be careful not to usurp the roles of other branches of government, except where constitutional rights are to be protected. Here, the trial judge had been guided by historical and contextual factors and had crafted a remedy that would protect and implement the minority rights, as well as maintain the appropriate respect for the proper roles of the other branches of government. He had vindicated the plaintiffs' rights and left the detailed means of complying with his Order in the hands of the government, while ensuring prompt compliance through the portion requiring reports from the government. The Order also avoided future expense on the part of the plaintiffs, requiring them to launch further proceedings had the government not acted promptly.

The Court also provided some guidance regarding the meaning of the words *appropriate and just in the circumstances* contained in subsection 24(1) of the *Charter*. Such a remedy

- is one that meaningfully vindicates the rights and freedoms of the claimant, relevant to the experience of the claimant and addresses the circumstances in which the right was infringed or denied

- must employ means which are legitimate within the framework of our constitutional democracy and strive to respect the relationships and separation of functions among the legislature, the executive and the judiciary, without departing unduly or unnecessarily from the role of the courts in adjudicating disputes

- is a judicial remedy which vindicates the right while invoking the function and powers of a court, without leaping into decisions and functions for which the court's design and expertise are manifestly unsuited

- is a remedy that, after ensuring that the right of the claimant is fully vindicated, is also fair to the party against whom the order is made, without imposing substantial hardships unrelated to securing the right

- must be allowed to evolve in order to play its intended role in the myriad of cases in which subsection 24(1) may be applicable, to include novel and creative features when compared to traditional and historical remedial practice.

The majority agreed in some respects with the dissenting judges as to a certain lack of clarity and precision in the trial judge's Order regarding the reporting process, although it stopped short of the dissenting judges' conclusion that it was so unclear that it should be declared invalid. Future orders of a similar nature could be more explicit and detailed, both as to the jurisdiction retained by the court and the procedure to be followed at reporting hearings. In *Charter* cases, the court has discretion to formulate the remedy that the court considers just and reasonable. There is no requirement to identify the single best remedy, even assuming that were possible.

The concluding observations regarding subsection 24(1) provide additional guidelines for future interpretation.

> Section 24(1) of the *Charter* requires that courts issue effective, responsive remedies that guarantee full and meaningful protection of *Charter* rights and freedoms. The meaningful protection of *Charter* rights, and in particular the enforcement of s. 23 rights, may in some cases require the introduction of novel

remedies. A superior court may craft any remedy that it considers appropriate and just in the circumstances. In doing so, courts should be mindful of their roles as constitutional arbiters and the limits of their institutional capacities. Reviewing courts, for their part, must show considerable deference to trial judges' choice of remedy, and should refrain from using hindsight to perfect a remedy. A reviewing court should only interfere where the trial judge has committed an error of law or principle.

This is an important clarification of the role of courts when they have issued orders or decisions. In some cases, when a judgment is rendered, the judge becomes what is referred to as *functus officio* (having performed the function) and is precluded from continuing to be involved with the matter. In others, as here, the judge may reserve a jurisdiction to follow up on the enforcement of the order and will not be limited to established and limited functions that predated the adoption of the *Charter*.

Health Service Waiting Times: Violation of Charter Rights?

Chaoulli v. Quebec (Attorney General) and Canada (Attorney General)
[2005] 1 S.C.R. 791

Who would have thought that hospital waiting times could be raised to a constitutional level and held to infringe both the Quebec and Canadian *Charters*? Certainly not the trial judge, who heard all the evidence, nor a unanimous three-judge bench of the Quebec Court of Appeal, nor three of the seven judges who heard the appeal in the Supreme Court of Canada. The outcome of the litigation, however, was determined by a bare majority of four judges of that Court.

The case came to the Supreme Court of Canada framed as an infringement of the claimants' *Charter* rights. Waiting times for medical treatment, they said, deprived them of their *Charter* rights to life, since there was an increased risk of dying while awaiting their turns for necessary services, as well as aggravation of any medical condition, including mental and emotional stress. Neither of the two claimants had personally experienced such conditions and were, essentially, representative claimants with sufficient standing to raise the issues before the courts. The provisions of the Quebec medical services legislation effectively prevented them from obtaining health insurance that would have enabled them to obtain private health or medical care. It was that prohibition, they claimed, that triggered their concern with the constitutionality of the legislation.

Despite the fact that the *Charter* interests were somewhat different-ly worded in the Quebec and Canadian statutes, as they related to the right to life, liberty, and the security of the person, the substance was essentially the same. The Quebec *Charter* had preceded the Canadian *Charter* by several years and had a quasi-constitutional status in Que-bec, whereas the Canadian *Charter* was embedded in and was part of the Constitution of Canada.

One of the judges comprising the majority wrote separate reasons for judgment which dealt only with the Quebec *Charter* and, having concluded that the legislation violated that statute, did not consider it necessary to go further and reach a conclusion on the Canadian *Char-ter*. The other three judges agreed with the analysis regarding the Que-bec *Charter*, but extended their consideration to the Canadian *Charter*, concluding that the Quebec legislation was also offside for purposes of the Canadian *Charter*. The result, given the view of the dissenting judg-es, is the somewhat anomalous position of three judges on each side, and a seventh who did not deal with the matter.

From a legal perspective, there were some difficulties, given the find-ings of fact reached by the trial judge. These difficulties were exposed quite clearly by the dissenting judges, who asserted that there was no basis for disagreement with those findings of fact. Normally there is considerable deference shown to such findings, since it was the trial judge who heard the evidence of the witnesses and who could best eval-uate their credibility, as well as the weight to be given to their evidence in relation to the matters before the court. Appellate court judges have not had the opportunity to hear and weigh that evidence. They should interfere very rarely and only when there has been a palpable error on the part of the trial judge. In this case, the majority judges appeared to come to different conclusions than had the trial judge and they reas-sessed portions of the evidence, an approach to which the dissenting judges took principled objection.

Health-care debates have a tendency to create more heat than light, particularly in the public forum, but also in court, and there were many quite pointed criticisms directed by the judges in relation to the views of their colleagues. For example:

These broad principles [of public and universal health care] have become hallmarks of Canadian identity. Any measure that might be perceived as compromising them has a polarizing effect on public opinion. The debate about the effectiveness of public health care has become an emotional one. The Romanow Report stated that the *Canada Health Act* has achieved an iconic status that makes it untouchable by politicians. ... The tone adopted by my colleagues [named] is indicative of this type of emotional reaction. It leads them to characterize the debate as pitting rich against poor when the case is really about determining whether a specific measure is justified under either the *Quebec Charter* or the *Canadian Charter*. I believe that it is essential to take a step back and to consider these various reactions objectively. The *Canada Health Act* does not prohibit private health care services, nor does it provide benchmarks for the length of waiting times that might be regarded as consistent with the principles it lays down, and in particular with the principle of real accessibility.

The minority did not take comments of that nature lying down:

> We note that our colleagues refer to the evidence before the trial judge rather than the view taken of that evidence by the trial judge. The trial judge reached a conclusion on the facts and deference is due to her view of that evidence. ... In any event, with respect, we accept the contrary conclusions of the trial judge and the Quebec Court of Appeal.

While it fell short of different armed camps on the Court, there were, on this issue, deep differences on the propriety of judicial intervention into matters of social policy and of changing factual conclusions reached by the lower courts, especially by the trial judge.

To begin with the majority outcome, the prohibition against obtaining health insurance was found to be unconstitutional, as a non-justifiable interference with the claimants' *Charter* rights. Delays resulting from the creation of waiting lists (effectively decisions relating to the allocation of state resources) added to the health risks. The path to the conclusion included some disagreements with the trial judge:

> As can be seen from the evidence, the arguments made in support of the position that the integrity of the public system could be jeopardized by abolishing the prohibition can be divided into two groups. The first group of arguments

relates to human reactions of the various people affected by the public plan, while the second group relates to the consequences for the plan itself.

... [discussion of what the witnesses said]

It is apparent from this summary that for each threat mentioned, no study was produced or discussed in the Superior Court. While it is true that scientific or empirical evidence is not always necessary, witnesses in a case in which the arguments are supposedly based on logic or common sense should be able to cite specific facts in support of their conclusions. The human reactions described by the experts, many of whom came from outside Quebec, do not appear to me to be very convincing, particularly in the context of Quebec legislation. ... The evidence that the existence of the health care system would be jeopardized by human reactions to the emergence of a private system carries little weight.

All four of the judges comprising the majority were concerned about the impact of delays on the rights to life and security of the person. The evidence, in their view, based on what was being done in other jurisdictions, showed that there was a wide variety of available measures and, in the case before them, the government had done nothing to show that the refusal to allow purchase of medical insurance was a minimum impairment of the protected right. As the discussion morphed into consideration of the Canadian *Charter*, the issue was framed more broadly.

The appellants do not seek an order that the government spend more money on health care, nor do they seek an order that waiting times for treatment under the public health care scheme be reduced. They only seek a ruling that because delays in the public system place their health and security at risk, they should be allowed to take out insurance to permit them to access private services.

The *Charter* does not confer a freestanding constitutional right to health care. However, where the government puts in place a scheme to provide health care, that scheme must comply with the *Charter*. We are of the view that the prohibition on medical insurance ... violates s. 7 of the *Charter* because it impinges on the right to life, liberty and the security of the person in an arbitrary fashion that fails to conform to the principles of fundamental justice.

Where the legislation imposed exclusivity, but the government then failed to provide public health care of a reasonable standard within a reasonable time, the government created circumstances that triggered section 7 of the Canadian *Charter*.

The dissenting judges were adamant that the protracted debate on public health care could not and should not be resolved as a matter of law by judges. How, they asked, could the debate be framed regarding a constitutional requirement to provide "reasonable" health services? Continuing, they posed further questions: what is a "reasonable" time and what would be the benchmarks? How short a waiting list is short enough? How many MRIs did the Constitution require? The majority did not identify a manageable constitutional standard. How can the public, judges, and even governments know how much health care would be "reasonable" enough to satisfy section 7 of the *Charter*?

> The evidence certainly established that the public health care system put in place to implement this policy [that contained in the *Canada Health Act*] has serious and persistent problems. That does not mean that the courts are well placed to perform the required surgery. The resolution of such a complex fact-laden policy debate does not fit easily within the institutional competence or procedures of courts of law.

The proper forum to determine the social policy of Quebec in the matter was, they said, the National Assembly. There was no principle of fundamental justice in the constitutional law of Canada that could dispose of the problem of waiting lists in the Quebec health system. The claimants' case did not rest on constitutional law, but on their disagreement with the Quebec government on matters of social policy.

Addressing the matter of arbitrariness, as discussed by the majority (and while not disagreeing with the general view that a law which arbitrarily violates the life or security of the person is unconstitutional), they said:

> Suffice it to say at this point that in our view, the appellants' argument about "arbitrariness" is based largely on generalizations about the public system

drawn from fragmentary experience, an overly optimistic view of the benefits offered by private health insurance, an oversimplified view of the adverse effects on the public health system of permitting private sector health services to flourish and an overly interventionist view of the role the courts should play in trying to supply a "fix" to the failings, real or perceived, of major social programs.

In the face of the growing level of expenditure on public health and whether it is sustainable, justified, or wise, everyone has opinions, but in the absence of a violation of a recognized principle of fundamental justice, the opinions that prevail, the judges said, should be those of the legislatures. They recognized that there were obviously waiting times and that management of them was a matter of serious public concern, but considered the proposed constitutional right to a two-tier system for those who could afford private medical insurance would "precipitate a seismic shift in health policy for Quebec," and they did not believe that such a shift was compelled by either of the *Charters*.

> We are not to be taken as disputing the undoubted fact that there are serious problems with the single-tier health plan in Canada. Our point is simply that bits of evidence must be put in context. With respect, it is particularly dangerous to venture selectively into aspects of foreign health care systems with which we, as Canadians, have little familiarity. At the very least, such information should be filtered and analysed at trial through an expert witness.

They remained, however, in the minority.

Given the context of waiting times for medical care, it is not without a certain irony that the parties in this case had to wait to get their decision—their legal care—from the Court for more than a year after the hearing!

Judicial Review and the Meaning of "Reasonable"

Dunsmuir v. New Brunswick   [2008] 1 S.C.R. 190

Dunsmuir was an employee in the New Brunswick Department of Justice and a Clerk in the Court of Queen's Bench, Trial Division. He had been subject to disciplinary procedures on a number of occasions and it was eventually decided that his particular skill set was not what his employer needed. He was then discharged, specifically not for cause, and given four months' pay in lieu of notice. He filed a grievance under the applicable legislation, complaining that the reasons for the employer's dissatisfaction were not made known, that he did not have a reasonable opportunity to respond to the employer's concerns, that the termination was without notice, due process, or fairness, and that the length of the notice period was inadequate.

The grievance was heard by an adjudicator appointed by the Labour and Employment Board, agreed to by the parties. The adjudicator decided that he had the right to determine whether the discharge was really for cause or not, although he eventually concluded that it was not. He ruled that Dunsmuir had been entitled to procedural fairness and quashed the dismissal, ordering him to be reinstated as of the date of the dismissal. In case his reinstatement order was to be quashed in the event of further proceedings, he found that eight months would be the appropriate notice.

Both the trial and appellate courts of New Brunswick overturned the reinstatement decision, for different reasons, and agreed with the additional notice period.

Judicial Review

When the matter reached the Supreme Court of Canada, it provided an obviously welcome opportunity for the Court to embark on a comprehensive consideration of the legal principles applicable to what is known as "judicial review." This is quite a different concept than the normal hierarchical process of appeal, from trial court to a court of appeal and, eventually, a possible appeal to the Supreme Court of Canada.

The Court began with a short primer:

> As a matter of constitutional law, judicial review is intimately connected with the preservation of the rule of law. It is essentially that constitutional foundation which explains the purpose of judicial review and guides its function and operation. Judicial review seeks to address an underlying tension between the rule of law and the foundational democratic principle, which finds an expression in the initiatives of Parliament and legislatures to create various administrative bodies and endow them with broad powers. Courts, while exercising their constitutional functions of judicial review, must be sensitive not only to the need to uphold the rule of law, but also to the necessity of avoiding undue interference with the discharge of administrative functions in respect of matters delegated to administrative bodies by Parliament and legislatures.

> By virtue of the rule of law principle, all exercises of public authority must find their source in law. All decision-making powers have legal limits, derived from the enabling statute itself, the common or civil law or the Constitution. Judicial review is the means by which the courts supervise those who exercise statutory powers, to ensure that they do not overstep their legal authority. The function of judicial review is therefore to ensure the legality, the reasonableness and the fairness of the administrative process and its outcomes.

The Court then noted that the present system of judicial review, developed over an extended period, had proven difficult to implement and that it needed to be simplified.

The current approach to judicial review involves three standards of review, ranging from correctness, where no deference is shown, to patent unreasonableness, which is most deferential to the decision maker, the standard of reasonableness *simpliciter* lying, theoretically, in the middle. In our view, it is necessary to reconsider both the number and definitions of the various standards of review, and the analytical process employed to determine which standard applies in a given situation. We conclude that there ought to be two standards of review—correctness and reasonableness.

That is all very well, but what do the terms now proposed really mean? In the former vocabulary, *patent unreasonableness* meant something so obvious that it could be seen on the face of the decision and *reasonableness simpliciter* implied that a more searching examination might be required before the decision could be considered unreasonable.

Reasonableness is a deferential standard animated by the principle that underlies the development of the two previous standards: certain questions that come before administrative tribunals do not lend themselves to one specific, particular result. Instead, they may give rise to a number of possible, reasonable conclusions. Tribunals have a margin of appreciation within the range of acceptable and rational solutions. A court conducting a review for reasonableness inquires into the qualities that make a decision reasonable, referring both to the process of articulating the reasons and to outcomes. In judicial review, reasonableness is concerned mostly with the existence of justification, transparency and intelligibility within the decision-making process. But it is also concerned with whether the decision falls within a range of possible, acceptable outcomes which are defensible in respect of the facts and law.

Another concept that needed consideration as part of the exercise was *deference* and what it means in the context of judicial review of the decisions of administrative tribunals. To whom is it owed, and to what extent is it owed? Indeed, why is it owed?

Deference is both an attitude of the court and a requirement of the law of judicial review. It does not mean that the courts are subservient to the determinations of decision makers, or that courts must show blind reverence to their interpretations, or that they may be content to pay lip service to the concept of reasonableness review while in fact imposing their own view. Rather, deference imports respect for the decision-making process of adjudicative bodies with regard to both the facts and the law. The notion for deference "is rooted in part in respect for governmental decisions to create administrative bodies with delegated powers." ... We agree ... that the concept of "deference as respect" requires of the courts "not submission but a respectful attention to the reasons offered or which could be offered to support a decision." ...

Deference in the context of the reasonableness standard therefore implies that the courts will give due consideration to the determinations of decision makers. ... a policy of deference "recognizes the reality that, in many instances, those working day to day in the implementation of frequently complex administrative schemes have or will develop a considerable degree of expertise or field sensitivity to the imperatives and nuances of the legislative regime." ... In short, deference requires respect for the legislative choices to leave some matters in the hands of administrative decision makers, for the processes and determinations that draw on particular expertise and experiences, and for the different roles of the courts and administrative bodies within the Canadian constitutional system.

The matter of *correctness*, however, does not require the same degree of nuance.

As important as it is that courts have a proper understanding of reasonableness review as a deferential standard, it is also without question that the standard of correctness must be maintained in respect of jurisdictional and some other questions of law. This promotes just decisions and avoids inconsistent and unauthorized application of law. When applying the correctness standard, a reviewing court will not show deference to the decision maker's reasoning process; it will rather undertake its own analysis of the question. The analysis will bring the court to decide whether it agrees with the determination of the decision maker; if not, the court will substitute its own view and provide the correct answer. From the outset, the court must ask whether the tribunal's decision was correct.

Where the nuance enters the picture again is settling on the standard of review in individual cases. In general, questions of fact, discretion, and policy attract the standard of reasonableness, including questions where the legal issues cannot be extracted from the factual issues. While many legal issues attract the standard of correctness, there are nevertheless some that attract the more deferential reasonableness standard. Examples include cases where a privative clause (one which purports to limit or exclude any appeal from a decision) is part of the statute, as evidence that there was a legislative intent that interference by reviewing courts be minimized (although this does not mean that a privative clause is determinative). Others might be where a tribunal is interpreting its own statute or statutes closely connected to its function, where particular expertise has been developed, such as in labour law or in the nature of the particular question of law.

The Court also summarized the development of the concept of procedural fairness as an integral part of Canadian law.

The essential importance of the Court's decision in this case is its clarification of the proper approach to the review of decisions taken by administrative tribunals, of which there are many, at federal, provincial, and territorial levels. The mere fact of their creation indicates an intention that decisions, often determinative of rights and status, be handled by those tribunals. This does not exclude the fundamental jurisdiction of the courts to ensure that they act within the limits established or, if those limits have been exceeded, either by the actions of the tribunals or by an improper assertion of jurisdiction by the legislature itself, to ensure that the rule of law is applied.

Arbitrary Closing of Public Drug-Injection Sites

Canada v. PHS Community Services Society   [2011] 3 S.C.R. 134

The Downtown Eastside of Vancouver (DTES) is not the only area in the country which has a plethora of intravenous drug users, but it is certainly among the best-known. Classic recourses, such as criminal prosecution for drug use, had proved to be ineffective, leading municipal, provincial, and federal authorities in 2003 to create a safe-injection facility (Insite), the first government-sanctioned safe-injection site in North America, in which drug users could inject drugs without the fear of arrest and prosecution. The initiative was found to be an effective response to the spread of infectious diseases such as HIV/AIDS and hepatitis C, as well as the high rate of deaths from overdoses in the DTES.

Making Insite work required an exemption from the application of the criminal provisions of the *Controlled Drugs and Substances Act*, (*CDSA*) a federal statute. In the early years of the operation of Insite, the federal government had granted the exemption, but in 2008, it refused to extend the exemption. Since this would effectively prevent Insite from offering services, the claimants brought an action in the British Columbia courts, claiming that the *CDSA* was inapplicable to Insite, that its application to Insite violated their rights under section 7 of the *Charter*, or, alternatively, that the Minister's decision to refuse the extension violated their section-7 rights.

The statutory framework included the relevant portions of the CDSA, the division of powers under the *Constitution Act, 1867*, and the *Charter*.

The *CDSA* prohibits possession and trafficking:

> 4. (1) Except as authorized under the regulations, no person shall possess a substance included in Schedule I, II or III.

> 5. (1) No person shall traffic in a substance included in Schedule I, II, III or IV or in any substance represented or held out by that person to be such a substance.

It then goes on to contemplate the exemption by the Minister of Health for medical or scientific reasons, or for any purpose the Minister may deem to be in the public interest.

> 56. The Minister may, on such terms and conditions as the Minister deems necessary, exempt any person or class of persons or any controlled substance or precursor of any class thereof from the application of all or any of the provisions of this Act or the regulations if, in the opinion of the Minister, the exemption is necessary for a medical or scientific purpose or is otherwise in the public interest.

Under section 91(27) of the *Constitution Act, 1867*, the federal government has the undisputed power to legislate to enact criminal laws. The claimants and other intervenors in the litigation would argue (unsuccessfully) that the *CDSA* infringed provincial powers in relation to health matters (not so explicitly stated—specific references are to hospitals and other institutions), property, and civil rights and, generally, all matters of a merely local or private nature in the province. Finally, the *Charter* provisions invoked were sections 1 and 7:

> 1. The *Canadian Charter of Rights and Freedoms* guarantees the rights and freedoms set out in it subject only to such reasonable limits prescribed by law as can be demonstrably justified in a free and democratic society.
> ...
> 7. Everyone has the right to life, liberty and security of the person and the right not to be deprived thereof except in accordance with the principles of fundamental justice.

There could have been little doubt that the *CDSA* was, in its "pith and substance," criminal law, nor that a valid federal law would become invalid if it affected a provincial subject, such as health. In addition, the *CDSA* did not grant any leeway to the provinces, since the exemptions from its application were to be determined solely by the federal minister. The Court did not accept the argument, based on jurisdictional immunity, that decisions as to health care are so core to the provincial health-care jurisdiction that they are protected from federal intrusion. In the emergent practice of cooperative federalism, as well as the dominant approach that permits concurrent federal and provincial legislation in respect of a matter, provided that each is directed at a legitimate aspect, the doctrine of jurisdictional immunity was not a preferred approach, nor one to be intensively relied upon. As the Court noted, "in areas of overlapping jurisdiction, the modern trend is to strike a balance between the federal and provincial governments, through the application of pith and substance analysis and a restrained application of federal paramountcy." The latter concept requires that, if there is a conflict between a federal and a provincial law, the federal law prevails to the extent of the inconsistency. The criminal law provisions were, accordingly, valid, and they applied to Insite.

The Canadian government raised a somewhat strange argument, given its extensive experience with the *Charter* to date. It said that "one part of the Constitution cannot be abrogated or diminished by another part of the Constitution." This led to the proposition that if the *CDSA* were to be valid and applicable, permitting *Charter* claims to succeed would therefore be an internal contradiction within that same Constitution. It is not at all clear why the Attorney General of Canada would have allowed such an argument to be raised in the Supreme Court of Canada. In any event, it was put to a swift end.

> More broadly, the principle that one part of the Constitution cannot be abrogated or diminished by another part of the Constitution is of no assistance in dealing with division of power issues on the one hand, and *Charter* issues on the other. There is no conflict between saying a federal law is validly adopted under s. 91 of the *Constitution Act, 1867*, and asserting that the same law, in purpose or effect, deprives individuals of rights guaranteed by the *Charter*. The *Charter* applies to all valid federal and provincial laws. Indeed, if the

CDSA were *ultra vires* [beyond the powers of] the federal government, there would be no law to which the *Charter* could apply. Laws must conform to the constitutional division of powers and to the *Charter*.

Having disposed of that contention, the Court then considered the *Charter* aspects. The "possession" (of drugs) rules in the *Criminal Code* were broad enough to reach the Insite staff, absent the exemption provided in section 56 of the *CDSA*.

One of the fundamental aspects of litigation in Canada is the generally high degree of deference afforded to the findings of fact by trial judges and courts. Here, the Court made it clear that the findings it noted had been made and that the same information supporting those findings had been available to the Minister.

The trial judge's key findings in this regard are consistent with the information available to the Minister, and are those on which successive federal Ministers have relied in granting exemption orders over almost five years, including the facts that: (1) traditional criminal law prohibitions have done little to reduce drug use in the DTES; (2) the risk to injection drug users of death and disease is reduced when they inject under the supervision of a health professional; and (3) the presence of Insite did not contribute to increased crime rates, increased incidents of public injection, or relapse rates in injection drug users. On the contrary, Insite was perceived favourably or neutrally by the public; a local business association reported a reduction in crime during the period Insite was operating; the facility encouraged clients to seek counselling, detoxification and treatment. Most importantly, the staff of Insite had intervened in 336 overdoses since 2006, and no overdose deaths had occurred at the facility. ... These findings suggest not only that exempting Insite from the application of the possession prohibition does not undermine the objectives of public health and safety, but furthers them.

This set up the position that the Minister's decision not to grant the exemption was arbitrary, as well as grossly disproportionate in proportion to any legitimate government interest. Failure to grant the exemption was not in accordance with the principles of fundamental justice.

It is arbitrary, undermining the very purposes of the *CDSA*, which include public health and safety. It is also grossly disproportionate: the potential denial of health services and the correlative increase in the risk of death and disease to injection drug users outweigh any benefit that might be derived from maintaining an absolute prohibition on possession of illegal drugs on Insite's premises.

The remedy was not to strike down the provisions, but to find a solution that was tailored to the particular circumstances, which was to order the Minister to grant the necessary exemption. It was not desirable to go any further, since it might not be beyond possibility that, at some time in the future, there could be constitutionally acceptable reasons not to grant such an exemption.

This case is one that was successful, but on a completely different basis than the parties had thought was the central point of the appeal.

The main issue, as the appeal was argued, was the constitutionality of the *CDSA* itself. I have concluded that, properly interpreted, the statute was valid. This leaves the question of the Minister's decision to refuse an exemption. A preliminary issue arises whether the court should consider this issue. In the special circumstances of this case, I conclude that it should. The claimants pleaded in the alternative that, if the *CDSA* were valid, the Minister's decision violated their *Charter* rights. The issue was raised at the hearing and the parties afforded an opportunity to address it. It is therefore properly before us and the Attorney General of Canada cannot complain that it would be unfair to deal with it. Most importantly, justice requires us to consider this issue. The claimants have established that their s. 7 rights are at stake. They should not be denied a remedy and sent back for another trial on this point simply because it is the Minister's decision and not the statute that causes the breach when the matter has been pleaded and no unfairness arises.

The moral of the story is that you never know for certain how or why you may win—or lose —an appeal.

Fighting for Language Rights

Attorney General of Quebec v. Blaikie et al. [1979] 2 S.C.R. 1016

In 1977, Quebec adopted a statute that had as its object emasculation of the use of the English language in official legislative and court proceedings.

Chapter III of Title I of the *Charter of the French Language*, entitled "The Language of the Legislature and of the Courts," reads as follows:

7. French is the language of the legislature and the courts in Quebec.

8. Legislative bills shall be drafted in the official language. They shall also be tabled in the Assemblée nationale, passed and assented to in that language.

9. Only the French text of the statutes and regulations is official.

10. An English version of every legislative bill, statute and regulation shall be printed and published by the civil administration.

11. Artificial persons addressing themselves to the courts and to bodies discharging judicial or quasi-judicial functions shall do so in the official language, and shall use the official language in pleading before them unless all the parties to the action agree to their pleading in English.

12. Procedural documents issued by bodies discharging judicial or quasi-judicial functions or drawn up and sent by the advocates practicing before them shall be drawn up in the official language. Such documents may, however, be drawn up in another language if the natural person for whose intention they are issued expressly consents thereto.

13. The judgments rendered in Quebec by the courts and by bodies discharg-

ing judicial or quasi-judicial functions must be drawn up in French or be accompanied with a duly authenticated French version. Only the French version of the judgment is official.

Quebec's litigious position was that it was entitled to enact the legislation on the basis of section 92(1) of what was then the *British North America Act, 1867* (*BNA Act*), which provided:

> 92. In each Province the Legislature may exclusively make laws in relation to Matters coming within the Classes of Subjects next hereinafter enumerated; that is to say—
> 1. The Amendment from Time to Time, notwithstanding anything in this Act, of the Constitution of the Province, except as regards the Office of Lieutenant Governor.

The claimants, Peter Blaikie, Roland Durand, and Yoine Goldstein, relied principally on section 133 of the same statute, which provided:

> 133. Either the English or the French language may be used by any Person in the Debates of the Houses of Parliament of Canada and of the Houses of the Legislature of Quebec; and both those languages shall be used in the respective Records and Journals of those Houses; and either of those Languages may be used by any Person or in any Pleading or Process in or issuing from any Court of Canada established under this Act, and in or from all or any of the Courts of Quebec.

> The Acts of the Parliament and of the Legislature of Quebec shall be printed and published in both those languages.

The claimants took initial action in the Quebec Superior Court that same year, seeking a declaration that the provisions noted above were *ultra vires* (beyond the powers of) the Legislature of Quebec because they were in direct violation of s. 133 of the *BNA Act*, the provisions of which could not be unilaterally modified by the Legislature. The Chief Justice of that court, in extensive and detailed reasons, upheld the challenge and granted the requested declaration on January 23, 1978. Quebec then appealed to the Quebec Court of Appeal, which, exceptionally, sat in a seven-judge bench (normally it sits in panels of three judges and, occasionally, in important cases, five judges). This court unanimously rejected Quebec's appeal. Neither of the Quebec courts found it necessary to deal with the argument, raised in a companion case heard at the same time, that the impugned provisions were also incompatible with the Quebec *Charter of Human Rights and Freedoms*, given the unconstitutionality already determined vis à vis the *BNA Act*. Quebec then obtained leave to raise the constitutional aspect of its case before the Supreme Court of Canada, which, in turn sat with a full bench. The Supreme Court unanimously, in a single judgment issued in the name of the Court, rejected the Quebec appeal. Every one of the seventeen judges who sat at the various levels agreed that the impugned provisions of the *Charter of the French Language* were beyond the powers of the Quebec legislature. Eleven of the seventeen judges were from Quebec.

The reasons for judgment were much shorter than most rendered by the Supreme Court in recent years, no doubt in part because they were a single set of reasons, and because, in part, the Quebec courts had dealt with the issues in considerable detail. Indeed, in many respects the Court was essentially content to rely on the reasons given in the Quebec Superior Court, as fortified by the Quebec Court of Appeal.

Nevertheless, the critical point was clear, even though overall reasons for the Court's judgment of the Court were perhaps somewhat more convoluted than was necessary. Section 133 of the *BNA Act* is an entrenched provision, which not only forbids modification by unilateral action of Parliament or of the Quebec Legislature, but also provides a guarantee to members of Parliament or members of the Quebec Legislature and to litigants in the courts of Canada or of Quebec that they are entitled to use either French or English in parliamentary or legislative assembly debates or in pleading (including oral argument) in the courts of Canada or of Quebec. The Supreme Court, once having stated that conclusion, declared that there was no reason to expand further on such a principal issue.

Parliament was entitled to enlarge the protection extended by section 133, should it choose to do so, but neither Parliament nor the Quebec Legislature could contract or shrink such protection. And it was, precisely, a contraction of those guarantees or requirements that the

Quebec Legislature had purported to enact through its unilateral adoption of the impugned provisions of the *Charter of the French Language*.

That *Charter*, also made reference to "regulations" issued under the authority of Acts of the Quebec Legislature. Regulations are a form of subsidiary legislation, increasingly used as a means of expediting the objects sought to be achieved by Acts (or statutes). Regulations can be adopted by Cabinet action and subsequent publication, without the lengthier and potentially more contentious process of enacting a statute. The Supreme Court held that such actions would truncate the protection granted by section 133 if account were not taken of the growth of delegated legislation.

As to language to be used in and by the courts, the term *Courts of Quebec* was taken to mean not only those courts in which the judges are federally appointed, but also those in which the judges are provincially appointed. The reference to quasi-judicial bodies in the *Charter* provisions then led the Supreme Court to consider some of the modern agencies operating outside of, but essentially parallel to, the formal court system. Just in case you may not think that judicial prose cannot occasionally be impenetrable, this is how the Court said, in effect, the same principle applies to the tribunal system as well:

> It is not a long distance from this latter class of tribunal to those which exercise judicial power, although they are not courts in the traditional sense. If they are statutory agencies which are adjudicative, applying legal principles to the assertion of claims under their constituent legislation, rather than settling issues on the grounds of expediency or administrative policy, they are judicial bodies, however some of their procedures may differ not only from those of Courts but also from those of other adjudicative bodies. In the rudimentary state of administrative law in 1867, it is not surprising that there was no reference to non-curial adjudicative agencies. Today, they play a significant role in the control of a wide range of individual and corporate activities, subjecting them to various norms of conduct which are at the same time limitations on the jurisdiction of the agencies and on the legal position of those caught by them. The guarantee given for the use of French or English in Court proceedings should not be liable to curtailment by provincial substitution of adjudicative agencies for Courts ...

Two Privy Council cases were cited to justify this conclusion. One was the analogy of the "living tree capable of growth and expansion within its natural limits" contained in the *Persons* case [see page 215] and the second (coming from a reference case on Privy Council appeals) in which it was said, "... it is ... irrelevant that the question is one that might have seemed unreal at the date of the *British North America Act*. To such an organic statute the flexible interpretation must be given which changing circumstances require."

> Although there are clear points of distinction between these two cases and the issue of the scope of s. 133, in its reference to the Courts of Quebec, they nonetheless lend support to what is to us the proper approach to an entrenched provision, that is, to make it effective through the range of institutions which exercise judicial power, be they called courts or adjudicative agencies. In our opinion, therefore, the guarantee and requirements of s. 133 extend to both.

> It follows that the guarantee in s. 133 of the use of either French or English "by any person or in any pleading or process in or issuing from ... all or any of the Courts of Quebec" applies to both ordinary Courts and other adjudicative tribunals. Hence, not only is the option to use either language given to any person involved in proceedings before the Courts of Quebec or its other adjudicative tribunals (and this covers both written and oral submissions) but documents emanating from such bodies or issued in their name or under their authority may be in either language, and this option extends to the issuing and publication of judgments or other orders.

This was an important assertion of English-language rights in the face of the unilateral discriminatory step taken by the Quebec government to deliberately weaken those rights and to attempt to justify the operative language as constitutionally compliant. It was important to take swift action in the face of such discrimination and equally important that every judge who considered the matter, including those from Quebec, shared the same view of its constitutional invalidity. It was also clear that the framers of the Canadian constitution correctly anticipated the possibility of precisely such conduct when they negotiated the principles of Confederation.

Can Pregnant Women Be Forced to Undergo Medical Treatment?

Winnipeg Child and Family Services (Northwest Area) v. D.F.G. [1997] 3 S.C.R. 925

D.F.G. was five months pregnant with her fourth child. She was addicted to solvent sniffing and two of her previous children, then wards of the state, had been born permanently disabled as a result of her addiction. The plaintiff government agency [Winnipeg Child and Family Services (Northwest Area)] applied to a superior court judge for an Order that D.F.G. be placed in the custody of the agency and detained in a health centre for treatment until the birth of her unborn child. Although such an Order had never previously been granted, the superior court judge saw no reason why the power of the court to issue protective orders of such nature could not be extended to protect unborn children. Two days after the Order was issued, it was stayed and ultimately set aside by the Manitoba Court of Appeal. D.F.G.'s child was born (apparently healthy) in December. The agency appealed the Order requesting the Supreme Court of Canada to overturn the Manitoba Court of Appeal's judgment setting aside the order. D.F.G. argued, on the other hand, that the appeal should be dismissed on the basis that the courts had no power to order a mother into custody against her will for the purpose of protecting her unborn child.

By a seven-to-two majority, the Supreme Court dismissed the appeal on the grounds that such an Order for the protection of the fetus would require changes to the law which could not properly be made by the courts and which should, instead, be left to the legislature. The dissenting judges thought that the common law should be sufficiently adaptable to deal with such novel situations and that, should the legislatures be too slow to respond to such circumstances, the courts should not hesitate to step in to protect persons unable to protect themselves.

The majority framed the situation and legal issues as follows:

> [D.F.G.] points out that damage to the fetal nervous system occurs in the early stages of pregnancy long before the order was sought or made, that at an earlier stage of her pregnancy she had voluntarily sought treatment but had been turned away due to lack of facilities, that when asked to take treatment she agreed and only later refused because she had fallen into a state of intoxication, and that once taken to the hospital, she remained until discharged, although the custodial order requiring her to remain had been stayed. This is not a story of heroes and villains. It is the more prosaic but all too common story of people struggling to do their best in the face of inadequate facilities and the ravages of addiction. This said, the legal question remains: assuming evidence that a mother is acting in a way which may harm her unborn child, does a judge, at the behest of the state, have the power to order the mother to be taken into custody for the purpose of rectifying her conduct? It is on this footing that I approach the case.

The two legal issues were, first, whether tort law (as it existed or may be properly extended by a court) permits detaining a pregnant woman against her will in order to protect her unborn child from conduct that might harm the child, and, second, whether the power of the court to make orders for the protection of children (using its *parens patriae* jurisdiction—meaning to act in the place of a parent or the parents) permits the same thing.

Existing tort law did not support the Order. Common law did not recognize a legal status for unborn children. The fetus was not a legal person and possessed no legal rights. Therefore, in terms of tort law, although it might be possible to claim for damages to the fetus, the courts could not deal with such a claim (brought in the name of the child) until after its birth. The question then became whether the existing tort law could be judicially extended. Normally, such extensions are incremental, applying existing principles to new circumstances. The Court was unwilling to grant the requested extensions.

> The changes which the agency asks this Court to make to the law of tort may be summarized as follows:
>
> 1. Overturn the rule that rights accrue to a person only at birth (the "live birth" rule);
> 2. Recognize a fetal right to sue the mother carrying the fetus;
> 3. Recognize a cause of action for lifestyle choices which may adversely affect others;
> 4. Recognize an injunctive remedy which deprives a defendant of important liberties, including her involuntary confinement.
>
> The proposed changes to the law of tort are major, affecting the rights and remedies available in many other areas of tort law. They involve moral choices and would create conflicts between fundamental interests and rights. They would have an immediate and drastic impact on the lives of women as well as men who might find themselves incarcerated and treated against their will for conduct alleged to harm others. And, they possess complex ramifications impossible for this Court to fully assess, giving rise to the danger that the proposed order may impede the goal of healthy infants more than it would promote it. In short, these are not the sort of changes which common law courts can or should make. These are the sort of changes which should be left to the legislature.

As to the inherent power of the courts to order detention and treatment of a pregnant woman for the purpose of preventing harm to an unborn child, the majority was similarly unwilling to extend the law of *parens patriae* that far, for much the same reason, noting that no other court, when confronted with arguments in favour of that extension, had accepted such a position. Given the magnitude of such changes, as well as their potential ramifications, the changes to the law sought on the appeal were, the Supreme Court concluded, best left to the wisdom of the legislature.

Although the two judges in the minority were thoroughly outvoted, their approach was interesting because it diametrically opposed the classic and conservative majority position. The common law had been sufficiently flexible over the centuries to meet changing circumstances as they arose: such flexibility was required in this appeal. The opposing judges recognized three questions: What were the rights of the pregnant woman? Did an unborn fetus have independent rights? Did the state have a separate right to intervene to prescribe proper medical treatment in achieving the birth of a healthy child as opposed to standing by at the birth of a permanently and seriously handicapped child with no future other than as a permanent ward of the state?

The "live-birth" rule was, these judges maintained, outdated:

> Historically, it was thought that damage suffered by a foetus could only be assigned if the child was born alive. It was reasoned that it was only at that time that damages to the live child could be identified. The logic for that rule has disappeared with modern medical progress. Today by the use of ultrasound and other advanced techniques, the sex and health of a foetus can be determined and monitored from a short time after conception. The sophisticated surgical procedures performed on the foetus before birth further belies the need for the "born alive" principle.

The "born-alive" rule is an evidentiary presumption of the common law, a legal anachronism rooted in "rudimentary medical knowledge that has long since been overtaken by modern science and should be set aside for purpose of this appeal." If that rule was not followed, the courts could intervene.

> This means that a superior court, on proper motion, should be able to exercise its *parens patriae* jurisdiction to restrain a mother's conduct when there is a reasonable probability of that conduct causing serious and irreparable harm to the foetus within her. While the granting of this type of remedy may interfere with the mother's liberty interests, in my view, those interests must bend when faced with a situation where the devastating harm and a life of suffering can easily be prevented. In any event, the interference is always subject to the mother's right to end it by deciding to have an abortion.
>
> ...
>
> Once the mother decides to bear the child the state has an interest in trying to ensure the child's health. What circumstances permit state intervention?

The "slippery slope" argument was raised that permitting state intervention here would impose a standard of behaviour on all pregnant women. Questions were raised about women who smoked, who lived with a smoker, who ate unhealthy diets, etc. In response to the query of where a reasonable line should be drawn it was submitted that the pen should not even be lifted. This approach would entail the state to stand idly by while a reckless and/or addicted mother inflicts serious and permanent harm on to a child she had decided to bring into the world.

The majority of the Court had relied on precedent—no other court had, in the past, agreed with arguments for extension of the law requested in this case. The minority position was that rigid application of precedents of questionability (such as the "born-alive" principle) without inquiry into the purpose of the particular rule could lead the law to recommit the errors of the past.

> The common law boasts that it is adaptable. If so, there is no need to cling to notions rooted in rudimentary medical and scientific knowledge of the past. A foetus should be considered within the class of persons whose interests can be protected through the exercise of the *parens patriae* jurisdiction.

Clearly, standards would have to be applied and intervention would likely occur in severe cases only. It would be necessary to define, but on a case-by-case basis, the applicable criteria and limitations, the procedure, the parties who should have standing [who can participate] in any proceedings, making certain that any confinement must be for purposes of treatment and not punishment, having evidence of the probable harm anticipated, and so forth.

The conclusions of the minority were challenges for society as a whole, eloquently and compellingly stated:

> I do not believe our system, whether legislative or judicial, has become so paralysed that it will ignore a situation where the imposition required in order to prevent terrible harm is so slight. It may be preferable that the legislature act but its failure to do so is not an excuse for the judiciary to follow the same course of inaction. Failure of the court to act should occur where there is no jurisdiction for the court to proceed. Outdated medical assumptions should

not provide any licence to permit the damage to continue. Where the harm is so great and the temporary remedy so slight, the law is compelled to act.

...

It seems fundamentally unfair and inexplicable for this Court to hold that a foetus, upon live birth, can sue for damages to recompense injuries suffered *in utero*, yet have no ability to obtain a remedy preventing that damage from occurring in the first place. This is one of the clearest of cases where monetary damages are a singularly insufficient remedy. If our society is to protect the health and well-being of children, there must exist jurisdiction to order a pre-birth remedy preventing a mother from causing serious harm to her foetus. Someone must speak for those who cannot speak for themselves.

Both the majority and the minority seem to have been addressing the legislative branches of government, the majority doing so in deferential terms, showing where action lay, while the minority was clearly advocating remedial legislative action.

Mandatory Drug Testing in Dangerous Workplaces: Allowed or Not Allowed?

CEPU v. Irving Pulp & Paper, Limited [2013] S.C.C. 34

This appeal arose out of a drug policy adopted by Irving Pulp & Paper, Limited ("Irving") with respect to its operations in Saint John, New Brunswick. There was no dispute that those operations involved hazardous chemicals and gases, heavy machinery and equipment, high-pressure boilers and steam lines, and high-voltage electric lines. Nor was there any doubt that even in normal operations, the mill was a dangerous environment, presenting risks not only to the employees, but to the public, to property, and to the environment. The workplace was essentially unionized and the workplace interests were governed by a process of collective bargaining. Where an employer decides to implement a program, such as a safety program, outside of the bargaining process, it is generally required to do so within the scope of "management rights" as contained in the appropriate collective agreement. In the case of Irving, this clause provided:

> 4.01. The Union recognizes and acknowledges that it is the right of the Company to operate and manage its business subject to the terms and conditions of this agreement.

Between 1991 and 2006, Irving had no formal policy regarding alcohol and drug use at the mill. In 2006, it unilaterally adopted a "Policy on Alcohol and Other Drug Use" under the management-rights clause, without any negotiations with the union. The policy imposed mandatory alcohol testing for employees holding positions designated by Irving as "safety sensitive." With respect to alcohol, there was a universal random-testing component, pursuant to which 10 percent of the employees in safety-sensitive positions could be randomly selected for unannounced breathalyzer tests over the course of a year. A positive test, over a specified threshold, could attract significant disciplinary action. Refusal to submit to testing was grounds for immediate dismissal. The policy did not provide for random drug testing, although such testing was permitted in safety-sensitive positions for drug or alcohol use after an accident in the workplace and where there was a reasonable basis to suspect alcohol or drug use or possession.

Matters were brought to a litigious head when an employee member of the Union was selected for testing. As it happened, the employee was a teetotaller who had not had a drink since 1979. His inclusion in the class of workers in safety-sensitive positions was undisputed. The breathalyzer test showed a blood-alcohol level of zero. The Union filed a grievance on his behalf, challenging only the random alcohol testing aspect of the policy. Interestingly enough, the balance of the testing policy was not challenged. Under that, employees were subject to mandatory testing if there was reasonable cause to suspect the employee of alcohol or other drug use in the workplace, after direct involvement in a work-related accident or incident, or as part of a monitoring program for any employee returning to work following voluntary treatment for substance abuse.

The matter was referred to arbitration pursuant to the collective agreement. The arbitral board ruled in favour of the Union, but the decision was set aside upon judicial review and the New Brunswick Court of Appeal dismissed the Union's appeal against that determination. On further appeal to the Supreme Court of Canada, the Court was divided six to three on the outcome, with the majority agreeing that the decision of the arbitrator had been reasonable and that tests devised by the lower courts which had overturned the arbitral decision were incorrect. The minority agreed that reasonableness was the proper standard of review, although it believed that the board decision was not reasonable. By way of set-up to its conclusion, the majority noted:

It may be tempting to suggest that dangerous unionized workplaces should be beyond the reach of the collective bargaining regime, freeing an employer from both the duty to negotiate with the union and from the terms of the collective agreement. This suggests, Cassandra-like and evidence-free, that collective bargaining is the altar on which public and workplace safety is sacrificed and that only employers have the capacity to address these concerns. But the reality is that the task of negotiating workplace conditions, both on the part of unions and management, as well as the arbitrators who interpret the resulting collective agreement, has historically—and successfully—included the delicate, case-by-case balancing required to preserve public safety concerns while protecting privacy. Far from leaving the public at risk, protecting employees—who are on the front line of any danger—necessarily also protects the surrounding public. To suggest otherwise is a counter-intuitive dichotomy.

What seemed to strike the majority as a determinant in the particular circumstances was that there was no evidence that unionized workplaces that were dangerous had suffered any, let alone a disproportionate number of accidents resulting from collective-bargaining safety measures. Nor, it found, was there any balancing of the privacy interests of the employees.

Dangerousness of the workplace, despite being relevant, should be only the beginning of the required inquiry, and not (without evidence such as a general problem of substance abuse) an automatic justification for unilateral imposition of unfettered random testing, with disciplinary consequences. The evidence before the board regarding substance abuse was that there had been eight documented alcohol-related incidents at the mill over a fifteen-year period, which was not regarded as a reflection of a significant problem with alcohol abuse. The majority concluded that there was a "very low incremental risk of safety concerns based on alcohol-related impaired performance of job tasks at the site."

While the employer had argued that deterrence was a major benefit of random alcohol testing, the board was not satisfied that there was any evidence of a deterrent effect at the mill. The only evidence supporting the employer's view was that of its expert witness, who described deterrence as the main theoretical goal of random alcohol testing policies, but had no information about this particular workplace. In the board's view, the lack of any positive test results in almost two years of random alcohol testing was equally consistent with the opposite conclusion: that there was no workplace alcohol abuse to deter.

The other side of the balance was the employees' right to privacy. The board had accepted that the testing involved significant inroads on privacy, effecting a loss of liberty and personal autonomy, both of which are at the heart of the right to privacy. The majority concurred.

> In the end, the expected safety gains to the employer in this case were found by the board to range "from uncertain ... to minimal at best," while the impact on employee privacy was found to be much more severe. Consequently, the board concluded that the employer had not demonstrated the requisite problems with dangerousness or increased safety concerns such as workplace alcohol use that would justify universal random testing. Random alcohol testing was therefore held to be an unreasonable exercise of management rights under the collective agreement. I agree.

This was not, however, to say that employers can never impose random tests in a dangerous workplace, should this represent a proportionate response in light of both legitimate safety concerns and privacy interests in appropriate circumstances. Otherwise, the employer must show reasonable cause before subjecting employees to potential disciplinary consequences.

The final cautionary note regarding characterization of the arbitral decision as "reasonable" or not was to observe:

> The board's decision should be approached as an organic whole, without a line-by-line treasure hunt for error. ... In the absence of finding that the decision, based on the record, is outside the range of reasonable outcomes, the decision should not be disturbed. In this case, the board's conclusion was reasonable and ought not to have been disturbed by the reviewing courts.

The minority was concerned, despite a jurisprudential background of deference to specialized labour arbitrators, with their specialized knowledge, about entrusting those arbitrators with a policy-making function that potentially carried serious repercussions for public safety and the environment.

> But the fact that the *public interest*—not merely that of employer and employee—is relevant in cases such as this one may counsel a reassessment of the legislative choice to delegate policy-making for drug and alcohol testing to the collective bargaining process and to labour arbitrators. It is one thing for employers and employees to negotiate a balance as they see fit with respect to their own privacy and safety. It is a different matter, however, to leave the public interest to the vicissitudes of the bargaining table. Of course, it would be counterintuitive to suggest that employees do not care for their own safety or, indeed, the safety of their neighbours. The point is simply that employees, employers, and the public may each strike the balance between privacy and safety differently. And where disputes between employers and employees emerge, it is not immediately apparent to us why an adjudicative body that is expert in the resolution of private labour disputes, but not in weighing broader considerations concerning the safety and environmental interests of the public at large, is best positioned to serve as the guardian of the public interest. Indeed, nothing in the relevant legislation even requires, let alone suggests, that labour arbitrators should assume this role.

However strongly the minority might feel about the appropriateness of legislative direction in such matters, that decision was one to be taken by the legislature, not by the courts. On the other hand, the minority drew a distinction between judicial abdication and judicial restraint and, to the extent that a particular arbitral award is unreasonable (which it thought the present one was), it remained liable to being set aside on judicial review.

The basic disagreement with the majority position was that the board had departed from the court-supported concept of arbitral consensus by raising the threshold of evidence that Irving was required to introduce in order to justify its policy of random alcohol testing, and had provided no explanation for having done so. With no explanation, the minority was unable to understand why the board had thought it was reasonable to do what it had done. Thus, in the circumstances of the case, its decision fell outside the range of reasonable defensible outcomes. Other cases had applied the evidentiary standard (before which an employer could impose random alcohol testing) of demonstrating that there was a "problem" with alcohol use, whereas the board in this case had elevated that requirement to a "significant problem" or a "serious" problem. The board had also required that the evidence of alcohol use be "tied" or "causally linked" to "accident, injury or near-miss history" at the mill, a position for which there was no support in the arbitral jurisprudence.

> In any case, to require that an employer tie alcohol use to actual incidents at the mill, as the board in this case did, is not only unreasonable, it is patently absurd. The arbitral cases recognize that evidence of alcohol use at an inherently dangerous facility such as the Irving mill—where the impact of a catastrophic failure could extend well beyond the safety of workers—is "a problem" enough.
>
> Taking these two points together, it is beyond question that the board in this case applied an evidentiary standard unknown to the arbitral jurisprudence. And it is the application of that higher standard which, in our view, dictated the board's decision in this case. As such, this is not a matter of quibbling with a few arguable statements or intermediate findings in the board's reasons—the higher evidentiary standard is *the* basis for the board's ultimate conclusion.

Though it had purported to apply the accepted test from the arbitral jurisprudence, the board had, in fact, departed from it and had compounded the unreasonableness of that finding by reasoning in an unreasonable manner. Although judicial deference is owed to decisions of labour arbitration boards, the minority concluded with the statement that "deference ends where unreasonableness begins."

In the majority decision, the privacy interests trumped the public-safety interests. For the minority, it was the reverse and, having lost the particular outcome, it was clearly speaking to the legislatures, effectively urging them to consider broader policy issues that might not best be handled in individual collective-bargaining processes.

An Early Look at Nuisance

Drysdale v. Dugas [1896] 26 S.C.R. 20

This is an early, but very important, decision of the Court (which has been cited by many courts around the world) dealing with the use of one's property and the consequences of causing nuisance to one's neighbours.

Dugas was the owner of two residential properties on St. Denis Street in Montreal. He resided in one of them and rented the other. In 1890 and 1891, Drysdale constructed a large stable immediately adjoining the rented property and about twenty-five feet from the house occupied by Dugas, in which he conducted the business of a livery stable keeper, having some twenty-eight or thirty horses. Dugas brought an action claiming that the offensive odours and the noise of the horses had caused him damage. Drysdale denied the fact of any nuisance and also pleaded that the stable had been built for carrying on a business necessary in a large city like Montreal, that it had been built using the most approved methods in relation to ventilation and drainage. He also established that Dugas had acquired the rented property after the stable had been built, arguing that he already knew about the stable and could not thereafter complain about it.

The lower courts agreed with Dugas and awarded him damages in respect of both properties. There was no doubt, on the evidence, that he had suffered inconvenience and discomfort in the enjoyment of the house he occupied by reason of the offensive smells caused by

Drysdale's stable. His property rights in the rented house had been depreciated due to the same cause, as well as the noise from the horses in the stable, particularly during the night. The rental from that property had been diminished as a result.

Responsibility for damages includes all abuses of proprietary rights, even the most absolute. All such rights, the Court held, "must, according to the general principles of all systems of law, be subject to certain restrictions subordinating the exercise of acts of ownership to the rights of neighbouring proprietors." This was identified as much a rule of the French law of Quebec as of the common law of England. One of the Quebec judges on the Court had summarized the French and Canadian authorities and the Chief Justice canvassed the English authorities.

> As a general proposition occupiers of lands and houses have a right of action to recover damages for any interference with the comfort and convenience of their occupation. In applying the law, however, regard is to be had, in determining whether the acts complained of are to be considered nuisances, to the conditions and surroundings of the property. It would be of course absurd to say that one who establishes a manufactory in the use of which great quantities of smoke are emitted, next door to a precisely similar manufactory maintained by his neighbour, whose works also emit smoke, commits a nuisance as regards the latter, though if he established his factory immediately adjoining a mansion in a residential quarter of a large city, he would beyond question be liable for damages for a wrongful use of his property to the detriment of his neighbour.

There was a very pithy statement by a judge in an earlier case to make the point: "That may be a nuisance in Grosvenor Square which would be none on Smithfield market."

Even though the rental property had been acquired by Dugas after the stable had been built, the house had been built long before the stable existed. The Court was crystal-clear: "This circumstance as to the date of [Dugas'] acquisition of title can make no difference in his rights to object to the nuisance." The defence that the stable was a necessity in the city was not accepted. Similarly, the fact that Drysdale had acted with extreme care and caution in carrying on his business did not constitute a justification of the nuisance of which Dugas had complained.

There was, therefore, an interference with the personal comfort and enjoyment of the respondent [Dugas] as respects his own house number 122, entitling him to recover damages. And there was also a like interference with the enjoyment of house number 118 by the respondent's tenants which depreciated the respondent's property by reducing the rental, for all of which damages were recoverable.

The case had been heard by a panel of six judges. An even number of judges is normally something the Court tries to avoid, in case there is an equal division of opinion—nothing looks worse than a non-decision. The only dissenting judge on the appeal did not get involved in any detailed analysis of the legal issues, but said that the practical impact of the judgment of the majority was to declare that it would be illegal to maintain a public stable for horses anywhere within the limits of the city of Montreal, since it was impossible that any such stable could be more perfect than Drysdale's. Since it was not possible for the Court to pronounce such an illegality, he thought the appeal should be allowed.

While the legal principles were well-established, we should not forget that the year was 1896, well before municipal regulation and major zoning categories were established, which can have the practical effect of avoiding some of the more obvious examples of nuisance. If you buy a property today in a residential zone, you know perfectly well that you cannot build a factory on it, and if you buy in an industrial zone you will not get permission to build a residence. There are even more variations that will diminish the prospect of nuisance, such as industrial zones, light industrial, commercial, single-family residential, height restrictions, and many others with which we are familiar.

Interestingly enough, however, many of the principles underlying such modern land-use regulation were presaged by some of the old cases mentioned by the Court. Statements from two, in particular, are interesting.

Where a locality is devoted to a particular trade or manufacture carried on by the traders or manufacturers in a particular and established manner, not constituting a public nuisance, judges and juries would be justified in finding, and may be trusted to find, that the trade or manufacture so carried on in that locality is not a private or actionable wrong.

and

> If a man lives on a street where there are numerous shops, and a shop is opened next door to him, which is carried on in a fair and reasonable way, he has no ground of complaint because to himself individually there may arise much discomfort from the trade carried on in that shop.

These examples were, of course, quite different from the building of a horse stable in the midst of a residential area and it is not difficult to see how the Court came to its conclusion regarding the damages suffered by Dugas.

Modern variations on the *Drysdale v. Dugas* model tend to be where someone has bought property known to be at the end of an airport runway or beside an autoroute and then complains about the noise.

Responsibility for Damages Caused by Things Under One's Care

Shawinigan Carbide Co. v. Doucet [1909] 42 S.C.R. 281

Jean Doucet was a workman employed by the Shawinigan Carbide Company at its facilities in Shawinigan Falls, Quebec. The mill manufactured calcium carbide, which is produced by the fusion of carbon and unslaked lime in an electric furnace. Shawinigan had two types of furnaces, one in which the constituents of the carbide were reduced to a liquid state and run off at stated intervals (known as the experimental furnace), and the other in which the crucible containing the fused product is removed and replaced by another (the Willson furnace). In the experimental furnace, the ports were sealed by mortar, except when the liquid was being run off. At those intervals, the mortar plug was pierced and the orifice cleaned out. When the run was completed, the opening was resealed. Doucet's job was to tap one of the furnaces and to clear the opening. On July 27, 1906, there was an accident. Doucet and his assistant came on duty at 7:00 p.m. for the night shift. The last of the day shift had charged the furnace and left a quantity of mortar ready for use. About twenty minutes after coming on duty, Doucet opened the furnace and drained the liquid, cleaned the opening, and proceeded to close one of the openings with a plug of mortar, placing it on the bottom of the opening. As he pressed it home with a long poker with a circular iron disc at the end, an explosion occurred, accompanied by a discharge of flaming liquid carbide that burned him severely and permanently blinded him.

This was long before the days of workmen's compensation legislation. Shawinigan denied responsibility for the accident. Doucet was forced to take legal action. He claimed $10,000 and was awarded $4,000. Shawinigan appealed to the Superior Court of Quebec, sitting in review, which reversed the judgment. Doucet then appealed to what was then called the Court of King's Bench, Appeal Side (now the Quebec Court of Appeal), which allowed his appeal and restored the judgment at trial. Shawinigan then appealed to the Supreme Court of Canada, which dismissed the appeal. After four successive court hearings, Doucet was finally entitled to damages in the amount of $4,000. In real terms, it was probably in the range of three times his annual earnings.

There seemed to have been little doubt that the explosion was caused by contact of the carbide in the furnace with water or water vapour from the mortar used to plug the openings in the furnace. The trial judge had found that the explosion could not have been the result of fault or neglect on the part of Doucet. He had no discretion as to the work required nor the manner in which he was to carry it out, and was injured in the course of discharging his duties in the manner in which he had been instructed to do them. Telegraphing to some extent, the direction in which the law might eventually move, one of the judges noted:

> Moreover, I would note *en passant*, that, to me, they seem to establish that, as found by the learned trial judge, and the majority of the judges in the Court of King's Bench, the things which caused the explosion, though the plaintiff [Doucet] was actually engaged with them, were not under his control or care, but were under the control and care of the defendants [Shawinigan]. They all belonged to them and were in use for their immediate purposes and profit. They had the direction and control of the manufacturing operations. The plaintiff was an unskilled workman—a servant acting in conformity to orders. I entertain no doubt that, upon the true construction of [the applicable provision], these things were in the control of the defendants.

There was no evidence of fault on the part of Shawinigan (although such evidence might have been available), so the Court could not base an award of damages on that basis and was left with having to interpret the generally stated principles of responsibility for damages under the

Civil Code of Lower Canada. The key language regarding fault and responsibility for things under care and control were Articles 1053 and 1054.

> 1053. Every person capable of discerning right from wrong is responsible for the damage caused by his fault to another, whether by positive act, imprudence, neglect or want of skill.

> 1054. He is responsible not only for the damage caused by his own fault, but also for that caused by the fault of persons under his control and by things which he has under his care;

> We have to show that portions of the provision have been omitted. The responsibility attaches in the above cases only when the person subject to it fails to establish that he was unable to prevent the act which has caused the damage.

What was interesting about the case was that in their analysis, two of the five sitting Supreme Court of Canada judges expressed the view that the applicable provision of what was then the Civil Code of Lower Canada established the presumption of liability for damages caused by things under one's control or care. The previous standard had been that, in a claim based on Article 1054, unless a plaintiff was able to show negligence on the part of the defendant, a claim for damages necessarily failed.

> There are other decisions of the Quebec courts ... in which it has been held that the effect of article 1054 C.C., is that, upon proof by the plaintiff that his injuries were caused by things under the care of the defendant, a presumption arises that such injuries are ascribable to the fault of the defendant, and the burden of proof is shifted, with the result that the defendant will be responsible in damages, unless he shews that he could not (presumably by the exercise of reasonable care and skill) have prevented the occurrence.

This seemed an unattractive outcome and led to a review of the law prior to the *Civil Code* and to French precedents, as well as to a comparison of the particular language used in the *Civil Code* with prior and other similar legislation, and eventually to the following observation:

Yet it seems to me that to hold that the defendant is responsible for damage caused by things under his care only when it is proved by the plaintiff that he has been negligent or at fault is to give no effect to the concluding words of the first paragraph of the article, because fault imputable to the defendant must be either that of himself or of persons under his control, and damage caused by such fault is expressly declared actionable by the earlier clauses of the paragraph. Notwithstanding that judges for whose opinions I entertain the very greatest respect have taken a different view of the proper construction of the first paragraph of article 1054 C.C., so far as it relates to cases of damage caused by things under the care of the defendant, I am of opinion that the terms of this paragraph are so clear and unambiguous that it is impossible to refuse to give effect to them merely because the responsibility to which they subject defendants may be unusually onerous.

The case did not ultimately require a definitive resolution of the position of the two judges, since Shawinigan had produced no evidence to show that the explosion was the fault of Doucet, or of some major defect, or that it was a pure accident, or that it had occurred without fault imputable to itself. It was enough that, absent such proof and without evidence of fault or negligence, the defendant would be responsible for damages shown to have been caused by things under his care.

Within the next dozen years, in a series of subsequent cases, the *Shawinigan* principle moved to be the position of the Court as a whole and was approved by the Privy Council. Absent proof on the part of a defendant that all reasonable precautions to avoid the damage had been taken, a presumption of responsibility was established. This proved to be a major breakthrough in making it possible to obtain relief for victims suffering damages as a result of "things," as opposed to personal fault on the part of someone causing damage. This would eventually become part of the civil law itself when the Civil Code of Quebec was redrafted.

Abuse of Power by Elected Officials

Roncarelli v. Duplessis [1959] S.C.R. 121

This is a fundamental case which underlines the importance of the rule of law and makes public officials responsible for arbitrary acts beyond their proper responsibilities.

The parties to the appeal were Frank Roncarelli, who sued the all-but-invincible Premier of Quebec, Maurice Duplessis, in damages. Not unlike John A. Macdonald, who did the same at the federal level, Duplessis also arranged to have himself appointed Attorney General of Quebec.

Roncarelli, a Jehovah's Witness in Montreal, operated a restaurant on fashionable Crescent Street, which he had inherited from his father, who had operated it since 1912. In connection with the restaurant, there had always been a liquor permit, held initially by Roncarelli's father and latterly by Roncarelli. The proselytizing activities of the Jehovah's Witnesses attracted vigorous opposition and some violence from the predominantly Roman Catholic population in Quebec. Distributors of printed matter by adherents of the sect were arrested and charged with violations of municipal by-laws of selling wares without a license. Roncarelli, who was not involved in any such activities, nevertheless put up bail for almost four hundred of those arrested, who would otherwise have been kept in jail pending payment of bail. Nothing he did could have been pertinent to his fitness or unfitness to hold a liquor license.

From the jaded perspective of the Quebec authorities, however, he was someone using the profits from the use of his Quebec liquor license to promote the disturbance of settled (read, Roman Catholic) beliefs and to arouse community disaffection. The head of the Liquor Commission, Edouard Archambault, telephoned Duplessis to advise him that Roncarelli was involved in the granting of bail to the Witnesses. Duplessis told the official to be sure of the identity of Roncarelli as both the furnisher of bail and as the holder of the liquor license, both of which were confirmed by a private investigator hired by the Commission. A further telephone call occurred, as a result of which Roncarelli's liquor license was immediately revoked, an order clearly given by Duplessis as a means to halt the activities of the Jehovah's Witnesses. Roncarelli was being punished for his role by revoking an existing license, as well as being forever barred from obtaining one, as a warning to others that they too could be stripped of provincial "privileges."

> It is then wholly as a private citizen, an adherent of a religious group, holding a liquor licence and furnishing bail to arrested persons for no other purpose than to enable them to be released from detention pending determination of the charges against them, and with no other relevant considerations to be taken into account, that he is involved in the issues of this controversy.

> The complementary state of things is equally free from doubt. From the evidence of Mr. Duplessis and Mr. Archambault alone, it appears that the action taken by the latter as the general manager and sole member of the Commission was dictated by Mr. Duplessis as Attorney-General and Prime Minister of the province; that the step was taken as a means of bringing to a halt the activities of the Witnesses, to punish the appellant for the part he had played not only by revoking the existing licence but in declaring him barred from one "forever," and to warn others that they similarly would be stripped of provincial "privileges" if they persisted in any activity directly or indirectly related to the Witnesses and to the objectionable campaign. The respondent [Duplessis] felt that action to be his duty, something which his conscience demanded of him; and as representing the provincial government his decision automatically that of Mr. Archambault and the Commission.

The question was whether there was legal redress available where there had been the exercise of executive control (by the Premier) over the appointee to a statutory public function (the Liquor Commission) to deliberately and intentionally destroy the vital business interests of a citizen.

The trial judge held that Duplessis was liable and ordered a modest payment of damages to Roncarelli. The Quebec Court of Appeal reversed that decision. The full Supreme Court of Canada heard the further appeal and, by a margin of six to three, restored the judgment of the trial judge, increasing the award of damages to $25,000. The majority concluded that there was ample evidence to sustain the finding of fact by the trial judge, namely that the cancellation of the permit was the result of an order given by Duplessis to the head of the Liquor Commission. (Appellate courts seldom interfere with findings of fact made by trial judges—they were not present to hear and observe the witnesses and make decisions as to their credibility—and therefore give a high degree of deference to such findings.) The majority also concluded that Duplessis was not acting in the exercise of any of his official powers. This was a particularly important finding, since it meant that Duplessis could not benefit from the formal protection provided in the Quebec Code of Civil Procedure regarding acts done by public officials in the exercise of their duties. His actions were so far outside his statutory powers and duties that his personal liability was engaged. The dissenting judges did not share that view.

The following extract comes from the reasons for judgment of Justice Ivan Rand, one of the better writers on the Court.

> ... what could be more malicious than to punish this licensee for having done what he had an absolute right to do in a matter utterly irrelevant to the *Liquor Act*? Malice in the proper sense is simply acting for a reason and purpose knowingly foreign to the administration, to which was added here the element of intentional punishment by what was virtually vocation outlawry.
>
> It may be difficult if not impossible in cases generally to demonstrate a breach of this public duty in the illegal purpose served; there may be no means, even if proceedings against the Commission were permitted by the Attorney-General, as here they were refused, of compelling the Commission to justify a refusal or revocation or to give reasons for its action; on these questions I make no observation; but in the case before us that difficulty is not present: the reasons are openly avowed.

The act of the respondent [Duplessis] through the instrumentality of the Commission brought about a breach of an implied public statutory duty toward the appellant; it was a gross abuse of legal power expressly intended to punish him for an act wholly irrelevant to the statute, a punishment which inflicted on him, as it was intended to do, the destruction of his economic life as a restaurant keeper within the province. Whatever may be the immunity of the Commission or its member for an action in damages, there is none for the respondent. He was under no duty in relation to the appellant and his act was an intrusion upon the functions of a statutory body. The injury done by him was a fault, engaging liability within the principles of the underlying public law of Quebec ... That, in the presence of expanding administrative regulation of economic activities, such a step and its consequences are to be suffered by the victim without recourse or remedy, that an administration according to law is to be superseded by action dictated by and according to the arbitrary likes, dislikes and irrelevant purposes of public officers acting beyond their duty, would signalize the beginning of disintegration of the rule of law as a fundamental postulate of our constitutional structure. An administration of licences on the highest level of fair and impartial treatment to all may be forced to follow the practice of "first come, first served," which makes the strictest observance of equal responsibility to all of even greater importance; at this stage of developing government it would be a danger of high consequence to tolerate such a departure from good faith in executing the legislative purpose.

Duplessis had argued that he had proceeded in good faith and that his role, notwithstanding the clear fact that he had ordered the revocation of the license, was merely giving advice. The argument was dispatched very easily.

"Good faith" in this context, applicable both to the respondent and the general manager, means carrying out the statute according to its intent and for its purpose; it means good faith in acting with a rational appreciation of that intent and purpose and not with an improper intent and for an alien purpose; it does not mean for the purposes of punishing a person for exercising an unchallengeable right; it does not mean arbitrarily and illegally attempting to divest a citizen of an incident of his civil status.

Two other judges responded to the argument that, as Attorney General, Duplessis had the responsibility to suppress or to prevent crimes and offences, which he could do by instituting legal proceedings or by other methods. The judges thought this amounted to the contention that Duplessis was free to use any methods he might choose, and that on suspicion of what he thought would be an offence, he could sentence a citizen to economic ruin without trial. That was considered to be a very dangerous proposition and one "completely alien to the legal concepts applicable to the administration of public office in Quebec, as well as in the other provinces of Canada."

This proved to be one of the classic cases stating and applying the rule of law to public officials, limiting arbitrary actions and holding them personally responsible for damages caused by their improper conduct. Duplessis had been a very powerful political figure in Quebec, and it had taken great courage on the part of Roncarelli to institute proceedings against him, plus perseverance on the part of counsel to wring the admission from Duplessis that he had, in fact, ordered the revocation of the permit, as well as the intellectual leadership of the scholar, poet and political activist, Frank Scott, who argued the case before the Court.

Duplessis was dead in less than nine months from the date of the judgment of the Court. Roncarelli died in relative poverty, employed by a railway company. Duplessis had, despite the loss in this case, achieved his desire to ruin Roncarelli financially. The courts, including the Supreme Court of Canada, fell woefully short of making Roncarelli whole from the damage caused to him.

A Prosecutor Must Never "Win" or "Lose"

Boucher v. The Queen [1955] S.C.R. 16

Ovila Boucher was convicted of the 1951 murder of Georges Jabour in Lévis County, Quebec, following a trial by judge and jury. His conviction had been upheld by a unanimous decision of the Quebec Court of Queen's Bench, Appeal Side (now the Quebec Court of Appeal). Leave to appeal to the Supreme Court was granted. Three grounds for appeal were argued.

The first was that the trial judge's charge to the jury regarding the overall burden of proof in criminal matters of proving guilt beyond all reasonable doubt had been deficient. In fact, that portion of the charge had been even more favourable to the accused than the usual standard. The second was that the trial judge had not explained to the jury the additional test in cases based largely on circumstantial evidence that not only must the evidence be consistent with the guilt of the accused, but it must also not be inconsistent with any other rational conclusion on the facts.

Both of these principles are well-established foundations of criminal law and problems tend to arise when trial judges set off on their own to use different language to explain concepts already decided by the courts on many other occasions. As to the first argument, the Court provided a gentle reminder that it is always best not to stray from settled language. As to the second point, the Court noted it had not been experiments with the language so much as a complete failure even to raise the matter before the jury.

But the real importance of this case as part of Canadian criminal law relates to the proper role of prosecuting [Crown] attorneys.

When addressing the jury, the prosecuting attorney had made statements of fact and inflammatory comments regarding the accused. One particular portion pertained to the overall approach to laying criminal charges:

> But the Crown is not here for the pleasure of condemning innocent persons. It is the duty of the Crown, when a matter like this arises, no matter what matter, and even more in a grave matter, to do all the investigations possible, and if in the course of these investigations with our experts we come to the conclusion that the accused is not guilty or that there is a reasonable doubt, it is the duty of the Crown, gentlemen, to say so or if we arrive at the conclusion that he is not guilty, not to arrest him. Here, this is what we did.
>
> When the Crown investigated that evidence, it was not with the intention of condemning the accused, it was with the notion of giving him justice. [unofficial translation]

The prosecuting attorney's concluding remarks to the jury were as follows:

> Every day we see more and more crimes than ever, robberies and many others. At least someone who commits armed robbery does not make his victim suffer like Boucher made Jabour suffer. It was a revolting crime by a man in the full prime of life, an athlete, against an old man of 77 years who was not capable of defending himself. I have some respect for those who rob when at least they have given a chance to their victims to defend themselves, but I have no sympathy, and I ask you to have none, no sympathy for these cowards who strike people, their friends—Jabour was perhaps not a friend, but he was a neighbour, at least they knew each other—in a cowardly manner, with blows from an axe. And, if you return a verdict of guilty, for once it will give me almost pleasure to request the death penalty against him. [unofficial translation]

All of the judges of the Court regarded these comments as excessive, although two of them thought that no substantial miscarriage of justice resulted. All the other judges were sufficiently concerned that they decided a new trial was warranted under the circumstances, because it could not be assumed that the jury would have reached the same conclusion had the statements not been made. The underlying principle of the role of the Crown in criminal prosecutions should be that the Crown neither wins nor loses. The Crown's responsibility is to bring the relevant facts to the attention of the court and to allow the decisions to be made by the court.

Somewhat different perspectives were expressed by members of the Court, although there was substantial agreement regarding the necessary outcome.

> There are a number of other passages in the address of this counsel to the jury which I do not find it necessary to quote as I think they can be fairly summarized by saying that counsel made it clear to the jury not only that he was submitting to them that the conclusion which they should reach on the evidence was that the accused was guilty, a submission which it was of course proper for him to make, but also that he personally entertained the opinion that the accused was guilty.

> There is no doubt that it is improper for counsel, whether for the Crown or the defence to express his own opinion as to the guilt or innocence of the accused.

> The grave objection to what was said by counsel is that the Jury would naturally and reasonably understand from his words first quoted above that he, with the assistance of other qualified persons, had made a careful examination into the facts of the case prior to the trial and that if as a result of such investigation he entertained any reasonable doubt as to the accused's guilt a duty rested upon him as Crown counsel to so inform the Court. As, far from expressing or suggesting the existence of any such doubt in his mind, he made it clear to the jury that he personally believed the accused to be guilty, the jury would reasonably take from what he had said that as a result of his investigation outside the court room Crown counsel had satisfied himself of the guilt of the accused. The making of such a statement to the jury was clearly unlawful and its damaging effect would, in my view, be even greater than the

admission of illegal evidence or a statement by Crown counsel to the jury in either his opening address or closing address of facts as to which there was no evidence.

Another, more contextual and visceral, approach was:

Many, if not the majority of, jurors acting, it may be, for the first time, unacquainted with the language and proceedings of courts, and with no precise appreciation of the role of the prosecution other than as being associated with government, would be extremely susceptible to the implications of such remarks. So to emphasize a neutral attitude on the part of the Crown representatives in the investigation of the facts of a crime is to put the matter to unsophisticated minds as if there had already been an impartial determination of guilt by persons in authority. It is the antithesis of the impression that should be given to them: they only are to pass on the issue and to do so only on what has been properly exhibited to them in the course of the proceedings.

It is difficult to reconstruct in mind and feeling the court room scene when a human life is at stake; the tensions, the invisible forces, subtle and unpredictable, the significance of a word may take on, are sensed at best imperfectly. It is not, then, possible to say that this reference to the Crown's action did not have a persuasive influence on the jury reaching their verdict. The irregularity touches on one of the oldest principles of our law, the rule that protects the subject from the pressures of the executive and it has its safeguard in the independence of our courts. It goes to the foundation of the security of the individual under the rule of law.

It cannot be over-emphasized that the purpose of a criminal prosecution is not to obtain a conviction, it is to lay before a jury what the Crown considers to be credible evidence relevant to what is alleged to be a crime. Counsel have a duty to see that all available legal proof of the facts is presented: it should be done firmly and pressed to its legitimate strength but it must also be done fairly. The role of the prosecutor excludes any notion of winning or losing; his function is a matter of public duty than which in civil life there can be none charged with greater responsibility. It is to be efficiently performed with an ingrained sense of the dignity, the seriousness and the justness of judicial proceedings.

From a practical perspective, an additional difficulty was that the statements of the Crown counsel were statements of fact, rather than argument. One of the judges noted that the facts stated by the prosecuting attorney were completely irrelevant and that if the attorney had elected to attempt to state them as a witness under oath, the evidence would have been rejected. Because these statements were made as part of argument, the otherwise inadmissible "facts" were nevertheless effectively submitted to the jury with the purpose of affecting their consideration. They were calculated to leave the impression that, before the accused was arrested, the Crown and its experts had made a thorough investigation and satisfied themselves that he was guilty beyond a reasonable doubt. Having slipped this statement in as part of the argument, there could be no possibility of any cross-examination to test the accuracy of those facts asserted.

This is a fundamental protection of the rights of persons accused of a crime and, while there are no doubt occasional transgressions, the clear duty of Crown counsel to conduct themselves in a special and responsible manner has been articulated in unequivocal terms by the highest court in the land.

Since the time of this decision in 1954, there have been significant changes to the rules regarding disclosure of evidence in the possession of the Crown to the defence, not only of evidence proposed to be used, but also of evidence that it may elect not to use, and which may prove favourable to the accused. Failure to make such full disclosure may lead to reversal of any conviction or a new trial.

Obscenity: Going to Bat for the Lady Chat

Brody, Dansky, Rubin v. The Queen [1962] S.C.R. 681

In 1959, Parliament amended section 150 of the *Criminal Code*, to add paragraph (8)

> For the purposes of the Act, any publication a dominant characteristic of which is the undue exploitation of sex, or sex and any one or more of the following subjects, namely, crime, horror, cruelty and violence, shall be deemed to be obscene.

The amendment was intended to codify at least certain elements of a common-law definition of obscenity that had been developing for more than a century and was likely intended to be the operating definition of obscenity for Canadian usage, although there was some division of opinion as to whether there might still be some vestiges of the common law still in play. For purposes of this particular case, however, the new statutory provision was the applicable test.

The book, *Lady Chatterley's Lover*, written by D. H. Lawrence, was first published in 1928 in Italy. Other editions were published in expurgated form, in which what was thought to be objectionable material was removed. Shortly before the *Criminal Code* was amended, an unexpurgated version was published. Several copies of it were seized in Quebec in November 1959, and several copies of it were also seized on the basis of a complaint under the *Criminal Code*. The Court of Sessions of the Peace ordered the books to be forfeited as obscene. The Quebec Court of Appeal (then Court of Queen's Bench) unanimously upheld that decision. An appeal was launched to the Supreme Court of Canada. The full bench of nine judges heard the case and, by a five-to-four majority, the work was declared not to be obscene.

At least three major Canadian literary figures were involved in the case. Hugh MacLennan and Morley Callaghan provided expert evidence as to the literary merits of the work and poet and constitutional scholar, F. R. Scott, (who also argued the *Roncarelli v. Duplessis* appeal—see page 149) argued the case. There was no dispute that the book contained a good deal of graphic descriptions of sex (at least fifteen) and many of the so-called four-letter words.

The majority began its treatment of the case as follows:

> The inquiry must begin with a search for a dominant characteristic of the book. The book may have other dominant characteristics. It is only necessary to prove that the undue exploitation of sex is a dominant characteristic. Such an inquiry necessarily involves a reading of the whole book with the passages and words to which objection is taken read in the context of the whole book. Of that there can be no doubt. No reader can find a dominant characteristic on a consideration of isolated passages and isolated words. Under this definition the book must now be taken as a whole. It is not the particular passages and words in a certain context that are before the Court for judgment but the book as a complete work. The question is whether the book as a whole is obscene, not whether certain passages and certain words, part of a larger work, are obscene.
>
> A search for a dominant characteristic of the book also involves an inquiry into the purpose of the author. What was he trying to do, actually doing, and intending to do? Had he a serious literary purpose or was his purpose one of base exploitation? ... One cannot ascertain a dominant characteristic of a book without an examination of its literary or artistic merit, and this, in my opinion, renders admissible the evidence of the author and others on this point. Evidence concerning literary and artistic merit has been excluded in England on the ground of relevancy and a supposed rule excluding evidence of opinion on the very fact which is before the Court for decision. ...

The test of the admissibility of this kind of opinion evidence under the present definition in the Code must be whether it is relevant to the determination of a dominant characteristic in the book. I can well understand that some judges and juries might think that such evidence would not help them to a decision and that others might be of the opposite opinion. I would join the second group. I can read and understand but at the same time I recognize that my training and experience have been, not in literature, but in law and I readily acknowledge that the evidence of the witnesses who gave evidence in this case is of real assistance to me in reaching a conclusion.

The evidence all pointed in a single direction. The witnesses and the many reviews of the book that were filed were unanimous in their opinions that it was a true and sincere representation of an aspect of life as it appeared to Lawrence, who had well-defined views of the organization of modern industrial society and its impact on the relations between man and woman. The theme of adultery and the assertion (whatever its merit) that there is an important connection between societal organization and the sexual relations between man and woman did not give the book the dominant characteristic as contained in the *Code*.

But I do not think that there is undue exploitation if there is no more emphasis on the theme than is required in the serious treatment of the theme of a novel with honesty and uprightness. That the work under attack is a serious work of fiction is to me beyond question. It has none of the characteristics that are often described in judgments dealing with obscenity—dirt for dirt's sake, the leer of the sensualist, depravity in the mind of the author with an obsession for dirt, pornography, appeal to a prurient interest, etc. The section recognizes that the serious-minded author must have freedom in the production of a work of genuine artistic and literary merit and the quality of the work, as the witnesses point out and common sense indicates, must have real relevance in determining not only a dominant characteristic but also whether there is undue exploitation. I agree with the submission of counsel for the appellant that measured by the internal necessities of the novel itself, there is no undue exploitation.

Whether the question of undue exploitation was to be measured by the internal necessities of the novel itself or by offence against community standards, the novel did not offend. A variation on this theme was expressed by one of the judges forming part of the majority.

> Having read the publication which is now before us as a whole and having considered the evidence of the experts called for the defence and the extensive, critical and other material having to do with the book which has been filed, I have little doubt that D. H. Lawrence deliberately selected sex as a dominant characteristic of *Lady Chatterley's Lover* and that one of the chief messages which he sought to convey was that there is nothing shameful or dirty about the natural functions of the body and that the ultimate physical fulfilment of love between the sexes is a thing of tenderness and beauty having no aspects of obscenity or pornography. It may be said with justice that the author has, in several isolated passages, employed language and depicted scenes which, standing alone, unduly exploit sex, but the opinion is widely held by men of high literary qualifications that this book as a whole constitutes an outstanding contribution to 20th-century English literature and the passages to which I refer must be regarded as an integral part of the wider theme. Although sex is a dominant characteristic of the book and although there are isolated passages which, read alone, unduly exploit sex, it does not appear to me to follow that these passages, read as part of the whole book, have the effect of making the undue exploitation which they contain a dominant characteristic of the publication so as to bring it within the provisions of s. 150(8) of the *Criminal Code*. Nor do I think that any significant segment of the population is likely to be depraved or corrupted by reading the book as a whole.

This was a sensible outcome and reflected a well-organized effort by the defence, which provided expert evidence that obviously assisted the judges forming the majority of Court in reaching their conclusion, combined with little evidence produced by the Crown, other than the book itself. It would have been anomalous indeed had Canada been the only western country that declared such an extraordinary work to be obscene.

Bearing in mind that the decision is now well over a half-century old, and that it was vigorously opposed by four judges of the Court, it is worth examining some of the dissenting comments in order to get a better flavour of the vehemence with which their opinions were expressed.

By reason of war wounds, the husband of Lady Chatterley was rendered impotent and, in order, as in substance the author puts it, that the wife should not be frustrated, she approached Mellors, the husband's gamekeeper, who was separated from his wife. In fact, she led him to the relationship that is afterwards set out in such great detail. There is not merely a description of one episode only, but of several, and it is sufficient to state that all of them are set forth in great detail that might have been expected in the Greece and Rome of ancient times.

More...

The author then minutely describes with unholy satisfaction more than fifteen adulterous scenes in the hen-house, the brush wood of the nearby fields, or the living quarters of the game keeper. Nothing is left even to the most vivid imagination. All the episodes are brutally described, and the conversation between the two lovers is of a low and vulgar character. Words are used that no decent person would dare to speak without, in my view, offending the moral sense of anyone who believes in the ordinary standards of decency, self-respect and dignity.

And more ...

This edition of the book contains no less than fifteen pornographic and adulterous episodes which decency has always forbidden ministerial and judicial officers to recite textually in the written opinion they gave as to its character. This edition is accurately described in the following excerpt from the interdiction pronounced in respect thereto by the United States Postmaster General:

> The book is replete with descriptions in minute detail of sexual acts engaged in or discussed by the book's principal characters. These descriptions utilize filthy, offensive and degrading words and terms. Any literary merit the book may have is far outweighed by the pornographic and smutty passages and words, so that the book taken as a whole, is an obscene and filthy work.

Whether admissible or not, expert evidence, so much relied upon by the appellants, as to the literary merit of Lawrence's works, is clearly ineffective to change this view of the book. The unexpurgated edition speaks for itself.

In light of this level of condemnation, imagine the courage of Lawrence in daring to write and publish a work of its importance, knowing the probable reaction in many parts of society. Great art always pushes the envelope.

Rape: Mistake of Fact as a Defence?

Pappajohn v. The Queen [1980] S.C.R. 120

The appellant was convicted of rape. His conviction was upheld by a majority of the Court of Appeal for British Columbia. The dissenting judge in that court considered that the trial judge had failed to put to the jury the possible defence of mistake of fact (that the accused may have had an honest belief that the complainant had consented to intercourse), and that such a failure amounted to misdirection, calling for a new trial.

The complainant was a successful real-estate agent employed by a well-known and well-established firm in Vancouver. The accused, a businessman anxious to sell his home, had listed it with the complainant's firm and she was to be responsible for the matter on behalf of the firm. She met the accused by appointment for lunch at a restaurant in the downtown area, to discuss the sale of the house. The lunch lasted from 1:00 until 4:00 or 4:30. During that time a good deal of alcohol was consumed by both parties, although each seemed to be capable of functioning normally. When they left the restaurant, the accused drove the complainant's car, while she sat in the front passenger seat. They went to the accused's house to consider further aspects in connection with the proposed sale. Up to the time of arrival at the house, the accounts of complainant and accused contained no significant variations.

Thereafter, there was complete divergence. It is appropriate to use the language of the Court to describe the facts.

The complainant, after describing the events of the early afternoon in the restaurant, said that upon entering into the house where discussions were to take place regarding its sale, the appellant seized her and pushed her down the hallway to the bedroom. She resisted his pushing and tried to reason with him. He said that he was going to break her and began, as soon as the bedroom was reached, to remove her blouse. She said she protested and screamed and grew hysterical and tried to reason with him but was not fighting him in a physical way. When he continued to remove her blouse, she realized he was going to rape her. She tried to escape but he threw her onto the bed and she became totally hysterical. She just lay on the bed and screamed. She then said she tried to rise from the bed but he held out his arm and told her to remove his cufflinks, she refused and then she tried to escape. He pushed her back onto the bed, removed her skirt, nylons and panties, but not her brassiere and slip. She remained on the bed screaming, then she observed that he was undressed, although she did not actually recall him undressing. She described various conversations in which she told him she was not able to take birth control pills and was without any contraceptive protection. She said that she and the man she lived with were attempting to have a baby and she was at that time ovulating. This information came, she said, from her lover who was a gynaecologist and he later gave evidence confirming these matters. She tried to persuade the appellant to desist but he would not be put off and finally had intercourse with her against her will. She said that the appellant had told her he would not ejaculate in her and she described three short acts of intercourse all against her will in which no ejaculation occurred. After some time the appellant left the bed and got a bow tie from a drawer and a sashcord from a dressing gown. Again, against her will, he tied the bow tie over her mouth as a gag and tied her hands behind her back. She struggled against this and threw herself from the bed onto the floor. He put her back on the bed and while her hands remained tied had intercourse again from the rear. During all this time she said she was at times pleading and reasoning with him, at times hysterical and screaming, and at times endeavouring to avoid and escape him. She said at one stage when she saw him get the tie and cord that she decided he was going to kill her. Shortly after the incident of falling off the bed, and by this time three hours had elapsed, she said that he left the room. She seized the opportunity to escape and fled from the house naked with her hands still tied behind her back. She ran down an alley and pounded at the door of a nearby house. She was admitted and the police were called. During all this period, she insisted that she did not consent to any of the acts of intercourse. She insisted that she was hysterical, fearful and helpless in his hands and she escaped as soon as she could.

The appellant's version was quite different. Again, in the words of the Court:

> The appellant, in giving evidence on his own behalf, said that upon arrival at the house, he entered and went immediately to the bathroom. On his return to the front of the house, he led the complainant into the living room. They sat on a couch and began to kiss. During this episode, she removed her necklace and left her car keys on a table in the living room. They then moved into the bedroom where she consented to the removal of her clothes. He agreed that she refused to undo his cufflinks but he undressed and they then had intercourse with her consent. He admitted to three occasions and admitted that he had no ejaculations. The whole performance, while with her consent, was not very successful. He admitted getting the tie to gag her and the cord to bind her, saying it was done as an act of bondage to stimulate sexual activity. He said that when bound she suddenly threw herself from the bed and was hysterical and screaming. He said that he put her back on the bed. He left to find a cigarette and on his return she had gone. He did not know where. He waited for some time then put some clothes on and had a look around the house and the yard but could not find her. He insisted that everything was done with her consent. She made no serious resistance to his advances beyond making such coy inquiries as "George, what are you doing?" He said he would not have forced her if she had resisted, that she made no objection to his advances, and, that when she threw herself from the bed he desisted from any further efforts at intercourse and did not have intercourse after that event.

Once the defence had closed its case, but before the trial judge had begun his charge to the jury, and in the absence of the jury, the appellant's counsel argued that on the facts of the case, the trial judge should put the defence of mistake of fact to the jury. If the appellant entertained an honest, though mistaken, belief that the complainant was consenting to the acts of intercourse as they occurred, the necessary *mens rea* [guilty intent] would not have been present and the appellant would be entitled to an acquittal. The trial judge found no evidence of any sufficient weight to do so. On the basis of the evidence, the issue was consent or no consent, and the jury, as the deciders of fact, would have to decide which version of the facts they preferred, the complainant's or the appellant's. The burden was also on the Crown to prove its case beyond a reasonable doubt, so all the appellant had to do was to raise a reasonable doubt in the minds of the jury. That he failed to do so was evidenced by his conviction.

The Court found that although the trial judge must draw to the attention of the jury and put before them fairly and completely the theory of the defence, this does not mean that he or she is bound to put every defence that may be suggested by counsel, especially if there is no evidence on which a particular defence may rest. If such evidence is not present, the defence should not be put to the jury, since it would only create unnecessary confusion.

> With that thought in mind, and bearing in mind that the object of judicial search must be evidence of a mistaken but honest belief in the consent of the complainant, one must first ask the question "Where is this evidence to be found?" It cannot be found in the evidence of the complainant. She denies actual consent and her evidence cannot provide any support for a mistaken belief in consent. Her conduct, according to her description, is that of a terrified, hysterical, non-consenting woman who resisted the appellant's advances, albeit unsuccessfully, and when able fled from the house in search of assistance. Turning then to the evidence of the appellant, it immediately becomes apparent that his evidence speaks of actual consent, even cooperation, and leaves little if any room for the suggestion that she may not have been consenting but he thought she was. The two stories are, as has been noted above, diametrically opposed on this vital issue. It is not for the trial judge to weigh them and prefer one to the other. It is for him in this situation, however, to recognize the issue which arises on the evidence for the purpose of deciding what defences are open. In this situation, the only realistic issue which can arise is the simple issue of consent or no consent. In my opinion, the trial judge was correct in concluding that there simply was not sufficient evidence to justify putting the defence of mistake of fact to the jury. He left the issue of consent and that was the only one arising on the evidence.

Clearly, one of the concerns of the Court was that if it were necessary to charge the jury in this case on the defence of mistake of fact, it would be necessary to do so in every case where a complainant denies consent and an accused asserts it.

> Where the complainant says rape and the accused says consent, and where on the whole of the evidence, including that of the complainant, the accused and the surrounding circumstances, there is a clear issue on this point, and where the accused makes no assertion of a belief in consent as opposed to an actual consent, it is unrealistic in the absence of some other circumstance or circumstances ... to consider the judge bound to put the defence on the evidence before him ...

This is not to say, therefore, that such a defence is unavailable in Canadian law. It can be a defence when it prevents an accused from having the *mens rea* that the law requires for the crime with which he is charged, allowing an accused who acts innocently pursuant to a flawed perception of the facts and who nevertheless commits the "criminal" act, to escape criminal liability. But, it is not an automatic defence that the jury must consider in all cases.

Rape, according to a well-known text on criminal law, is aimed at the protection of women from forcible subjection to non-marital sexual intercourse. (The case before the Court did not call for it to consider the circumstances of possible rape within a marital relationship.) The suggested defence should be available when there is an honest belief in consent, or an absence of knowledge that consent has been withheld.

> In relying upon consent as a defence, the appellant invites the trier of fact to find in all the circumstances that she did consent (i.e., to reject her testimony). In relying on honest belief, he is suggesting that even if she did not consent, he nonetheless proceeded in the mistaken but honest belief that she had been willing. Though the offence was committed, he is not responsible, for he lacked the requisite intention. In most cases it is difficult to imagine that consent and honest belief can offer alternative defences. If there is no consent in fact, rare is the case in which a man will, nonetheless, believe that it was given.

The outcome in this appeal prevented possible erosion of the protection of women against rape. It is a defence that often has the effect of putting the female victim on trial.

The Battered-Wife Defence

R. v. Lavallée [1990] 1 S.C.R. 852

In the early hours of August 31, 1986, following an argument, Angelique Lyn Lavallée shot and killed Kevin Rust with a single shot to the back of his head with a .303 calibre rifle as he was leaving their bedroom, following a boisterous party from which most of the guests had already left. She was twenty-two years old and had been living with Rust for three or four years.

Although Lavallée did not give evidence at her trial, there was abundant evidence from others regarding a pattern of violence and physical abuse. Between 1983 and 1986, Lavallée had made several trips to hospital for treatment of injuries, which included severe bruises, a fractured nose, multiple contusions, and a black eye. At least one of the attending physicians on one occasion did not believe her explanation that the injuries were the result of falling from a horse. Others had seen Rust beating her. On the evening of the murder, she said, in the statement to the police who arrested her:

> OK and then he went out and I was sitting on the bed and he started going like this with his finger [the appellant made a shaking motion with an index finger] and said something like "You're my old lady and you do as you're told" or something like that. He said "wait till everybody leaves, you'll get it then" and he said something to the effect of "either you kill me or I'll get you" that was what it was. He kind of smiled and then he turned around. I shot him but

I aimed out. I thought I aimed above his head and a piece of his head went
that way.

There was no doubt that Lavallée had fired the shot, nor that she had
been physically abused on many occasions. Her defence to the charges
laid was that of self-defence. The provision of the *Criminal Code* that
provides for such a defence reads:

> 34. ...
>
> (2) Every one who is unlawfully assaulted and who causes death or grievous
> bodily harm in repelling the assault is justified if
>
> (a) he causes it under reasonable apprehension of death or grievous bodily
> harm from the violence with which the assault was originally made or with
> which the assailant pursues his purposes, and
>
> (b) he believes on reasonable and probable grounds, that he cannot other-
> wise preserve himself from death or grievous bodily harm.

The case before the Supreme Court of Canada arose from the expert
evidence given by a psychiatrist with extensive professional experience
in the treatment of battered wives. He had, at the request of defence
counsel, prepared a psychiatric assessment of Lavallée, the substance
of which was that she had been terrorized by Rust to the point of feeling
trapped, vulnerable, worthless and unable to escape the relationship
despite the violence. At the same time, he noted that the continuing
pattern of abuse put her life in danger and that the shooting was a final
desperate act by a woman who sincerely believed that she would be
killed that night. His opinion was based on four hours of formal inter-
views with Lavallée, the police report of the incident, hospital reports
documenting her visits to emergency departments, and an interview
with her mother. It was also based (and this is part of what created difficulties for the courts) on things told to the psychiatrist for which there
was no admissible evidence and which were not contained in the statement to the police.

The Crown, after the psychiatrist had testified and been cross-exam-
ined, attempted to have his evidence removed from the jury's consideration because it was based at least in part on the fact that some of the
evidence on which he relied in reaching his conclusions was not before

the court. The trial judge thought that the evidence could remain, provided that the charge to the jury (the trial judge's instructions as to the applicable law and summary of the evidence properly before the jury) raised the importance of the jury understanding what was and what was not based on facts properly brought before it. The jury acquitted Lavallée, but a majority of the Manitoba Court of Appeal overturned the verdict and sent the case back for retrial, essentially on two grounds: that the evidence of the psychiatrist's evidence should not have been before the jury and that the charge to the jury had been defective.

This gave rise to a consideration of the role of expert evidence. Generally, if the subject matter of the inquiry is such that ordinary people are unlikely to form a correct judgment about it unless assisted by persons with special knowledge, then an expert witness is brought in. This would include technical information, scientific theory, engineering matters, pathology, and, in this case, psychiatric or psychological testimony, all predicated on the likelihood that the average person may not have sufficient knowledge to draw the proper inferences from the facts before him or her. The Crown position was, in effect, that the judge and jury were thoroughly knowledgeable about human behaviour and that nothing further was needed. The Court rejected that position.

> Expert evidence on the psychological effect of battering on wives and common law partners must, it seems to me, be both relevant and necessary in the context of the present case. How can the mental state of the appellant [Lavallée] be appreciated without it? The average member of the public (or of the jury) can be forgiven for asking: Why would a woman put up with this kind of treatment? Why should she continue to live with such a man? How could she love a partner who beat her to the point of requiring hospitalization? We would expect the woman to pack her bags and go. Where is her self-respect? Why does she not cut loose and make a new life for herself? Such is the reaction of the average person confronted with the so-called "battered wife syndrome." We need help to understand it and help is available from trained professionals.

It went on to review the developments in the law, which had formerly sanctioned the abuse of women within marriage as an aspect of "ownership" of women by their husbands. While the legislative initiatives had moved a long way to correct the historical abuses, there has by no means been a complete reversal of the concept of matrimonial subjugation.

> However, a woman who comes before a judge or jury with the claim that she has been battered and suggests that this may be a relevant factor in evaluating her subsequent actions still faces the prospect of being condemned by popular mythology about domestic violence. Either she was not as badly beaten as she claims or she would have left the man long ago. Or, if she was battered that severely, she must have stayed out of some masochistic enjoyment of it.

The Court went on, in the context of the "reasonable" requirement in the self-defence provision, to observe that if it strained credulity to imagine what the "ordinary man" would do in the position of a battered spouse, it was probably because men do not typically find themselves in that position. "Some women do, however. The definition of what is reasonable must be adapted to circumstances which are, by and large, foreign to the world inhabited by the hypothetical 'reasonable man.'"

It then considered some of the typical and chilling elements of the battered-wife syndrome as contained in the psychiatrist's opinion and sources on which he had relied in forming his opinion of the psychological state of Lavallée. This included the cyclical nature of the violence, the escalation of it, the predictive features, including apparent remorse on the part of the male, the belief by the woman that thinks she can improve the man, traumatic bonding, and the deterioration of the situation that may lead to a final action.

> Where evidence exists that an accused is in a battering relationship, expert testimony can assist the jury in determining whether the accused had a "reasonable" apprehension of death when she acted by explaining the heightened sensitivity of a battered woman to her partner's acts. Without such testimony I am sceptical that the average fact-finder would be capable of appreciating why her subjective fear may have been reasonable in the context of the relationship. After all, the hypothetical "reasonable man" observing only the final incident may have been unlikely to recognize the batterer's threat as potentially lethal. Using the case at bar as an example the "reasonable man" might have thought, as the majority in the Court of Appeal seemed to, that it was

unlikely that Rust would make good on his threat to kill the appellant that night because they had guests staying overnight.

The issue is not, however, what an outsider would have reasonably perceived but what the accused reasonably perceived, given her situation and her experience.

In a self-defence trial, the issue is not whether the defendant is a battered woman, but whether in the circumstances it was justifiable that she killed her husband. It is the jury that must decide whether, as a matter of fact, the perceptions and actions of the accused were reasonable. It is important to note that no jury is compelled to accept the expert opinions that are offered about the effects of battering on the mental state of victims in general or on the particular accused, since that evidence does not supplant the function of the jury. On the other hand, the Court concluded that fairness and the integrity of the trial process demanded that the jury have the opportunity to hear them.

Rather than exclude the whole of the expert's report, where part of it may have been based on facts not proven in court, the duty of the trial judge was not to exclude the report, but to caution the jury "that the weight attributable to the expert testimony is directly related to the amount and quality of admissible evidence on which it relies." The Court was satisfied that the trial judge had made that sufficiently clear to the jury and that a new trial was not warranted on the basis of his charge to the jury.

The cautionary element with respect to expert evidence is that, precisely because the subject matter of that evidence is generally not something with which a judge or jury is likely to be familiar, special care must be taken to avoid being fooled by "quacks" masquerading as experts, or experts who lose track of their proper function of independent expertise and who become, in effect, advocates for the position of a party to the litigation. In this case, there seemed to be no suggestion of either possibility and no contrary evidence was offered by the Crown. The persuasiveness of the evidence was undoubtedly the reason why, after hearing and cross-examining on it, the Crown sought to have it removed from consideration by the jury.

Hate Propaganda: Does Prosecution Violate the Accused's Charter Rights?

Regina v. Keegstra [1990] 3 S.C.R. 697

James Keegstra was a high school teacher in Alberta, who was dismissed in 1982. Two years later, he was charged under the *Criminal Code* for unlawfully promoting hatred against an identifiable group by communicating anti-semitic statements to his students. He described Jews using terms such as *treacherous, subversive, sadistic, money-loving, power hungry, child killers, revolutionists, imposters, communists, secret, sneaky, manipulative,* and *deceptive.* His classes were told that Jewish people seek to destroy Christianity and were responsible for depressions, anarchy, chaos, wars, and revolution. According to him, Jews "created the Holocaust to gain sympathy" and, in contrast to the open and honest Christians, were said to be deceptive, secretive, and inherently evil. Indeed, he maintained that anyone Jewish must be evil and that anyone evil must be Jewish. He expected his students to reproduce his teachings in assignments and on exams. If they did so, they got good marks; if they did not, their marks were poor. Keegstra was convicted by a jury in a trial before the Alberta Court of Queen's Bench (the provincial superior court).

The applicable provision of the *Criminal Code* was section 319, which read:

(2) Every one who, by communicating statements, other than in private con-

versation, wilfully promotes hatred against any identifiable group is guilty of

(a) an indictable offence and is liable to imprisonment for a term not exceeding two years; or

(b) an offence punishable on summary conviction.

(3) No person shall be convicted of an offence under subsection (2)

(a) if he establishes that the statements communicated were true;

(b) if, in good faith, he expressed or attempted to establish by argument an opinion on a religious subject;

(c) if the statements were relevant to any subject of public interest, the discussion of which was for the public benefit, and if on reasonable grounds he believed them to be true; or

(d) if, in good faith, he intended to point out, for the purpose of removal, matters producing or tending to produce feelings of hatred towards an identifiable group in Canada.

...

(6) No proceeding for an offence under subsection (2) shall be instituted without the consent of the Attorney General.

Prior to his trial, Keegstra attempted to have the charge quashed [dismissed] on a number of grounds, chiefly that the *Criminal Code* provision was unconstitutional because it unjustifiably infringed on his freedom of expression as guaranteed by section 2(b) of the *Charter*, which, together with the introductory language in section 1, provided:

1.   The *Canadian Charter of Rights and Freedoms* guarantees the rights and freedoms set out in it subject only to such reasonable limits prescribed by law as can be demonstrably justified in a free and democratic society.

2.   Everyone has the following fundamental freedoms:

...

(b) freedom of thought, belief, opinion and expression, including freedom of the press and other media of communication;

These types of pre-trial motions are quite common, especially in criminal matters, where defence lawyers may not want the facts to come before juries or judges and attempt to win cases on procedural grounds to the point that justice in many cases of criminal law has become far more procedural than substantive.

His motion was rejected. He proceeded to trial and was convicted. On appeal to the Alberta Court of Appeal, however, the appeal was allowed, that Court determining that the *Charter* had been violated. That led to the appeal before the Supreme Court of Canada, which, in a very lengthy four to three decision, reversed the Court of Appeal decision and restored the conviction.

This was not an easy case to decide. None of the members of the Court supported the hate propaganda spewing from Keegstra and all of them were equally offended by it.

> Hatred is predicated on destruction, and hatred against identifiable groups therefore thrives on insensitivity, bigotry and destruction of both the target group and the values of our society. Hatred in this sense is a most extreme emotion that belies reason; an emotion that, if exercised against members of an identifiable group, implies that those individuals are to be despised, scorned, denied respect and made subject to ill-treatment on the basis of group affiliation.

The problem was not that anyone wanted to excuse or minimize the infandous conduct of a person responsible for exposing young students to that propaganda, but rather how to deal with it in the context of the fundamental *Charter* guarantee of freedom of expression. Was it appropriate to criminalize the conduct, or were there other more appropriate measures?

Both the majority and the minority relied upon and referred to the 1966 *Report of the Special Committee on Hate Propaganda in Canada*, the opening paragraph in the Preamble of which stated:

> This Report is a study in the power of words to maim, and what it is that a civilized society can do about it. Not every abuse of human communication can or should be controlled by law or custom. But every society from time to time draws lines at the point where the intolerable and the impermissible collide.

In a free society such as our own, where the privilege of speech can induce ideas that may change the very order itself, there is a bias weighted heavily in favour of the maximum of rhetoric whatever the cost and consequences. But that bias stops this side of injury to the community itself and to individual members or identifiable groups innocently caught in verbal cross-fire that goes beyond legitimate debate.

The Committee recommended amendments to the *Criminal Code*, including the provision now before the Court, namely the wilful promotion of hatred. The constitutional question was whether freedom of expression, whatever that meant, was infringed by the *Criminal Code* and how competing interests might co-exist with the freedom guaranteed by section 1 of the *Charter*. The Canadian courts had long protected freedom of expression, well before the advent of the *Charter* and even before the 1960 *Canadian Bill of Rights*.

The pre-*Charter* jurisprudence emphasized the importance of political expression because it was a challenge to that form of expression that most often arose under the division of powers and the "implied bill of rights," where freedom of political expression could be related to the maintenance and operation of the institutions of democratic government. But political expression is only one form of the great range of expression that is deserving of constitutional protection because it serves individual and societal values in a free and democratic society.

There was little doubt on the part of both the majority and the minority of the Court that subsection 319(2) of the *Criminal Code* infringed the freedom of expression entrenched in section 2(b) of the *Charter*, despite the fact that it included hate propaganda. This led to examining whether that infringement was justifiable under section 1 of the *Charter* as a reasonable limit in a free and democratic society and here was where the majority and minority parted company.

The analytical framework in *Oakes* (see page 50) had already made its mark and was used again in this case. The Court was willing to examine U.S. jurisprudence on the U.S. equivalent of the *Charter* protection (the well-known First Amendment to the U.S. Constitution), from which there was much to be learned, but it was also careful to reserve space for the uniquely Canadian vision of a free and democratic society and, therefore, should not hesitate whenever necessary to depart from the path taken in the U.S. The objective of the *Criminal Code* provision was summarized as follows:

> Parliament has recognized the substantial harm that can flow from hate propaganda, and in trying to prevent the pain suffered by the target group members and to reduce racial, ethnic and religious tension in Canada has decided to suppress the wilful promotion of hatred against identifiable groups. The nature of Parliament's objective is supported not only by the work of numerous study groups, but also by our collective historical knowledge of the potentially catastrophic effects of the promotion of hatred. ... Additionally, the international commitment to eradicate hate propaganda and the stress placed upon equality and multiculturalism in the *Charter* strongly buttress the importance of this objective. I consequently find that the first part of the test under s. 1 of the *Charter* is easily satisfied and that a powerfully convincing legislative objective exists such as to justify some limit on freedom of expression.

The second *Oakes* test was proportionality—was the legislative response a reasonable limit on the freedom of expression in a free and democratic society? That analysis could not ignore the nature of the expression sought to be restricted. On the other hand, the Court had to guard against judging expression according to its popularity, while at the same time recognizing that it can be equally destructive of free-expression values to treat all expressions as equally crucial to the principles at the core of section 2(b) of the *Charter*.

> The suppression of hate propaganda undeniably muzzles the participation of a few individuals in the democratic process and hence detracts somewhat from free expression values, but the degree of this limitation is not substantial. I am aware that the use of strong language in political and social debate—indeed, perhaps even language designed to promote hatred—is an unavoidable part of the democratic process. Moreover, I recognize that hate propaganda is expression of a type which would generally be categorized as "political," thus putatively placing it at the very heart of the principle extolling freedom of expression as vital to the democratic process. Nonetheless, expression can work

to undermine our commitment to democracy where employed to propagate ideas anathemic to democratic values. Hate propaganda works in just such a way, arguing as it does for a society in which the democratic process is subverted and individuals are denied respect and dignity simply because of racial or religious characteristics. This brand of expressive activity is thus wholly inimical to the democratic aspirations of the free expression guarantee.

Concluding that the principle of proportionality was respected, the majority noted that *wilfully* imposes a difficult burden for the Crown to meet, that Parliament can use the criminal law to prevent the risk of serious harm (here to the target group), that *promotes* means more than simple encouragement or advancement of the subject matter, the exclusion of private conversation, and the need for there to be a target. Nor should the proportionality consideration force a government, in every circumstance, to rely solely on a mode of intervention least likely to interfere the least with a *Charter* freedom.

The minority was concerned that virtually nothing should trump the right of free expression and worried about the "chilling effect" that might result from legislation limiting expression. The mere suppression of expression by the state might imply that there is some truth to what is being suppressed. The power of the authorities to invoke the legislation might be abused. Other remedies might be more appropriate and effective than the severity of criminalization. It concluded that such criminalization did not impair free speech to the minimum extent permitted by its objectives.

Death Penalty: No Extradition

United States v. Burns [2001] 1 S.C.R. 283

Glen Sebastian Burns (a Canadian) and a co-accused Atif Ahmad Rafay (a non-Canadian) were sought by the United States for the brutal murder of three members of the family of the co-accused, who apparently thought his financial prospects would be improved if all the other family members were dead. Burns was thought to be the physical murderer, having used a baseball bat as the murder instrument, and the described circumstances were particularly horrific. The crime had been committed in the state of Washington and the U.S. authorities wanted the suspects extradited from Canada in order to stand trial for the murders. Washington was a state in which convicted murderers could face the death penalty, either by lethal injection or, at the option of the convicted criminal, by hanging. The federal Minister of Justice ordered the extradition without attaching any conditions regarding capital punishment. The British Columbia Court of Appeal held that failure to attach conditions violated the *Charter* rights of the accused, and the matter found its way to the Supreme Court of Canada.

Exercise of the power to extradite persons is, essentially, a matter of discretion under the various extradition agreements between Canada and other countries and the courts generally accord considerable deference to ministerial decisions on matters of public policy. The Minister had relied on two previous decisions of the Court in which extradition without conditions had been authorized, even where it was likely that the persons extradited would face the death penalty. Both were well-publicized cases. One involved an American citizen (Joseph John Kindler) convicted of the brutal murder of a witness scheduled to testify against him in a burglary case. He was convicted of the murder. The jury recommended the death penalty, but Kindler escaped to Canada and was eventually captured. Judicial review of the "surrender" order (by which he would be surrendered to the U.S. authorities) was dismissed, even though the death penalty was no longer a mere possibility. The other was Charles Chitat Ng, a Hong Kong-born British subject who moved to the U.S. He was arrested in Calgary following the shooting of security guards who tried to arrest him for shoplifting. After his identity was established, he was extradited to California, where he was tried and convicted of eleven murders during a "spree of sexual torture and murder. The Minister was held by the Court to have the power, though not the duty, to extradite without assurances.

The approach developed by the Court was to attempt to implement a balancing process that would keep the global context squarely in mind and, even in the cases in which the Court allowed extradition without conditions, it nevertheless recognized that there might be circumstances that could vitiate an order for surrender. The Court decided that the approach used in those cases—the balancing process—was still the correct manner of proceeding.

It is inherent in the *Kinder* and *Ng* balancing process that the outcome may well vary from case to case depending on the mix of contextual factors put into the balance. Some of these factors will be very specific, such as the mental condition of a particular fugitive. Other factors will be more general, such as the difficulties, both practical and philosophic, associated with the death penalty. Some of these factors will be unchanging; others will evolve over time. The outcome of this appeal turns more on the practical and philosophic difficulties associated with the death penalty that have increasingly preoccupied the courts and legislators in Canada, the United States and elsewhere than on the specific circumstances of the respondents in this case. Our analysis will lead to the conclusion that in the absence of exceptional circumstances, which we refrain from trying to anticipate, assurances in death penalty cases are always constitutionally required.

The real crux of the matter was that there had been, since the earlier cases, considerable widespread evolution in generalized resistance to the death penalty. An increasing number of countries had abolished the penalty and many, while still having it as part of their law, had stopped carrying out the sentences. Canada had played an active role internationally, advocating for abolition of capital punishment. There had been too many cases of miscarriage of justice, where the accused—and convicted individuals—had eventually been exonerated and released. None of these cases could have been remedied if the death penalty had already been carried out. Examining the context of Canada's position, the Court concluded that aversion to the death penalty had become embedded as a fundamental element in Canadian principles of fundamental justice.

One of the challenges for the Court was to bridge the possible gap between the power of the Minister to exercise discretion under the extradition treaty with the U.S. and its own responsibility to declare, in appropriate circumstances, the exercise of that discretion to be unconstitutional. It undertook an extensive review of experiences in Canada, the U.S., and the U.K., concluding that, despite the safeguards for protection of the innocent, where fugitives are sought to be tried for murder in a state which retains the death penalty, the history of such miscarriages of justice weighed heavily in the balance against extradition without assurances.

> The distinction between "general public policy" on the one hand and "the inherent domain of the judiciary as guardians of the justice system" is of particular importance in a death penalty case. The broader aspects of the death penalty controversy, including the role of retribution and deterrence in society, and the view that capital punishment is inconsistent with the sanctity of human life, are embedded in the basic tenets of our legal system, but they also reflect philosophic positions informed by beliefs and social science evidence outside "the inherent domain of the judiciary." The narrower aspects of the controversy are concerned with the investigation, prosecution, defence, appeal and sentencing of a person within the framework of the criminal law. They bear on the protection of the innocent, the avoidance of miscarriages of justice, and the rectification of miscarriages of justice when they are found to exist. These considerations are central to the preoccupation of the courts,

and directly engage the responsibility of judges "as guardian[s] of the justice system." We regard the present controversy of Canada and the United States over possible miscarriages of justice in murder convictions ... as falling within the second category, and therefore as engaging the special responsibility of the judiciary for the protection of the innocent.

Having reviewed the factors for and against unconditional extradition, the Court concluded that to order extradition of the particular fugitives in this case without obtaining assurances that the death penalty would not be imposed would violate the principles of fundamental justice.

It is true that if assurances are requested, the respondents will not face the same punishment regime that is generally applicable to crimes committed in Washington State, but the reality is that Washington requires the assistance of Canada to bring the respondents to justice. Assurances are not sought out of regard for the respondents, but out of regard for the principles that have historically guided this country's criminal justice system and are presently reflected in its international stance on capital punishment.

The resulting constitutional principle has been expressed as a general rule, that extradition without assurances violates the constitutional rights of the fugitive, absent exceptional circumstances. The burden of demonstrating the exceptional circumstances that justify not obtaining the assurances rests with the Minister and it is safe to assume that it will not be one easily discharged, especially if resistance to capital punishment continues to develop.

The final analysis of the Court was to determine whether the violation of the respondents' *Charter* rights (extradition to face the death penalty) could be upheld under section 1 of the *Charter* as reasonable and demonstrably justifiable in a free and democratic society. This proved not to be a difficult call, since the Court had already noted that it would be rare for a violation of the fundamental principles of justice to be justifiable under section 1. Although not foreclosing the possibility that there might be situations in which the Minister's objectives were so pressing and there were no other way to achieve those objectives other than through extradition without assurances that a violation might be justified, no such justification existed in the present case.

The Court also dealt with the suggestion that Canada might become a "safe haven" for persons committing murders in states that impose the death penalty.

> International criminal law enforcement including the need to ensure that Canada does not become a "safe haven" for dangerous fugitives is a very legitimate objective, but there is no evidence whatsoever that extradition to face life in prison without release or parole provides a lesser deterrent to those seeking a "safe haven" than the death penalty, or even that fugitives approach their choice of refuge with such an informed appreciation of tactics. If Canada suffers the prospect of being a haven from time to time for fugitives from the United States, it likely has more to do with geographic proximity than the Minister's policy on treaty assurances. The evidence as stated is that Ministers of Justice have on at least two occasions (since *Kinder* and *Ng*) refused to extradite without assurances, and no adverse consequences to Canada from those decisions were brought to our attention. The respondents pointed out that "[s]ince the execution by the United States of two Mexican nationals in 1997, Mexican authorities have consistently refused to extradite anyone, nationals or non-nationals, in capital cases without first seeking assurances."

Readers, therefore, who may face extradition from Canada to the United States on charges of murder can rest assured that they will not face execution—merely life imprisonment with no possibility of parole.

Juries Decide the Facts: the Judge Determines the Law

R. v. Latimer [2001] 1 S.C.R. 3

F̲ew Canadian trials and appeals have attracted as much attention as
that involving Robert Latimer. The set-up paragraph in the decision
of the Supreme Court of Canada identifies all of the issues arising from
his second trial.

> This appeal arises from the death of Tracy Latimer, a 12-year-old girl who had
> a severe form of cerebral palsy. Her father, Robert Latimer, took her life some
> seven years ago. He was found guilty of second degree murder. This appeal
> deals with three questions of law arising from his trial. First, did the trial judge
> mishandle the defence of necessity, resulting in an unfair trial? Second, was
> the trial unfair because the trial judge misled the jury into believing it would
> have some input into the appropriate sentence? Third, does the imposition
> of the mandatory minimum sentence for second degree murder constitute
> "cruel and unusual punishment" in this case, so that Mr. Latimer ... should
> receive a constitutional exemption from the minimum sentence?

A unanimous bench of seven judges answered all three questions in
the negative. The Court acknowledged that the questions arising in Latimer's case had divided Canadians and sparked a national discourse,
and that its judgment would not end that discourse.

There was no serious dispute regarding the facts. The cerebral palsy, caused by neurological damage, was severe and permanent. Tracy Latimer was quadriplegic, immobile, bedridden much of the time, and had the mental capacity of a four-month-old baby. She could communicate only by means of facial expressions, laughing and crying. Despite the anti-epileptic medications she took, she suffered five to six seizures per day. She was thought to suffer a great deal of pain, which could not be reduced because the pain medication conflicted with the anti-epileptic medication. Spoon-feeding, was difficult because of her inability to swallow, and Tracy was losing weight. The Latimers rejected a feeding tube as intrusive and a first step toward artificial preservation of their daughter's life. Her breathing difficulties had increased and she would have to undergo repeated surgeries, of which she had already had several, causing her considerable pain. She was not, however, terminally ill.

> Tracy was scheduled to undergo further surgery on November 19, 1993. This was to deal with her dislocated hip and, it was hoped, to lessen her constant pain. The procedure involved removing her upper thigh bone, which would leave her lower leg loose without any connecting bone; it would be held in place only by muscle and tissue. The anticipated recovery period for this surgery was one year.

> The Latimers were told that this procedure would cause pain, and the doctors involved suggested that further surgery would be required in the future to relieve the pain emanating from various joints in Tracy's body. According to the appellant's wife, Laura Latimer, further surgery was regarded as mutilation. As a result, Robert Latimer formed the view that his daughter's life was not worth living.

> ...

> On October 12, 1993, after learning that the doctors wished to perform this additional surgery, the appellant decided to take his daughter's life. On Sunday, October 24, 1993, while his wife and Tracy's siblings were at church, Robert Latimer carried Tracy to his pickup truck, seated her in the cab, and inserted a hose from the truck's exhaust pipe into the cab. She died from the carbon monoxide.

Latimer was twice convicted of murder. On the first charge, for first-degree murder, he was convicted of second-degree murder, but a new trial was ordered when it became clear that the prosecutor in the case had interfered with the jury-selection process. Latimer was convicted of second-degree murder again.

The legal defence of necessity is rarely applied and is quite narrow in its range. There are three elements that must be present: imminent peril or danger, the accused must have no reasonable legal alternative to the course of action undertaken, and there must be proportionality between the harm inflicted and the harm avoided. The Court stated that the trial judge, before the jury is left with consideration of the defence of necessity, must determine that there is sufficient evidence to give "an air of reality" to each of the three requirements. If there is no such air of reality, the defence should not be left to the jury. In this case, the Court held that there was no air of reality to any of the three requirements. The trial judge had been correct to remove the defence from the jury.

The related challenge regarding the necessity defence was whether removing it after the defence counsel had requested a ruling on its availability was a proper course of action by the trial judge. Counsel had two versions of his jury address on Latimer's behalf: one raised necessity, the other did not. The trial judge said he would rule on the matter after the submissions. This led to a *Charter* argument that Latimer did not have a fair trial because he did not know the case he had to meet. The Court did not accept that submission. First, there was no broad right to have all rulings on the availability of defences occur prior to closing submissions. Second, the right to respond to the Crown's case is not the same as a right to respond to rulings of the trial judge. Clearly, it would have been preferable for the trial judge to have ruled earlier, especially since, as the Saskatchewan Court of Appeal had noted, not a single one of the requirements for necessity had an air of reality to it.

Perfection is not, however, a requirement for measuring trial fairness. A trial, especially a criminal trial, and a murder trial at that, is a dynamic and fast-moving drama, in which the trial judge has a particularly demanding role to fill. There is no blueprint or cookie-cutter model that applies to all such trials. Here, removal of the defence did not amount to an ambush, nor did it catch him unaware. It had also been removed during the course of the first trial and the first appeal. There was no unfair trial in the subsequent trial, the appeal from which was now before the Court.

It seems clear that the jury was concerned about the penalty that would result from conviction of Latimer. During the course of its deliberations, it sent a note to the trial judge inquiring, in part, whether it could offer input on sentencing. The trial judge replied that the jury was not to concern itself with the matter of penalty, but solely on the question of guilt. He then added, "it may be that later on, once you have reached a verdict, you—we will have some discussions about that [penalty]."

> The appellant argues that the jury was misled into believing it could make a recommendation on sentence. The trial judge might have confined himself to telling the jury not to concern itself with the penalty. But his vague suggestion ("it may be that later on ... we will have some discussions about that") cannot be taken to have seriously misled the jury into believing that it would determine the sentence. In fact the jury could and did offer its input on sentence by virtue of s. 745.2 of the *Criminal Code*, which requires a trial judge to ask the jury if it wishes to recommend more than the 10-year minimum before parole eligibility for second degree murder. It seems likely that the trial judge had this provision in mind when he suggested the jury could "have some discussions" about the sentence. Read in the context of the trial judge's repeated insistence that the jury focus on the issue of guilt, not penalty, it is clear that his comment about discussing the sentence later on did not render the trial unfair.

In the Latimer circumstances, it is not impossible that the judge and the jury had quite different ideas in mind in relation to the inquiry.

The jury was probably fully aware of the mandatory sentence for second-degree murder and might well have been looking for some way out of what it knew was likely to be the sentence, hence the question sent to the trial judge. It may have drawn some incorrect comfort from the response it received, thinking, perhaps, that a lower minimum sentence might have been possible on the basis of recommendations from the jury. Juries are, in the end, human, and the jury might even have been willing to find a way to acquit Latimer if there were to be no possible way to avoid the minimum sentence. That is, of course, completely wrong as a matter of legal theory, however true it may be in human terms.

That concept is known as *jury nullification*. The Court was not prepared to support an argument that the accused was entitled to rely on some broad right to jury nullification and held that there was no unfair trial as a result of the trial judge having undermined that power: guarding against it is a desirable and legitimate exercise for a trial judge and no prejudice was caused to the accused.

The remaining issue was whether the mandatory minimum sentence was cruel and unusual punishment ("whether the punishment prescribed is so excessive as to outrage the standards of decency").

> It is not for the court to pass on the wisdom of Parliament with respect to the gravity of various offences and the range of penalties which may be imposed upon those found guilty of committing the offences. Parliament has broad discretion in proscribing conduct as criminal and in determining proper punishment. While the final judgment as to whether punishment exceeds constitutional limits set by the *Charter* is properly a judicial function, the court should be reluctant to interfere with the considered views of Parliament and then only in the clearest of cases where the punishment prescribed is so excessive when compared with the punishment prescribed for other offences as to outrage standards of decency.

The difference between first- and second-degree murder is relevant only for purposes of sentencing. Both require a verdict of guilt for murder. Here the Court found that the minimum mandatory sentence was not grossly disproportionate. It found nothing in the circumstances that diminished the degree of Latimer's criminal responsibility, and, while acknowledging the matter was not free of debate, declared that the sentence was not out of step with valid penological goals or sentencing principles.

Having decided all this, the Court then telegraphed some concerns and possibilities. One was the choice of Parliament as to the use of minimum sentences in criminal matters, in the face of considerable differences of opinion on the wisdom of such sentences. The "telegraph" was a reference to the royal prerogative of mercy, contained in the *Criminal Code* itself.

Where the courts are unable to provide an appropriate remedy in cases that the executive sees as unjust imprisonment, the executive is permitted to dispense "mercy," and order the release of the offender. The royal prerogative of mercy is the only potential remedy for persons who have exhausted their rights of appeal and are unable to show that their sentence fails to accord with the *Charter*.

But the prerogative is a matter for the executive, not the courts. The executive will undoubtedly, if it chooses to consider the matter, examine all the underlying circumstances surrounding the tragedy of Tracy Latimer that took place on October 24, 1993, some seven years ago. Since that time Mr. Latimer has undergone two trials and two appeals to the Court of Appeal for Saskatchewan and this Court, with attendant publicity and consequential agony for him and his family.

The Court could easily have bailed out of the matter with its legal conclusion on the sentence. Was it sending a message, in carefully coded language, to the Executive?

DNA Evidence: Balancing Identification of the Guilty with Exoneration of the Innocent

R. v. S.A.B. [2003] 2 S.C.R. 678

The claimant in this case was a fourteen-year-old girl, who discovered that she was pregnant. She advised her mother that the accused, who had been living with the family for several months, had sexually assaulted her. She had an abortion and the police seized foetal tissue for blood sampling. They then proceeded to obtain, on an *ex parte* basis (i.e., without involvement or notice to the other party), a warrant to seize a blood sample from the accused, and took such a sample. A paternity-test analysis was then made to compare the blood sample of the accused with that of the foetal tissue. The accused was arrested and charged with sexual assault and sexual exploitation. The evidence presented at trial established the probability that he was not the father to be at 1 in 10 million. Leaving aside the predictable (but unsuccessful) argument that the expert opinion on the matter was unreliable, the accused challenged the constitutionality of the applicable provisions of the *Criminal Code* on the basis that they violated sections 7 and 8 of the *Canadian Charter of Rights and Freedoms*. He was convicted of sexual assault, but acquitted of sexual exploitation. The Court of Appeal of Alberta upheld the conviction and the matter reached the Supreme Court of Canada, where, in a unanimous judgment, the Court dismissed the appeal.

The legislation under attack was contained in the *Criminal Code*, which authorizes the search and seizure of DNA for investigative purposes. This is accomplished by means of search warrants for purposes of seizing bodily substances for purposes of forensic DNA testing. A search warrant is obtained on the basis of an *ex parte* sworn application to a provincial court judge, who is entitled to grant a warrant only if there are reasonable grounds to believe (a) that the particular offence has been committed, (b) that a bodily substance has been found (among others) in the body of any person associated with the commission of the offence, (c) that the person targeted by the warrant was a party to the offence, and (d) the forensic DNA analysis of a bodily substance from that person will provide evidence about whether the bodily substance in (b) was from that person. There are additional factors and precautions involved, including the requirement to inform the person from whom the sample will be taken, the contents of the warrant, the nature of the investigative process by which the samples are to be taken, the purpose of taking the samples, the authority to use as much force as is necessary in executing the warrant and the possibility that the results may be used in evidence. The person may be detained for a period that is reasonable in the circumstances and the privacy of the person is to be respected in a reasonable manner. Additional provisions deal with the limited use of the samples and, if the person is acquitted, or if there are discharges, withdrawals of charges, or stays, the subsequent destruction of negative samples.

Section 8 of the *Charter* provides that everyone has the right to be secure against unreasonable search or seizure. The Court had previously held that a reasonable search must be one "(a) authorized by law; (b) the law itself must be reasonable; and (c) the manner in which the search was carried out must be reasonable." The appellant's attack in this case focussed on the reasonableness aspect, namely whether the statutory scheme providing for DNA warrants was reasonable, that the legislation was not minimally intrusive, it operated on reasonable grounds alone and it allowed for *ex parte* applications in all cases.

Inquiries under section 8 of the *Charter* require a balancing of the interests of privacy with the government's interest in advancing its goals, including law enforcement.

MADE IN COURT

Generally, the proper balancing of these interests requires that there be a system of prior authorization through the issuance of a warrant by a decision maker capable of balancing the interests at stake and acting judicially. The DNA warrant scheme clearly fulfills these requirements by providing a detailed procedure under which a warrant is issued by a judicial officer. Significantly, [*Code* section reference] provides that the application to obtain a warrant must be made to a provincial court judge rather than, as is typical in obtaining other types of warrants, by making an application to a justice of the peace. This measure indicates Parliament's attentiveness to the seriousness of the interests at stake in obtaining a DNA warrant.

There was no doubt that the taking of bodily samples could involve significant intrusions on a person's privacy and human dignity, but the extent to which such an intrusion will be allowed will depend on the circumstances. In a pre-*Charter* case, the balance between those interests had been described as follows, where a search warrant had been issued authorizing a surgical operation of some complexity to remove a bullet from the shoulder of a robbery suspect:

Words much plainer than those used would be required to convince me that Parliament intended in this section to authorize the breaking open of the human frame by means of a search warrant. As I pointed out during the argument, if the police are today to be authorized to probe into a man's shoulder for evidence against him, what is to prevent them tomorrow from opening his brain or other vital organs for the same purpose. The investigation of crime would no doubt be thereby rendered easier, but I do not think that we can, in the name of efficiency, justify the wholesale mutilation of suspected persons.

The criminal law has always had to strike the precarious balance between the protection of society on the one hand and the protection of the rights of the individual members of such society on the other. Both rights are equally important, but any conflict between them must wherever possible be resolved in a manner most compatible with human dignity. The constant preoccupation of our Courts with the protection of the citizen against the state results in the Crown always having to bear the burden in any criminal prosecution. I am not the first Judge, and I trust that I shall not be the last, to decide that the possibility that some guilty person may escape the net of justice is not too high a price to pay for the right to live in freedom. If the Crown cannot prove its case against [the accused] without doing physical violence to his person then it is better that the case be not proved.

In my view, the Justice [of the Peace] had no jurisdiction, either by statute or at common law, to issue this warrant and it is my duty to interfere and prevent what I can only describe as a grotesque perversion of the machinery of justice and an unwarranted invasion upon the basic inviolability of the human person. Even if the operation were minor, and the evidence is that it is not, I would not be prepared to sanction it and I do not do so.

This balance, said the Court, in the present case, had been accommodated in the DNA warrant provisions of the *Criminal Code*.

While the taking of bodily samples under such a warrant clearly interferes with bodily integrity, the degree of offence to such physical integrity is relatively modest. Buccal swabs are quick and not very intrusive. Blood samples are obtained by pricking the surface of the skin, which is not particularly invasive and, with the exception of pubic hair, the plucking of hair is not a serious affront to privacy or dignity. The legislation also requires that the person authorized to take samples do so in a manner that respects the individual's privacy and is reasonable in the circumstances. For the Court, the various provisions contained in the statutory framework alleviated any concern that there would be an intolerable affront to the physical integrity of the person.

Regarding privacy concerns, the Court was also satisfied that the DNA Warrant provisions struck an appropriate balance between the public interest in effective criminal-law enforcement for serious offences and the rights of individuals to control the release of personal information, as well as the right to dignity and physical integrity. The samples are collected for a limited purpose. The samples are not such that they can be used to predict or identify markers for medical information (such as future conditions or tendencies) and may only be used for forensic purposes, to compare the sample taken with another existing sample. Indeed, it is an offence to use information obtained from a DNA analysis except in the course of investigation of the designated offence.

One particular aspect of the public interest is to arrive at the truth in the course of law enforcement, not only to bring offenders to justice, but also to avoid wrongful convictions. Many will be aware of the number of occasions in which DNA analysis has revealed that individuals convicted of offences, who may have been imprisoned for many years, were wrongfully convicted. Innocent parties may well have a strong personal interest in having a DNA analysis establish in advance that they are not guilty of the offence under investigation, before being put to the embarrassment and expense of a criminal trial. This aspect, too, is a considerable advantage to the criminal process.

The appellant in this case argued that DNA warrants should be a "last resort"—available only when the state cannot investigate effectively by using less-intrusive techniques, analogous to wiretap authorizations, which are given only when a court is satisfied that other investigative techniques have been unsuccessfully tried or are unlikely to succeed. The Court did not accept the argument.

> I see no reason to import, as a constitutional imperative, a similar requirement in the case of DNA warrants. There are obvious differences between the use of wiretaps as an investigative tool, and recourse to a DNA warrant. Wiretaps are sweeping in their reach. They invariably intrude into the privacy interests of third parties who are not targeted by the criminal investigation. They cast a net that is invariably wide. By contrast, DNA warrants are target specific. Significantly, DNA warrants also have the capacity to exonerate an accused early in the investigative process. Although it would have been open to Parliament to provide for the use of forensic DNA analysis as a last resort investigative technique, I see no reason to require, as a condition for constitutional compliance, that it be so. Moreover, as the Court of Appeal noted, the [*Criminal Code*] requirement of showing that the warrant is "in the best interests of the administration of justice" would prevent a judge from issuing a warrant where it is unnecessary to do so.

Finally, the Court concluded that the particular nature of the evidence did not offend the principle against self-incrimination, since not all compelled evidence violates the principle, which has a limited scope and requires different things at different times, guided by concerns of unreliable confessions or evidence and abuse of power by the state.

To conclude, the legislative scheme ... is sensitive to the various interests in play. On balance, the law provides for a search and seizure of DNA materials that is reasonable. In light of the high probative value of forensic DNA analysis, the interests of the state override those of the individual. Forensic DNA analysis is capable of both identifying and eliminating suspects, a feature that seriously reduces the risk of wrongful convictions. The DNA provisions contain procedural safeguards that protect adequately the multiple interests of the suspected offender. The DNA warrant scheme therefore complies with s. 8 of the *Charter*.

It seems clear that the Court was concerned with the *Charter* rights of the accused, but was also very much aware of the fact that forensic DNA analysis might avoid repetition of the many false convictions that had occurred in prior years, resulting, at least in part, from the unavailability of evidence of sufficient probative quality.

Division of Legislative Powers: the Canadian Constitutional Obsession

Citizens' and The Queen Insurance Cos. v. Parsons [1879-80] 4 S.C.R. 215

The efforts of insurance companies to avoid liability on a fire-insurance policy provided the Supreme Court of Canada with one of its early opportunities to reflect on the division of legislative authorities under the *British North America Act, 1867*. It is often said that the single greatest metaphysical concern for Canadians is whether a particular matter is a federal or a provincial responsibility. This case involved the question of whether insurance was a subject falling exclusively within the competence of the federal government as a matter of the regulation of trade and commerce under section 91 of the *Act* or whether it more properly belonged as a matter of property and civil rights or matters of local concern only, under section 92. The Court ended up divided on the outcome, with the majority holding that provincial legislatures also had the power, along with the federal government, to legislate on the subject matter of insurance.

The *BNA Act* was barely off the presses as a major constitutional statute, and the courts were feeling their way while trying to give meaning to the division of powers it contained. Many of the legislators then in office had been intimately involved in the pre-Confederation conferences, were quite familiar with the terms and constitutional philosophy of the American Constitution (which had been studied very carefully and which contained many subjects also dealt with in the Canadian constitution), and had followed the enactment of the *BNA Act* as it worked its way through the Imperial Parliament in Westminster. So the *Act* was not a completely alien statute arriving on Canada's doorstep unannounced. Nor was it an enactment drafted without knowledge of a particular geographic (and demographic) configuration of Canada at the time of Confederation and of a potentially significantly greater geography in future. By the time this case was heard, both Manitoba and British Columbia had been admitted to Confederation.

The relative immediacy of the new constitution allowed the Court to reflect on the relationships between the legislative capacities of the two levels of government, as well as the need to reconcile possible areas of overlap. From the outset the principle was acknowledged that each level of government possessed legislative sovereignty "as independent and exclusive in the one as in the other over the matters respectively confided to them, and the power of each must be equally respected by the other, or *ultra vires* legislation [i.e., legislation beyond the legal power of each to enact, and thereby void] will necessarily be the result." The Court acknowledged that it may be difficult to draw the exact line between the powers of the federal parliament to regulate trade and commerce and the powers of the provincial legislatures over "local works and undertakings," "property and civil rights in the province," and "generally all matters of a merely local or private nature in the province." Where there may be a conflict, provincial legislation must yield to the supremacy of the federal parliament, while at the same time, taking property and civil rights as an example, the federal Parliament would only have the right to interfere for the purpose of legislating generally and effectually in relation to matters confided to the Parliament of Canada.

> I think the power of the Dominion parliament to regulate trade and commerce ought not to be held to be necessarily inconsistent with those of local legislatures to regulate property and civil rights in respect to all matters of a merely local and private nature, such as matters connected with the enjoyment and preservation of property in the province, or matters of contract between parties in relation to their property or dealings, although the exercise by the local legislatures of such powers may be said remotely to affect

matters connected with trade and commerce, unless, indeed, the laws of the provincial legislatures should conflict with those of the Dominion parliament passed for the general regulation of trade and commerce. I do not think the local legislatures are to be deprived of all power to deal with property and civil rights, because parliament, in the plenary exercise of its power to regulate trade and commerce, may possibly pass laws inconsistent with the exercise by the local legislatures of their powers—the exercise of the powers of the local legislatures being in such a case subject to such regulations as the Dominion may lawfully prescribe.

This was a perfectly reasonable approach to take, reflecting not only a legally satisfactory methodology, but also an eminently sensible practical allocation of legislative competence. This was the original analytical framework for determining where legislative jurisdiction should rest. Coming back to the matter of insurance, which was the specific legislative issue in the appeal, the Court concluded that the provincial statute attacked by the insurers as void (thus potentially relieving them of their obligation to pay on account of the losses of the insured) was not the regulation of trade and commerce—it was a contract of fire insurance as between the insurer and the insured—a contract of indemnity against loss or damage by fire. It was simply an exercise of the power of the local legislature for the protection of property in Ontario, and the civil rights of the proprietors thereof in Ontario.

If the legislative power of the provincial legislatures is to be restricted and limited, as it is claimed it should be, and the doctrine contended for in this case, as I understand it, is carried to its legitimate logical conclusion, the idea of the power of the local legislature to deal with the local works and undertakings, property and civil rights, and matters of a merely local and private nature in the province is, I humbly think, to a very great extent, illusory.

That, too, was an important observation, since it put to rest the thought that practically everything having any connection with trade and commerce could be subsumed under the general regulatory authority of the federal government. That would have made a complete mockery of the entire constitution. Another way of looking at the same question was the following:

In order to determine the meaning of these words [i.e., "regulation of trade and commerce"] in the second paragraph of section 91, they should not be read alone, but, on the contrary, they should be taken in connection with the whole of the provisions of the Constitutional Act, in order to arrive at a conclusion comfortable to the spirit of the Act and to give effect to all of its provisions. The object of the law-giver, in dividing the legislative powers between the Federal power and the provincial legislatures, was, as far as it was possible in the new order of things, to conserve to the latter their autonomy in so far as the civil law peculiar to each province was concerned. We would, however, arrive at a very different conclusion if we held that the words in paragraph two had the comprehensive meaning that they have literally. But it is evident that it would not be interpreting them correctly, as in the following paragraph of the same section their meaning is limited. If it had been the intention to give to this expression, "Regulation of trade and commerce," such an absolute meaning, why should certain subjects of legislation which certainly come under the power of regulating trade and commerce have been enumerated in the statute, such as navigation, ships and steamers, banks, bills of exchange, promissory notes, insolvency and bankruptcy; all subjects which, without this special enumeration, would be comprised within the power of regulating trade and commerce. The proper conclusion to draw, it seems to me, is that the general expression in this paragraph did not comprise, according to the Act itself, all that certainly form part of commerce, it certainly should not comprise a subject-matter which is only indirectly connected with commerce.

This is a legally sound approach to statutory construction and was an early identification of a fundamental principle of such analysis, namely being certain to understand a provision in the context of the entire statute, not just on the basis of words that can only be properly understood as part of the expression of an integrated legislative policy.

Much of Canadian constitutional history has been created by the courts, often with the Imperial Privy Council in a position of confirming or overturning judgment of the Supreme Court of Canada until appeals to it were abolished following the Second World War. By far the greatest number of decisions turned on the determination of whether particular legislation fell within the competence of the enacting body, whether federal or provincial. This case is an example of the kind of analysis necessary to make sense of what might appear to be conflicting jurisdictions, to identify the real subject matter of any particular enactment, and to determine the right response to legislative conflicts.

Judges in the earlier cases had to develop a feel for the nature of the considerations involved, particularly the balancing of federal and provincial interests. This challenge was made more difficult by the fact that Canadian judges were, after all, attempting to interpret a foreign statute, even if they might be familiar with a particular subject matter.

Over time, the statutory language in the Canadian constitution, which made it clear that the provincial governments possessed only those matters specifically granted to them, with all residual jurisdiction maintained by the federal government, became watered down considerably in favour of enlarged jurisdictions for the provinces. This can be contrasted with what happened in the United States, where the constitutional language granted the national government only those powers identified by the states, but where court decisions over time tended to enlarge the federal jurisdiction at the expense of the supposed residual powers retained by the states. Once appeals to the Privy Council were abolished, the Supreme Court of Canada began a long process of clawing back the original intention of the framers of the Constitution (see pages 204 and 209).

Trade and Commerce: Escaping from the Privy Council Bondage

Canadian Industrial Gas & Oil Ltd. v. Saskatchewan [1978] 2 S.C.R. 545

T his appeal arose from the actions in late 1973 by the Organization of Petroleum Exporting Countries (OPEC) to increase dramatically and unexpectedly the price of Middle East oil, which had a worldwide impact on the value of crude oil and refined petroleum products. Many have referred to this action and the consequences as the "energy crisis," a phenomenon the effects of which persist to this day. There was fallout throughout the world, reaching even to Saskatchewan, the government of which considered that the vital interests of its citizenry were affected. Its response in December 1973, was to enact legislation, the general purpose being to increase the provincial revenues by capturing the enhanced value of provincial oil from the producing companies.

This was done through two means. The first was by a "mineral income tax" on production revenues. This tax was 100 percent of the difference between the well-head price and a defined "basic well-head price," essentially the price per barrel prior to the energy crisis. The second was expropriation of all petroleum- and natural-gas-producing properties in the province and subjecting them to a "royalty surcharge" calculated in the same manner as the mineral income tax, but on the higher of the well-head price and the price per barrel determined by the Minister.

There were other complex aspects of the legislation, including regulations, which are not necessary for purposes of the present assessment of the appeal. As the majority observed, the "practical consequence of the application of the legislation is that the Government of Saskatchewan will acquire the benefit of all increases in the value of oil produced in that Province above the set basic well-head price fixed by the statute and regulations, which is approximately the same as that which existed in 1973 before the increase in world prices for oil."

Such action, as may be imagined, was a shock to the industry in Saskatchewan. The appellant was a producer of crude oil, having some 156,000 acres of all types of leases and other arrangements, which sold its entire production of crude oil at the well site, virtually all of which left the province by pipeline to be refined in eastern Canada or the United States. This was typical of the industry in Saskatchewan, which used only 1.8 percent of the crude oil produced in the province: all the rest was used in other provinces or in the United States.

The appellant launched an attack on the legality and constitutionality of the provincial scheme on two principal grounds: that the taxes were indirect taxes beyond the provisions of section 92(2) of the *British North America Act, 1867*, which allowed the provincial legislatures to "make laws in relation to matters coming within ... direct taxation within the Province in order to the raising of a revenue for provincial purposes," (this was before the patriation of the Constitution, which occurred in 1982) and, that the legislation as a whole was in relation to trade and commerce and, therefore, was within the exclusive jurisdiction of the federal parliament under section 91(2) of the *Act*.

The Saskatchewan courts upheld the validity of the legislation. Leave to appeal to the Supreme Court of Canada was granted, where the case was heard by the full Court. The appeal was allowed in a seven to two decision. The legislation was declared to be *ultra vires* [beyond the powers of] the Saskatchewan Legislature and the appellant was entitled to recovery of all amounts paid by way of mineral income tax and royalty surcharge, within interest from the date of payment.

Both of the grounds for appeal involved important points of Canadian constitutional law, and both had been the subject of earlier appeals. Seen from the perspective of the full landscape of such law, the real importance of the case is that it is part of the effort of the Canadian courts to recover from some of the decisions of the Privy Council, prior to the abolition of appeals to it in 1949, that had seriously weakened the default provisions of the *British North America Act, 1867,* that operated generally to leave to federal competence any matters not expressly granted to the provincial legislatures. Judicial change is seldom dramatic and marked by paradigm shift; it tends to be incremental. Accordingly, the Supreme Court's disassociation from the earlier decisions was gradual, but nevertheless intentional.

Saskatchewan cannot have been unaware that its confiscatory legislation would likely to be subjected to constitutional attack and it is likely not a coincidence that it called its tax a mineral "income" tax, so that it could argue that it was an income tax and therefore a direct tax, relying on earlier judicial authority to that effect. The classic distinction between a direct and an indirect tax is derived from *Principles of Political Economy* by John Stuart Mill:

> Taxes are either direct or indirect. A direct tax is one demanded from the very person who it is intended or desired should pay it. Indirect taxes are those which are demanded from one person in the expectation and intention that he shall indemnify himself at the expense of another, such are the excise or customs.

> The producer or importer of a commodity is called upon to pay a tax on it not with the intention to levy a peculiar contribution on him, but to tax through him the consumers of the commodity, from whom it is supposed that he will recover the amount by means of an advance in price.

The Fathers of Confederation were assumed to have been familiar with Mills' economic theories.

The minority of the Court concluded that the tax was direct, but the majority was of a different view.

> The mineral income tax and the royalty surcharge are taxes imposed in a somewhat unusual manner. The mineral income tax purports to be a direct tax upon income imposed upon the taxpayer, which he cannot pass on to his purchaser. The royalty surcharge, while carrying a different title, is the same in nature. What differentiates this legislation from other legislation imposing export taxes is that the true effect of the legislation is to impose a freeze on the actual income which the producer exporter can derive from the sale of

his product. All that he is permitted to retain on the sale of each barrel of oil is the basic well-head price. In addition to being subjected to an income freeze, he is compelled to sell his product at a price equivalent to what the Minister considers to be its fair value in order to obtain the funds necessary to meet the tax. This amount per barrel over and above the basic well-head price he must obtain from his purchaser as a part of the purchase price. In essence the producer is a conduit through which the increased value of each barrel of oil above the basic well-head price is channeled into the hands of the Crown by way of tax. The increase in value is itself the tax and it is paid by the purchaser of the oil.

It is contended that the imposition of these taxes will not result in an increase in the price paid by oil purchasers, who would have been required to pay the same market price even if the taxes had not been imposed, and so there could be no passing on of the tax by the Saskatchewan producer to his purchaser. On this premise it is argued that the tax is not indirect. This, however, overlooks the all important fact that the scheme of the legislation under consideration involves the fixing of the maximum return of the Saskatchewan producers at the basis well-head price per barrel, while at the same time compelling him to sell at a higher price. There are two components in the sale price, first the basic well-head price and the second the tax imposed. Both are intended by the legislation to be incorporated into the price payable by the purchaser. The purchaser pays the amount of the tax as part of the purchase price.

For those reasons, the taxation scheme did not constitute direct taxation within the province and was outside the scope of the provincial power in the *Act*.

Regarding the second argument, the federal power in relation to the regulation of trade and commerce, one that had been regularly eviscerated by the Privy Council, with the result that it was very difficult, in practice, for the country to "work," the Court had to be certain of the essential facts, which were relatively simple. The overwhelming majority of the Saskatchewan oil was destined for interprovincial or international trade. The legislation was, therefore, properly characterized as legislation "directly aimed at the production of oil destined for export [from the province] and has the effect of regulating the export price, since the purchaser is effectively compelled to obtain that price on the sale of the product." Accordingly, the statutory provisions and regulations were *ultra vires* the Saskatchewan legislature.

The fact that there were still dissenting judges unwilling to concede either that the tax was indirect and that oil, 98 percent of which was known to be destined for markets outside Saskatchewan, clearly involved interprovincial and international trade, shows the lingering effect of the Privy Council decisions and a judicial reluctance to move on from them as part of the new constitutional reality of Canada.

Trade and Commerce: Unravelling the Privy Council's Gordian Knot

General Motors of Canada Ltd. v. City National Leasing [1989] 1 S.C.R. 641

This important constitutional case arose from a squabble between City National Leasing (CNL) and General Motors of Canada (GM) about whether GM had practiced price discrimination in relation to GM cars purchased by CNL's competitors. CNL instituted civil proceedings against GM for breach of contract and damages, pursuant to a remedy provided in section 31.1 of the *Combines Investigation Act*. The constitutional point was that the creation of civil causes of action was a provincial matter, whereas the *Combines Investigation Act* was federal legislation. GM's initial response was to challenge CNL's action on the basis that section 31.1 was *ultra vires* (beyond the powers of) the federal Parliament. By the time the matter got to the Supreme Court of Canada, there were two constitutional questions: whether the *Combines Investigation Act* (in whole or part) was within the legislative competence of the federal Parliament under section 91(2) of the *Constitution Act, 1867*, (the Constitution had been patriated in 1982) and whether section 31.1 was within the same legislative competence. The provision read:

31.1 (1) Any person who has suffered loss or damage as a result of

(a) conduct that is contrary to any provision of Part V [of the Combines statute], or

(b) the failure of any person to comply with an order of the Commission or a court under this Act, may, in any court of competent jurisdiction, sue for and recover from the person who engaged in the conduct or failed to comply with the order an amount equal to the loss or damage proved to have been suffered by him, together with any additional amount that the court may allow not exceeding the full cost to him of any investigation in connection with the matter and of proceedings under this section.

The case is included in this collection as a further example of the Supreme Court's conscious effort to undo some of the damage to the trade and commerce powers conferred on the federal government under the *Constitution Act, 1867,* arising from earlier decisions of the Privy Council regarding those same powers. In that respect, the case is a companion case to *Canadian Industrial Gas* (see page 204) heard a dozen years before, although the Court was by now far readier to be overtly critical of the Privy Council's tendencies to attempt to limit those powers regarding the regulation of trade and commerce. On this occasion, there were no dissenting judges.

The *Combines Investigation Act* had been around for decades and there was no longer any dispute that it could be justified under the federal criminal power. Far less obvious was its legitimacy under the federal power of the regulation of trade and commerce, in respect of which the Privy Council decision in *Citizens' Insurance* (see page 199) had imposed certain limitations (political arrangements requiring the sanction of Parliament, regulation of matters of interprovincial concern, and, possibly, general regulation of trade affecting the whole Dominion) on the otherwise ordinary meaning of the words. Since that time, most of the jurisprudence had been confined to defining the boundaries of international and interprovincial trade and commerce, and not much attention had been devoted to the power over general trade and commerce affecting Canada as a whole. There had been a number of refusals to apply it in relation to the insurance industry, prices and profits, labour relations, marketing, and the prohibition of margarine.

The Supreme Court of Canada had previously characterized the Privy Council positions as "their Lordships' emphatic and reiterated allocation of 'the regulation of trade and commerce' to ... [a] subordinate and wholly auxiliary function. ..." By now, the Court was willing to incorporate far more critical comment into its judgment, quoting here from a 1969 academic consideration of the matter:

> The British North America Act was framed with a greater interest in central control than motivated the constitutional fathers to the south. Reaction in the founding provinces to the consequences of decentralized control in the United States has been well documented. The broad and unqualified language of section 91(2) reflected the basic interest that strength from economic unity replace the foundering provincial economies. Yet, as the American courts broadened their commerce clause until it meant essentially what the Fathers of Confederation had sought for Canada, so have the Privy Council and the Canadian courts reacted against the hopes of the framers of their constitution and have decentralized commercial control.

> At least until relatively recently the history of the interpretation of the trade and commerce power has almost uniformly reinforced the federal paralysis which has resulted from a series of Privy Council decisions in the years 1881–1896. The predominant view was that section 91(2) did not in any way go to either general commerce, contracts, particular trades or occupations, or commodities so far as those things might be interprovincial. The test for the local nature of a transaction was abstractly legal, divorced from commercial effect.

Since the abolition of appeals to the Privy Council there had been much more importance attached to the trade-and-commerce provision by the Supreme Court of Canada. This is not to say, however, that courts can simply legislate judicially to change previous outcomes of which they might not approve: they must wait for cases to come before them and find a way, grounded in legal principle, which will enable them to arrive at different conclusions. A balance must be found that reconciles the general trade-and-commerce federal power with the provincial power over property and civil rights, which "must lie between an all pervasive interpretation of s. 91(2) and an interpretation that renders the general trade and commerce power to all intents vapid and meaningless." Three hallmarks of valid federal legislation under such power were identified.

> First, the impugned legislation must be part of a regulatory scheme. Second, the scheme must be monitored by the continuing oversight of a regulatory agency. Third, the legislation must be concerned with trade as a whole rather than with a particular industry. Each of these requirements is evidence of a concern that federal authority under the second branch of the trade and commerce power does not encroach on provincial jurisdiction. By limiting the means which federal legislators may employ to that of a regulatory scheme overseen by a regulatory agency, and by limiting the object of federal legislation to trade as a whole, these requirements attempt to maintain a delicate balance between federal and provincial power.

Two additional requirements were also added, namely that the legislation should be of such a nature that the provinces jointly or severally would be constitutionally incapable of enacting, and that the failure to include one or more provinces or localities in a legislative scheme would jeopardize the successful operation of the scheme in other parts of the country. While not an exhaustive checklist, it does give an indication of validity under the trade-and-commerce power.

There followed a lengthy consideration of the proper approach to the constitutional examination: the statute as a whole first, or the particular provision of the statute being challenged. An invalid provision within a statute that is constitutionally valid is not automatically valid; it will depend on how well that provision is integrated into the legislative scheme and its importance in the efficacy of the legislation, as well as the degree to which the provision intrudes on the provincial powers (while recognizing that some intrusion is likely inevitable). Here, the impugned provision was only a remedial provision, designed to help enforce the substantive aspects of the legislation. It did not create a general cause of action, but was carefully limited by the provisions of the *Act*. Finally, the federal government is not constitutionally limited from creating rights of civil action when such measures are warranted.

As to the statute as a whole, the Court stated:

> From this overview of the Combines Investigation Act I have no difficulty in concluding that the Act as a whole embodies a complex scheme of economic

regulation. The purpose of the Act is to eliminate activities that reduce competition in the market-place. The entire Act is geared to achieving this objective. The Act identifies and defines anti-competitive conduct. It establishes an investigatory mechanism for revealing prohibited activities and provides an extensive range of criminal and administrative redress against companies engaging in behaviour that tends to reduce competition. In my view, these three components, elucidation of prohibited conduct, creation of an investigatory procedure, and the establishment of a remedial mechanism, constitute a well-integrated scheme of regulation designed to discourage forms of commercial behaviour viewed as detrimental to Canada and the Canadian economy.

The Court was clearly concerned with the regulation of trade in general, not the regulation of a particular industry or commodity. The undesirable effects of anti-competitive practices clearly transcended provincial borders; competition was not an issue of simply local concern but was crucially important for the national economy and could not be effectively regulated unless regulated nationally. Paying appropriate heed to the provincial powers, however, the Court noted:

> On the other hand, competition is not a single matter, any more than inflation or pollution. The provinces too, may deal with competition in the exercise of their legislative powers in such fields as consumer protection, labour relations, marketing and the like. The point is, however, that Parliament also has the constitutional power to regulate interprovincial aspects of competition.

Turning then to the validity of section 31.1, the Court determined that the provision must be sufficiently and functionally related to the scheme of the Act in order to be constitutionally justified. As part of the arsenal or remedies created to discourage anti-competitive practices, it merely served to reinforce other sanctions in the Act. It was a private remedy dependent on individual initiative, but was not creation of a general action for damages. It had been added to a package of amendments to the *Act* in 1975 to reflect recommendations to the effect that prevention and deterrence, rather than convictions, should be the primary goals of the legislation, part of which was the recommendation that a private right of civil action should be part of the enforcement provisions. The underlying concern was that the purely criminal constitutional foundation of the legislation contributed to the rigidity and "inflexibility of the law and its administration. Criminal offences must be proved beyond a reasonable doubt. Charges must be expressed and proven in the categorical manner specified in the statute." It was certainly true that the record of convictions to date had been lamentable. The American experience with private prosecutions had proven to have been an important element of deterrence. This was viewed as supportive of the decision favoured by the Court.

> While it is true that the Combines Investigation Act existed for decades without a provision equivalent to s. 31.1, I see no reason why remedies available for violations of the Acts should be frozen in time. There is no constitutional impediment to amending the remedies provisions of the Combines Investigations Act to conform with changing economic realities.

> For these reasons, I conclude that s. 31.1 is an integral part of the Combines investigation Act scheme regarding anti-competitive conduct. The relationship between the section and the Act easily meets the test for the section to be upheld. This finding should not be interpreted as authority for upholding all provisions creating private civil action that are attached to a valid trade and commerce regulatory scheme or any other particular type of scheme. Section 31.1 is carefully constructed and restricted by the terms of the Combines Investigation Act.

Bear in mind that this decision was rendered some forty years after abolition of appeals to the Privy Council. Judicial progress is not measured in minutes and, as is often noted, one does not turn the *Queen Mary* on a dime. The progress toward the recapture of what the Fathers of Confederation had in mind for the federal government has, however, been steady ever since 1949. That the recovery is not complete can be seen by the Court's decision to declare unconstitutional the creation of a single regulatory agency to govern the issuance and trading of securities in Canada. While that idea may make perfect sense on a conceptual and business sense, the Court refused to provide the idea with constitutional approval.

Is a Woman a "Person"?

Henrietta Edwards et al. v. Attorney General of Canada [1928] S.C.R. 276; [1930] A.C. 124

Sometimes the courts lead in the development of the law and sometimes they can stand in the way of progress. In October 1927, the federal government submitted a Reference case to the Court on the question of whether women could be considered as "qualified persons" who could be called (appointed) to the Senate. A petition had been filed in late August by a well-known group of political activist women, Henrietta Muir Edwards, Nellie L. McClung, Louise C. McKinney, Emily F. Murphy, and Irene Parlby (sometimes known in Canadian history as the "Famous Five"), as persons interested "in the admission of women to the Senate of Canada." Women had, by that time, already won the right to vote and were therefore legally qualified to hold public office, but the matter of whether they were "qualified persons" in relation to possible Senate appointment was still outstanding.

The federal government, instead of dealing with the whole issue as a political matter (which it clearly was), decided that it would submit a Reference to the Supreme Court of Canada, asking for its legal view. The statutory and political language of the day in relation to women varied from quaint to patronizing; while it undoubtedly enraged women at the time, it would be anathema to women today. The terms of the Reference, which asked whether the word *Persons* in section 24 of the *British North America Act, 1867*, included female persons, was introduced by the Minister of Justice, who stated that the law officers of the Crown "who have considered this question on more than one occasion" had expressed the view that only male persons could be summoned to the Senate, but that while he was not disposed to question that view, nevertheless considered that it would be an act of justice to the women of Canada to obtain the Court's opinion. The Minister allowed that the question was one of great public importance. The matter was heard on March 14, 1928, and the decision was rendered on April 24.

The Court was unanimous in holding that women were not "qualified persons" within the meaning of the provision and, therefore, not eligible for appointment to the Senate of Canada. It began with a general disclaimer that it was "in no wise concerned" with the desirability or the undesirability of the presence of women in the Senate, nor with any political aspect of the question submitted, having the duty to construe the provisions of the statute and to base an answer on that construction. There followed a series of propositions about statutory interpretation, almost all from cases decided by the English courts. The Court then moved on to a long line of decisions that made clear the principle that women were not entitled to exercise any public function. There were several references to reasons for this lack of status, clothed in such terms as it being founded on motives of decorum and a privilege of the sex, in respect of their dignity, and being excused from taking part in public affairs.

When considering the language of the *BNA Act*, the Court asked itself if the lengthy tradition of excluding women from public office had been changed by the Imperial Parliament when it used the word *persons*. It concluded that such a fundamental change (a striking constitutional departure from the common law) would not be made "furtively," and that when Parliament contemplates such a "decided innovation," it is never at a loss to make its intention unmistakable. It ducked and weaved unconvincingly around the English statute (don't forget that, at the time, the Canadian constitution, the *BNA Act, 1867*, was a statute of the Imperial Parliament) that declared that words in a statute referring to the masculine gender shall be deemed to include females unless the contrary is expressly provided.

Mr. Justice Duff (later the Rt. Hon. Sir Lyman Duff, Chief Justice of Canada) also concluded that women could not become senators, but took a different approach to the rest of the Court. He did not attach much importance to the use of the masculine personal pronoun, but took the view that what Parliament had in mind in respect of the Senate was something akin to the former legislative councils in the Canadas, as established in the enactments in 1791 (creating the separate jurisdictions of Upper and Lower Canada) and 1840 (creating a single province of Canada, divided into Canada East and Canada West). At that time, women could not have been part of any such legislative council, with the result that the same exclusion should apply to the Senate of Canada.

In the end, however, all five judges of the Court concurred in the outcome, even if for somewhat different reasons. It was a rather static conception of statutory interpretation, looking to the law of England at the time the *BNA Act, 1867*, was adopted. The public reaction to the judgment in Canada was one of outrage and the Supreme Court of Canada was ridiculed in the media, and the judges themselves were mocked. This was the first time the Court had been subjected to public ridicule.

In 1928, however, the Supreme Court of Canada was not the final court of appeal for Canadian matters. Its decisions could be appealed to the Judicial Committee of the Imperial Privy Council. Henrietta Muir Edwards did just that, applying for and being granted special leave for that purpose.

On October 18, 1929, having heard four days of argument by the parties, the Privy Council reversed the unanimous decision of the Supreme Court of Canada, a reversal received quite warmly in Canada, with the all-but-certain exception of the Supreme Court of Canada. The Privy Council's approach to the question was far more liberal and purposive than that of the Canadian court. On the general exclusion of women from all public offices, it noted:

> The exclusion of women from all public offices is a relic of days more barbarous than ours, but it must be remembered that the necessity of the times often forced on man customs which in later years were not necessary.

The Privy Council also agreed that the particular section in the *BNA Act, 1867*, should not be read as an independent enactment, but as part of the *Act* as a whole. It reviewed the history of Canada regarding the rights (or lack thereof) of women to vote or to hold public office. It went on to say that interpretation given by the Supreme Court of Canada would not be difficult where women were expressly excluded by statute from public office, but that where there was no such exclusion, and those entitled to be summoned or placed in public office are described under the word *person*, other considerations arose. It did not view the past history as conclusive.

> Over and above that, their Lordships do not think it right to apply rigidly to Canada of to-day the decisions and the reasons therefor which commended themselves, probably rightly, to those who had to apply the law in different circumstances, in different centuries, to countries in different stages of development.

The judgment of the Privy Council also contains one of the most judicially important observations in Canadian constitutional life:

> The British North America Act planted in Canada a living tree capable of growth and expansion within its natural limits. The object of the Act was to grant a Constitution to Canada.
>
> ...
>
> Their Lordships do not conceive it to be the duty of this Board—it is certainly not their desire—to cut down the provisions of the Act by a narrow and technical construction, but rather to give it a large and liberal interpretation so that the Dominion to a great extent, but within certain fixed limits, may be the mistress of her own house, as the Provinces to a great extent, but within certain fixed limits, are mistresses in theirs.

To be sure, it was much easier for the Privy Council to distinguish (differentiate between) cases decided in the English courts than for a Canadian court to do so, but it made the fundamental breakthrough observation that it was dealing with a constitution, which had to be permitted to grow and develop as the country grew and developed, a perspective that led it naturally to a broader outlook than dutiful repetition of historical precedent. Its approach to the question of women was not so much why they should be able to hold public office, as why not.

It found references to "males" in the *BNA Act* and used them as a platform to say that where Parliament had intended to mean males only, it had said so, and that when a reference was to "person," it extended to both male and female.

While it is perhaps disappointing that the Supreme Court of Canada did not reach the right conclusion on such an important constitutional and human-rights issue, especially when by the time it heard the Reference women were entitled to vote and to be candidates in all federal and provincial elections (except in Quebec), this may have been the result of paying too much deference to the English cases. Canadian courts may also not have had the global perspective of the Imperial courts, acting as the latter did, in appeals from throughout the world's largest empire.

In the long run, however, from a Canadian constitutional perspective it may have been better to have the Privy Council itself essentially volunteer the principle of the "living tree capable of growth and expansion" rather than to have invented the same principle in Canada and then have to wrest concurrence with the idea from a British court potentially resistant to any perceived diminution of Imperial prerogative.

Marital Breakdown: Wives Without Rights

Murdoch v. Murdoch [1975] 1 S.C.R. 423

There are some judgments which cannot be said to be legally wrong, despite the fact that they are so far from being just as to offend the conscience. This was a four to one decision of the Court, in which the real impact came not from the majority, but from the dissent, which set in motion family-law reforms across the country. The dissenting judge, Bora Laskin, then the junior judge on the panel, would go on to become Chief Justice of Canada.

The Murdochs were married in 1943 and worked as a couple on ranches in western Canada for several years. Later, with the assistance of some small family inheritances, they branched out into their own businesses, all of which were registered in the name of the husband, as was the family homestead. Some of the money came from the wife's side of the family, some from the husband's. The first property was used as a dude ranch, until it was sold and the husband realized a small profit on his share. While the dude ranch was being operated, the husband was away for some five months per year, employed by a stock association.

The wife performed all of the work necessary to operate the dude ranch while the husband was away, which included accompanying the guests on pack trips, on hunting and fishing hikes, as well as doing all the necessary chores around the ranch. She testified that she did "haying, raking, swathing, moving, driving trucks and tractors and teams, quietening horses, taking cattle back and forth to the reserve, dehorning, vaccinating, branding, anything that was to be done. I worked outside with him, just as a man would, anything that was to be done." The husband's version regarding her activities around the ranch was, "Oh, just about what the ordinary rancher's wife does. Most of them can do most anything." That answer seemed to influence the trial judge to conclude that the wife did nothing more than was normal in relation to the matrimonial regime.

The state of the law at that time was that, in the event of a marriage breakdown, if the wife had made only a "normal" contribution, she had no basis for claiming any interest in assets accumulated during the marriage that were registered in the husband's name. The other possible basis for a claim could have come from financial contribution. The salary paid to the couple in the early years of the marriage clearly included both of them and the portion of the price for the dude ranch contributed by the husband included some of that money. Subsequent acquisitions used the same money, contributions from the wife's bank account (which the husband claimed to have been loans from the wife's mother), as well as profits from intermediate sales, so there was no doubt that the wife also made more than nominal financial contribution. The trial judge did not deal with this matter, even though it was part of the record before him. He also did not mention that the household furniture had been purchased with the wife's money and that she had not been allowed to take any of that furniture with her when the couple separated.

It is worth a reminder here that appellate courts usually tend to afford considerable deference to findings of fact made by trial judges. They do so on the basis that they, the appellate courts, have not had the same opportunity as the trial judge to observe the witnesses, to assess their credibility, and to choose between conflicting versions of the facts or events. If a litigant wants to challenge findings of fact, there is a fairly steep hill to climb, and it must be shown that there has been an obvious and overriding error on the part of the trial judge. (This is unlike matters of law, where the trial judge, as well as any intermediate court of appeal, is held to an obligation of being correct and no deference is accorded to legal conclusions reached.) There are, of course, some hybrid situations, such as written evidence, uncontested evidence, and others where an appellate court is in just as good a position as a trial judge to conclude on the evidence. In my experience, however, appellate courts are more likely to find ways to deal with inconvenient facts than their statements about deference might suggest.

The situation was summarized as follows:

> The position between the parties at the time of their separation was, therefore, that the wife had contributed considerable physical labour to the building up of the assets claimed by the husband as his own and had also made a modest financial contribution to their acquisition. The legal question is whether she can now claim a one-half or any interest in them when the husband has legal title and possession, denies any arrangement for the sharing of the assets and the wife is unable to produce any effective writing to support a division in her favour.

> The legal proposition upon which the respondent husband rests is that his wife's work earned her nothing in a share of the assets in his name when it had not been recognized by him in a way that would demand an apportionment, that is by proof of an agreement or at least of a common intention that she would share in the acquisitions. In my view, this is to state too narrowly the law that should apply to the present case.

> The case is one where the spouses over a period of some fifteen years improved their lot in life through progressively larger acquisitions of ranch property to which the wife contributed necessary labour in seeing that the ranches were productive. There is no reason to treat this contribution as any less significant than a direct financial contribution, which to a much lesser degree she also made. The relations of husband and wife in such circumstances should not be allowed to rest on the mere obligation of support and shelter which arises from the fact of marriage, where the husband is able so to provide for an impecunious wife, nor on her statutory dower rights under the law of Alberta. They represent a minimum and reflect the law's protection for a dependent wife. I do not regard them as exhausting a wife's claim upon her husband where she has, as here, been anything but dependent.

There had been legislation in England and in some of the American states providing considerably enhanced protection for the property rights of married women, although nothing comparable to the circumstances in the present case had been adopted. Even the majority of the Court had seemed to recognize that some degree of evolution was on the way, although it was not willing to do anything to advance the law, nor to apply any particular ingenuity to finding a solution to an obviously unsatisfactory set of circumstances. The usual conundrum regarding provincial jurisdiction for legislation of this nature (property and civil rights) added to the complexity of having a legislated solution. As the dissenting judge stated:

> No doubt, legislative action may be the better way to lay down policies and prescribe conditions under which and the extent to which spouses should share in property acquired by either or both during marriage. But the better way is not the only way; and if the exercise of a traditional jurisdiction by the Courts can conduce to equitable sharing, it should not be withheld merely because difficulties in particular cases and the making of distinctions may result in a slower and perhaps more painful evolution of the principle.

> A Court with equitable jurisdiction on solid ground in translating into money's worth a contribution of labour by one spouse to the acquisition of property taken in the name of the other, especially when such labour is not simply housekeeping, which might be said to be merely a reflection of the marriage bond. It is unnecessary in such a situation to invoke present-day thinking as to the co-equality of the spouses to support an apportionment in favour of the wife. It can be grounded on known principles whose adaptability has, in other situations, been certified by the Court.

So, yes, legislation would undoubtedly be the best option, in which legislators could examine the most equitable policies, but, no, the courts need not await such legislation (assuming it might be forthcoming) in order to provide equitable justice in circumstances of this nature. How was this to be done under the applicable principles of law? One of the features of the law of trusts provided the key. Trusts are legal relationships in which the legal (or registered) owner of a property is different from the beneficial owner, and the legal owner is considered to hold the property on behalf of the beneficial owner, who can claim certain rights in it. Some trusts are contractual, where the legal owner (trustee) agrees to act in that capacity. A "resulting" trust can arise where someone takes title in someone else's name. The solution in this case was expressed in the following terms:

> The appropriate mechanism to give relief to a wife who cannot prove a common intention or to a wife whose contribution to the acquisition of property is physical labour rather than purchase money is the constructive trust which does not depend on evidence of intention. Perhaps the resulting trusts should be as readily available in the case of a contribution of physical labour as in the case of a financial contribution, but the historical roots of the inference that is raised in the latter case do not exist in the former. ... A constructive trust is imposed where a person holding title to a property is subject to an equitable duty to convey it to another on the ground that he would be unjustly enriched if he were permitted to retain it. ... The basis of the constructive trust is the unjust enrichment which would result if the person having the property were permitted to retain it.

Had the minority position been maintained by the full Court, the outcome would have been that the wife would have been declared to have a beneficial interest in the property and that the husband was under an obligation to convey that interest to her. The amount of the interest was not to be fixed arbitrarily, but referred back for inquiry and report.

Having such an inequitable situation exposed so graphically was a real eye-opener for the country as a whole, as was a failure of the country's highest court to deal equitably with the matter. It fell to the minority to be the conscience of fair treatment for married women who provided significant assistance in the acquisition of matrimonial assets. The decision can safely be said to have been the necessary stimulus to awareness of inherent inequities, and it led to major activism in favour of more comprehensive legislation in the field of family and matrimonial law.

The dissents of one era quite often become mainstream in the next. By 1978, the dissent effectively showed up as a minority opinion in the case of *Rothwell,* and evolved to form the majority opinion in *Becker v. Pettkus* in 1980, in which Rosa Becker, an unmarried woman in a twenty-year relationship, won a substantial award on the basis of the Court finding that there was a constructive trust in her favour. Despite the award, the matter ended badly. Pettkus refused to comply with the court order, and deliberately destroyed the business assets (beehives). Rosa Becker later committed suicide. The Supreme Court of Canada revisited the property division issue in 2011 in *Kerr v. Baranow* and concluded that a claim might exist on the basis of unjust enrichment, even where the conditions leading to a constructive trust did not exist. Most provinces now have extensive matrimonial property legislative schemes in place, but there are still possible gaps, as can be seen from the Court's 2013 decision in *Attorney General (Quebec) v. A* [see page 226].

De Facto Spouses: Some Have No Rights

Quebec (Attorney General) v. A   [2013] S. C. C. 5

This was a family-law case concerning the rights of *de facto* spouses in the province of Quebec. Initials have been used to protect the identities of the individuals involved, although it is the worst-kept secret in recent years.

The facts were not in dispute and the description that follows is taken from the headnote of the reported decision. A and B met in A's home country in 1992. A, who was seventeen years old at the time, was living with her parents and attending school. B, who was thirty-two, was the owner of a lucrative business. From 1992 to 1994, they travelled the world together several times a year. B provided A with financial support so that she could continue her schooling. In early 1995, the couple agreed that A would come to live in Quebec, where B lived. They broke up soon after, but saw each other during the holiday season and in early 1996. A then became pregnant with their first child. She gave birth to two other children with B, in 1999 and 2001. During the time they lived together, A attempted to start a career as a model, but she largely did not work outside of the home and often accompanied B on his travels. B provided for all of A's needs and for those of the children. A wanted to get married, but B told her that he did not believe in the institution of marriage. He said he could possibly envision getting married someday, but only to make a long-standing relationship official. The parties separated in 2002 after living together for seven years.

In February 2002, A filed a motion in court seeking custody of the children, accompanied by a notice to the Attorney General of Quebec stating that she intended to challenge the constitutionality of several provisions of the *Civil Code of Québec* (the "Code") in order to obtain the same legal regime for *de facto* spouses that existed for married spouses. In the circumstances, quite apart from the constitutional principles involved, there was a great deal of money at stake. The issue was whether a number of the *Civil Code* provisions infringed section 15(1) of the *Charter*, and if so, was any such infringement within the reasonable limit prescribed by law that can be demonstratively justified in a free and democratic society under section 1 of the *Charter*. By the time the appeal reached the Supreme Court of Canada, only the constitutionality of the *Civil Code* provisions remained in issue.

The full Court heard the case and was deeply divided on the outcome. The judgment was a Brazilian-rainforest-destroying 450 paragraphs. Five judges thought section 15(1) of the *Charter* was infringed and four did not. On the question of whether the Code provisions were reasonable limitations, the four dissenting judges said the question did not need to be answered, while of the five judges who thought there had been a infringement, one thought the limitation was reasonable, one thought not, and the other three considered that only one article of the Code was not justified. Quebec judges on the Court were on both sides of the division, as were judges from the common-law jurisdictions.

Arriving by somewhat differing directions at the same conclusion, the majority determined that the exclusion of *de facto* spouses from the economic protections afforded to formal spousal unions is a distinction based on marital status (an analogous ground under s. 15 of the *Charter*). Then, was that distinction discriminatory?

> That it imposes a disadvantage is clear, in my view: the law excludes economically vulnerable and dependent *de facto* spouses from protections considered so fundamental to the welfare of vulnerable married or civil union spouses that one of those protections is presumptive, and the rest are of public order, explicitly overriding the couple's freedom of contract or choice. The disadvantage this exclusion perpetuates is an historic one: it continues to deny *de facto* spouses access to economic remedies they have always been deprived

of, remedies the National Assembly considered indispensable for the protection of married and civil union spouses.

...

The National Assembly enacted economic safeguards for spouses in formal unions based on the need to protect them from the economic consequences of their assumed roles. Since many spouses in *de facto* couples exhibit the same functional characteristics as those in formal unions, with the same potential for one partner to be left economically vulnerable or disadvantaged when the relationship ends, their exclusion from similar protections perpetuates historic disadvantage against them based on their marital status.

There is no need to look for an attitude of prejudice motivating, or created by, the exclusion of *de facto* couples from the presumptive statutory protections. Nor need we consider whether the exclusions promot[ing] the view that the individual is less capable or worthy of recognition as a human being or citizen ... would be difficult to prove. There is no doubt that attitudes have changed towards *de facto* unions in Quebec, but what is relevant is not the *attitudinal* progress toward them, but the continuation of their discriminatory *treatment*.

The majority conceded that excluding *de facto* spouses from property and spousal-support regimes in Quebec was a carefully considered policy choice, one which was discussed and reaffirmed in family-law reforms beginning in 1980. That did not, however, act as a shield against constitutional scrutiny. What was relevant was that the resulting legislative choice and the carefully deliberate policy route, as well as the popularity of its outcome, were not an answer to the requirement of constitutional compliance.

Every other province has extended spousal support to unmarried spouses. They have set up different rules by requiring minimum periods of cohabitation before couples become subject to the regimes and have preserved the freedom of choice for couples to opt out. Some have extended the statutory division of property to unmarried spouses. Notwithstanding lack of a uniform position on division of property and the various thresholds, the Court noted that the existence of such alternatives to total exclusion for unmarried spouses in the rest of Canada might be instructive. Provincial dignity being what it is, however, there was a quick transition in the direction of provincial legislative authority:

> Quebec is, of course, in no way obliged to mimic any other province's treatment of *de facto* spouses. Quebec not only has a separate system of private law from the rest of Canada, it also has unique historical and societal values that it has a right to express through its legislation. The fact of these other regimes, however, can be helpful in determining that there *is* a less impairing way to fulfill the objective of preserving freedom of choice.

> The current opt *in* protections may well be adequate for some *de facto* spouses who enter their relationships with sufficient financial security, legal information, and the deliberate intent to avoid the consequences of a more formal union. But their ability to exercise freedom of choice can equally be protected under a protective regime with an opt *out* mechanism. The needs of the economically vulnerable, however, require presumptive protection no less in *de facto* unions than in more formal ones.

The dissenting judges viewed the matter as one of freedom of contract, in which persons are free to choose between marriage, civil union, and *de facto* unions. The legislature had decided to recognize the three types of conjugality. Each of the first two has certain mandatory characteristics and the third did not regulate the private relationship of *de facto* spouses on the basis that their individual autonomy and freedom should be respected. They remained free to establish the terms and conditions governing their relationship.

> As I mentioned above, the *Civil Code of Quebec* does not lay down the terms of the union of *de facto* spouses. The law imposes no duty of assistance and succour on them, and thus no obligation of support. The sharing of household expenses is left to their discretion; they are not required to contribute toward those expenses in proportion to their respective means. Nor are they required to choose the family residence together. No mandatory provisions apply to limit the exercise of their rights of ownership in the family residence. A *de facto* spouse who is the sole owner of the residence can therefore sell it or lease it without the other spouse's consent. A *de facto* union does not create

a family patrimony, is not subject to the legal matrimonial regime of partner-ship of acquests and does not entitle a spouse to a compensatory allowance.

A *de facto* spouse continues, both while living with the other spouse and after their relationship breaks down, to own any property he or she acquired be-fore or during their union. Any change in this situation must be consented to by the spouse whose rights are affected. ...

Since the *de facto* union is not subject to the mandatory legislative framework that applies to marriage and the civil union, *de facto* spouses are free to shape their relationships as they wish, having proper regard for public order. They can enter into agreements to organize their patrimonial relationships while they live together and to provide for the consequences of a possible break-down. ... Such agreements are commonly referred to as "cohabitation agree-ments."

Such spouses who might believe they were wronged when a relation-ship broke down would have available the general remedy of unjust en-richment to compensate for a contribution of property or services that enabled the other party to be in a better position than he or she would have been had they not lived together.

This view was rejected by the judges forming the majority, as noted above, but was a clearly drafted position and powerfully expressed.

At the end of the day, the methodology for remedying the s. 15 breach lies with the Quebec legislature. The Quebec scheme currently gives *de facto* spouses the choice of entering into a contract to enshrine certain protections, or marrying and receiving all the protections provided by law, or remain-ing unbound by any mutual rights or obligations. None of these choices is compromised by a presumptively protective scheme of some sort. It is en-tirely possible for Quebec to design a regime that retains all of these choices. Spouses who are aware of their legal rights, and choose not to marry so they can avoid Quebec's support and property regimes, would be free to choose to remove themselves from a presumptively protective regime. Changing the *default* situation of the couple, however, so that spousal support and division of property protection of some kind applies to them, would protect those spouses for whom the choices are illusory and who are left economically at the dissolution of their relationship.

The Chief Justice, the Rt. Hon. Beverley McLachlin, was also of the view that section 15 of the *Charter* had been violated, but concluded that the limit on equality rights of *de facto* spouses imposed by law was reasonable and justifiable in a free and democratic society. The goal of Quebec, an important policy goal, was to enhance the choice and autonomy of couples. Treating *de facto* spouses differently from married and civil-union spouses enhanced that goal and did so in a proportionate way. The fact that Quebec had chosen a different policy than other provinces was in keeping with its own history and social values did not make the law unconstitutional. She thus broke an uncomfortable tie between the minority on the section 15 question and the majority (of which she had effectively been part), saving the Quebec legislation from being invalidated as unconstitutional.

Damages for Abuse of Rights by Bank

Houle v. National Bank of Canada [1990] 3 S.C.R. 122

Picture this: your family and the family company have been doing business with the National Bank of Canada for some fifty-eight years. Over time, the company has arranged for a revolving line of credit of $700,000 and it has a letter of credit for an additional amount of $100,000. The bank has all kinds of security, including personal guarantees from the shareholders and even from the mother of the current shareholders. It also has security, under special provisions of the *Bank Act*, as well as by a separate trust deed, on all the assets of the company. The advances have all been evidenced by demand promissory notes. Some examples of the "customer-friendly" banking document language include:

> 4. In the event of failure by the *customer* to pay in full any advance or debt, the Bank is authorized to realize in whole or in part on the guarantees given by the *customer* and to sell in whole or in part the property (hereinafter referred to as the "*effects*") pledged or covered by these guarantees, and all of its proceeds, in such manner, at such time and at such place as the Bank, in the exercise of its absolute discretion, shall decide, without notice to the *customer* or to any person whatsoever, and without any obligation to place any advertisement or sell at public auction.

> 10. The Bank or its representative may at any time, without notice, force entry

to the property (real or personal) of the *customer* and the premises occupied by him in connection with the *effects* (except for the establishment of a warehouseman or carrier); it may effect entry therein, occupy and use the same without cost and to the exclusion of any other person, including the *customer*, until it has disposed of the *effects*. ...

The bank is also aware that you are negotiating with a third party for the sale of the shares of the company for $1 million. During the course of the negotiations, the company requested an increase in the line of credit to $900,000. Before agreeing to the increase, the head office of the bank engaged an accounting firm to review the financial condition of the company. Based on a verbal report from the accounting firm, the bank decided to call in the loan and realize on its security. A representative of the accounting firm went to the shareholders to tell them that the bank intended to call the loan, that notice to this effect would be served on them, but that if they were to invest further in the company, the bank would increase the line of credit. Over the course of a meeting which lasted an hour, no agreement was reached. The bank served the notice. The company assets were immediately seized by the bank and liquidated. The total elapsed time between first advising the company that a notice might be served and liquidation of the assets was three hours. The manager of the bank who looked after the company had been completely unaware of the actions taken by the head office.

The shares were later sold by the shareholders to the company with which they had been negotiating, but for $300,000. The shareholders instituted proceedings against the bank for $700,000 (the difference between what they had expected to receive on the sale of the shares and the amount they eventually received).

The trial judge found in favour of the shareholders. The bank was at fault for not giving the company enough time to meet the demand for repayment. The trial judge thought that this was an occasion on which it would be appropriate to "lift the corporate veil" to recognize that even though the contractual arrangements were between the bank and the company, the company was really only an intermediary between the bank and the shareholders. The Quebec Court of Appeal affirmed that judgment and the bank obtained leave to appeal to the Supreme Court of Canada.

A unanimous Court dismissed the bank's appeal. Central to its decision was the concept of abuse of rights, both contractual and extra-contractual, although the Court concentrated on contractual rights, where such abuse causes damage to persons who are not parties to contract. There was a lengthy review of the concept of abuse of rights, dating back to Roman law, then French law and later Canadian law (primarily for this appeal, Quebec civil law). This review showed clearly that the doctrine of abuse of contractual rights was "consistent with the fundamental principles of Quebec law, where good faith and reasonableness permeate the theories of rights and obligations, contractual ... as well as extra-contractual."

> But more fundamentally, the doctrine of abuse of contractual rights today serves the important social as well as economic function of a necessary control over the exercise of contractual rights. While the doctrine may represent a departure from the absolutist approach of previous decades, consecrated in the well-known maxim "*la volonté des parties fait loi*" (the intent of the parties is the governing factor), it inserts itself into today's trend towards a just and fair approach to rights and obligations. ... Such uncertainty which the doctrine of abuse of rights may bring to contractual relationships, besides being worth that price, may be counterbalanced by the presumption of good faith which remains basic in contractual relationships. Courts have so far demonstrated, in applying the doctrine, that they will only sanction marked departure from the general norm of behaviour acceptable in our society.

This led to a review of the criteria for determining whether there has been an abuse of contractual rights: was this to be restricted to malice and bad faith, or did it extend to unreasonable use of those rights? The answer was that both criteria could apply, although the jurisprudence was somewhat contradictory, earlier cases tending toward a more strict application based on malice and bad faith, with later cases favouring the less stringent standard of reasonableness. The next issue was whether liability for abuse of contractual rights was grounded in contract or delict (civil responsibility based on fault). This was important for the shareholders, since they were not contractual parties to the arrangements between the bank and the company, so that if the liability triggered by an abuse of the contract was solely contractual, only the contracting parties could make a claim. Again, there was some division on whether abuse of contractual rights should be restricted to the contractual basis or whether it could be a combination of both contract and delict.

> In summary, although contractual and delictual liability may coexist even in the context of a contract, delictual liability must arise independently of contractual obligations and all of the elements required to give rise to such liability must be found. In the context of an abuse of contractual rights, it is the right arising out of the contract itself which are exercised, and only the contracting parties possess these rights and the correlative obligation to exercise them reasonably. This obligation is derived exclusively from the contract. Consequently, when the fault alleged arises strictly from the abuse of a contractual right, then the liability must have its source in the contract.

> Conversely, since a claim for abuse of contractual rights is based solely on contractual grounds, the contracting parties alone have a right of action. From this flows the conclusion that the respondent shareholders in the present case, given that it was the company which contracted with the bank, have no right of action based on the contract, for the abuse by the bank of those contractual rights. Such action is only open to the company, a party to the contract. The company in the present case did not take action against the bank, given that it was sold shortly after the liquidation of the assets and the new purchaser released the bank of potential liability for its actions in the execution of the loan.

The Court had no issue with the bank's right to call the loan as soon as financial difficulties are noticed. Calling the loan was not in and of itself, an abuse of its contractual rights. The principle, however, of giving a debtor whose loan has been called a reasonable time to respond is very much part of the law. It is also a feature of the common law. By liquidating the company's assets just three hours after requesting payment of the loans, the bank deprived its customer of any chance to meet its obligations or to obtain financing from other sources.

> The bank acted, in my view, in a sudden, impulsive, and harmful manner, particularly considering that there was never any warning that the bank was

concerned about its loan. The effect of the bank's decision was the termination of over fifty years of business in three hours. With a low risk of losing money or security, at least in the short term, one is at a loss to understand why the bank did not at least wait until the negotiations had been completed with [the prospective buyer of the company shares] before exercising its securities. The record is silent on this. Therefore, I find that there was a flagrant abuse of the bank's contractual right to realize its securities after the demand for payment of its loan was not met.

I must note that the contract regarding the rights of the bank to realize its securities stipulates, in paragraph 4, [see above] that it can do so without notice. Nevertheless, this seemingly absolute right must be tempered by the principle of reasonable delay, and what constitutes the abuse of contractual rights in this case is the absence of such reasonable delay to allow the company to pay after it was put in default.

The Court did not agree with the lower courts about lifting the corporate veil. The independent legal personality of a corporation had been established at the beginning of the century and many persons chose the corporate form of carrying on business with the protection of limited liability. By choosing that form, to enjoy such benefits, the individual shareholders had to be prepared to accept the necessary consequences. One of these was that when the corporation is damaged, the shareholders have no separate recourse for whatever may be the indirect loss they suffer.

The difference here was that the shareholders had a direct, personal, financial interest at stake, of which the bank was fully aware. The potential value of their shares was damaged. The shareholders lost something "that was inches away from their grasp."

Having determined the fault of the appellate bank and the direct and certain damage suffered by the respondents, I have no difficulty in concluding that there was a direct relationship between the fault and the damage and that the actions of the bank directly caused the respondents' loss. It was inevitable under the circumstances that precipitous action, in liquidating the assets of the company, would cause damage to the respondents. The liquidation of the assets of a company can do nothing but decrease the bargaining power of any individual who is in the process of negotiating the sale of shares in that company, and this was exactly the result in this case. Consequently a causal link exists between the fault of the appellant bank and the damage to the respondent shareholders.

The facts of this case give rise to a legal obligation on the appellant to act reasonably towards the respondents in order to avoid prejudice. Banks are no different than any other member of society who must abide by the rules of good faith implicit in a contractual relationship and avoid any actions which might be in breach of a legal obligation of diligence regardless of any contractual relationship, as is the case here. Having determined that all of the elements of delictual liability are present in this case, independently from any contractual liability which may have existed between the parties to the contract, I conclude that the appellant has breached its legal obligation towards the respondents ... and must be found liable for the damages suffered by them....

The shareholders were fortunate, in this case, that the bank was aware of the negotiations to sell their shares. Without that fact, it would have been much more difficult for them to have recovered any damages whatsoever. In the end, however, the important legacy of this appeal is that abuse of rights is now well established as a ground for the recovery of damages and that abuse may occur when a person with rights does not exercise them reasonably.

Discrimination against Common-Law Spouses

Miron v. Trudel   [1995] 2 S.C.R. 418

This is a leading case in which the Court decided, albeit narrowly (five to four), that a provincial automobile insurance scheme that provided benefits to spouses—acknowledged to be persons legally married—discriminated against persons living in a common-law relationship.

John Miron and Jocelyne Valliere lived in such a relationship, and, with their children, functioned as an economic unit. Miron was injured in an automobile accident, as a passenger in an uninsured automobile driven by an uninsured driver. As a result, Miron was no longer able to work and could no longer contribute to the support of his family. Valliere had an insurance policy which extended benefits to the "spouse" of the policy holder. Miron made a claim under that policy for accident benefits for loss of income and damages. Not surprisingly, the insurer denied the claim: Miron was not married to Valliere, so he could not be her "spouse." That led to the litigation. Attempting to shortcut the process prior to a trial, the insurer made a preliminary motion to determine whether the word *spouse* appearing in the policy included common-law couples. It was clearly an issue that would be headed to the Supreme Court of Canada.

By the time the case reached the Court, it had been framed as discrimination against Miron in violation of section 15(1) of the *Charter*, which provides:

> Every individual is equal before and under the law and has the right to the equal protection and equal benefit of the law without discrimination and, in particular, without discrimination based on race, national or ethnic origin, colour, religion, sex, age or mental or physical disability.

None of the judges in the lower courts, nor, for that matter, in the Court, thought that the word *spouse* where it appeared in the insurance policy meant anything other than someone who was legally married.

Four judges on the Court decided that there was, in fact, discrimination within the meaning of the *Charter* language. Four decided that there was no such discrimination. Separate reasons, somewhat differently framed, given by the ninth judge, supported the conclusion that there was discrimination.

It is not sufficient to establish discrimination simply to allege that it has occurred. The Court has developed a process for analyzing discrimination cases, which was expressed in the following language:

> The analysis under s. 15(1) involves two steps. First, the claimant must show a denial of "equal protection" or "equal benefit" of the law, as compared with some other person. Second, the claimant must show that the denial constitutes discrimination. At this second stage, in order for discrimination to be made out, the claimant must show that the denial rests on one of the grounds enumerated in s. 15(1) or an analogous ground and that the unequal treatment is based on the stereotypical application of presumed group or personal characteristics. If the claimant meets the onus under this analysis, violation of s. 15(1) is established. The onus then shifts to the party seeking to uphold the law, usually the state, to justify the discrimination as "demonstrably justified in a free and democratic society" under s. 1 of the *Charter*.

The shift of onus is important. The claimant is in the best position to demonstrate that a benefit has been denied or a disadvantage has been suffered, as well as providing the basis for such treatment. If the claimant succeeds in demonstrating this, the burden then shifts to the state to defend the violation under section 1 of the *Charter*.

The state may attempt to differentiate on stereotypical grounds, but it must then be prepared to justify the discrimination if the law is to stand.

The Court was also clear that unequal treatment of and by itself, the mere fact of making a distinction, does not violate the *Charter*. To prove discrimination, the claimant is required to show that the unequal treatment is based on one of the grounds mentioned, or some analogous ground. As the Court noted,

> These grounds serve as a filter to separate trivial inequities from those worthy of constitutional protection. They reflect the overarching purpose of the equality guarantee in the *Charter*—to prevent the violation of human dignity and freedom by imposing limitations, disadvantages or burdens through the stereotypical application of presumed group characteristics rather than on the basis of individual merit, capacity, or circumstance.

On occasion, even distinctions made on the basis of the enumerated or analogous grounds may be found not to constitute discrimination, or to engage the purpose of the *Charter* guarantee. A distinction on such a ground that does not impose a real disadvantage in the social and political context of the claim may also not violate the *Charter*. The Court warned, however, that where such distinctions have been made, it may be hard to demonstrate that the distinction is not discriminatory. For example, if such a distinction is clearly irrelevant to the functional values of the legislation, the distinction will be discriminatory. The reverse is not necessarily true, namely that if the distinction is relevant, a claim of discrimination will be unsuccessful. Focus must be maintained on the "effect or impact of the distinction in the social and economic context of the legislation and the lives of the individuals it touches."

Following a lengthy backswing of identifying the nature and extent of the *Charter* analysis, the Court then turned to the analysis of the particular case. First, there was no doubt that there was a denial of equal benefit on the basis of Miron's marital status. Second, the categories of circumstances leading to discrimination are not closed, cannot be confined to historically disadvantaged groups and the *Charter* must retain a capacity to recognize new grounds of discrimination.

Looking at the matter of marital status, the Court noted that

> ... discrimination on the basis of marital status touches the essential dignity and worth of the individual in the same way as other recognized grounds of discrimination violative of fundamental human rights norms. Specifically, it touches the individual's freedom to live life with the mate of one's choice in the fashion of one's choice. This is a matter of defining importance to individuals. It is not a matter which should be excluded from *Charter*-consideration on the ground that its recognition would trivialize the equality guarantee.

It then went on to note that persons in unmarried relationships constitute an historically disadvantaged group that often suffered social disadvantage and prejudice, including social ostracism and denial of status and benefits. There might also be reasons beyond the control of an individual that could stand in the way of formal marriage, such as the law, reluctance of one partner to marry, and financial, religious, or social constraints. This led to the conclusion of a comparison with discrimination on the basis of religion, with its roots in the expression of moral disapproval of all sexual unions other than those sanctioned by church and state. This failed to align with current social values or realities. Many other statutes in Ontario and other provinces no longer distinguished between married partners and those cohabiting in a conjugal relationship, all of which suggest recognition of the fact that it was often wrong to deny equal benefit of the law simply because a person was not married. Its conclusion was that discrimination had been made out.

The dissenting members of the Court had determined that the purpose of the statutory language in issue was the promotion of marriage. The counter to this position was that the issue was not whether marriage was good, but whether it could be used to deny equal treatment on grounds that had nothing to do with true worth or entitlement due to circumstance.

Once discrimination had been found, the next step was to determine whether it could be "demonstrably justified in a free and democratic society." This involves two inquiries:

First, the goal of the legislation is ascertained and examined to see if it is of pressing and substantial importance. Then the court must carry out a proportionality analysis to balance the interests of society with those of individuals and groups. The proportionality analysis comprises three branches. First, the connection between the goal and the discriminatory distinction is examined to ascertain if it is rational. Second, the law must impair the right no more than is necessary to accomplish the objective. Finally, if these two conditions are met, the court must weigh whether the effect of the discrimination is proportionate to the benefit thereby achieved. ...

Examination of the goal of the legislation is vital in discrimination cases as elsewhere. Sometimes the legislative goal is apparent on the face of the legislation. Other times it may not be. Legislation aimed at effecting a less than worthy goal may be cloaked in the rhetoric of justice and reason. The task of the court in every case is to identify the functional values underlying the law.

The goal or functional value of the legislation here at issue is to sustain families when one of their members is injured in an automobile accident. When an adult partner in a family unit is injured, economic dislocation may not be far behind. If the injured partner is a wage-earner, the family income may be reduced or eliminated. If the injured party works in the home, it may be necessary to hire replacement services. In either case, the result is economic dislocation. This, in turn, can work great hardship on the family and its members. The goal of the legislation is to reduce this economic dislocation and hardship. This is a laudable goal. And given the frequency of injuries from motor vehicle accidents, it assumes an importance which can without exaggeration be described as pressing and substantial.

The state was unable to demonstrate that the chosen "group marker" was reasonably relevant to the legislative goal, having regard to available alternative criteria and the need to minimize prejudice within the group. The real functional value was financial interdependence, not marriage equivalence. The *Charter* violation was established.

It only remained for the Court to determine how to deal with the legislation. It could "read-in" appropriate amendments or issue a declaratory statement of invalidity for sufficient time to enable the legislature to remedy the violation. It decided on the exceptional remedy of retroactive amendment. The matter was then remitted to trial to determine whether Miron and Valliere met the requirements of the judicially amended legislation.

Damages for Breach of Fiduciary Responsibility to Indian Band

Guerin v. The Queen [1984] 2 S.C.R. 335

The appellant was the Chief of the Musqueam Indian Band. In 1955, 235 members of the band lived on a reserve located within the present boundaries of the city of Vancouver. The reserve comprised 416.5 acres of extremely valuable land, some of which was surplus to the current needs of the Band. The subject matter of the litigation that reached the Supreme Court of Canada was 162 acres leased, on behalf of the Band, by the Indian Affairs Branch of the federal government to the Shaughnessy Heights Golf Club in 1958. The action by the Band in 1984 was based on breach of trust.

To begin with, even in 1958, there was no doubt as to the value of the land. Offers to buy and to lease it had already been received. The Branch itself had noted that the reserve was "undoubtedly the most potentially valuable 400 acres in metropolitan Vancouver today." At that time the Club was looking for a new site, since its lease from the CPR would expire in 1960 and would not be renewed. In addition, a prominent real-estate firm, on behalf of a developer–client, was interested in a long-term lease. The principal wanted to arrange a meeting with the Chief of the Band to try to work out an arrangement. He was told by the Branch not to deal directly, but to do so only through Indian Affairs personnel. He followed that advice. The Band was never advised of any interest in the land except for that expressed by the Club.

The Band agreed that the land should be leased. They authorized an appraisal, which was done by an appraiser who was not a land-use expert. The valuation was quite low and the Band was never given a copy of it (even though it had paid for it). Even the Branch had difficulty in getting it. The Branch had discussions with the Club and reviewed the appraisal report with its representatives. The Branch was considering a lease to the Club at between $20,000 and $25,000 per year. At a meeting in 1957 with the Band Council, presided over by the Branch, the Club proposal was put to the Band in the most general of terms: 160 acres would be leased for an initial term of fifteen years with options for the Club for additional fifteen-year periods, "on terms to be agreed upon." The Branch already knew that the Club proposal was $25,000 per year for the first fifteen years with the rent for each successive renewal period being settled by mutual agreement or arbitration, except that there was a ceiling to the increase of 15 percent of the initial $25,000 rent (e.g., $3,750) and the Club had the right to remove all improvement upon termination of the lease. The valuator was never told of either condition by the Branch.

Negotiations between the Branch and the Band continued throughout most of 1957, during which the Band was not informed by the Branch of many of the key elements of the proposed lease and renewal terms. Because of the peculiarities of "Indian" title and the legal difficulties of reconciling it with the elements of legal ownership as generally understood, the mechanism for uniting the titles has been for Natives to surrender the lands to the Crown so that commercial leases or sales of the affected property can be effected. Thus the Band had to "surrender" the leased land to the Crown, which would then enter into the commercial transaction on behalf of the Band. The Band voted after extensive discussions with Branch.

The trial judge in the 1980s, who had heard and examined all of the evidence, made specific findings of fact that:

(a) Before the Band members voted, those present assumed or understood the golf club lease would be, aside from the first term, for 10-year periods, not 15 years.

(b) Before the Band members voted, those present assumed or understood there would be no 15% limitation on rental increases.

(c) The meeting was not told the golf club proposed it should have the right, at any time during the lease and for a period of up to 6 months after termination, to remove any buildings or structures, and any course improvements and facilities.

(d) The meeting was not told that future rent on renewal periods was to be determined as if the land was still in an uncleared and unimproved condition and used as a golf club.

(e) The meeting was not told that the golf club would have the right at the end of each 15-year period to terminate the lease on six month's prior notice.

Neither (d) nor (e) was in the original Club proposal and were not brought to the Band at any time for either comment or approval. The Band voted to approve the surrender, having heard no mention of details of the proposed lease to the Club. When the matter came to trial, the Crown's position was that once the surrender documents had been signed, the Crown could lease to anyone on whatever terms it saw fit.

As the Court noted thereafter:

> After the surrender there was considerable correspondence between [the Branch official] and personnel in the Indian Affairs Branch in Ottawa particularly over the more controversial provisions of the lease but none of the correspondence was communicated to the Band Council nor were they given a copy of the draft lease which would have drawn these controversial provisions to their attention. The trial judge stated: ...

> Put baldly, the band members, regardless of the whole history of dealings and the limited information imparted at the surrender meeting, were not consulted. But it was their land. It was their potential investment and revenue. It was their future.

> The learned trial judge accepted that the Chief, the Councillors and the Band members were wholly excluded from any further discussions or negotiations among the Indian Affairs personnel, the golf club officers and their respective solicitors with respect to the terms of the lease. The trial judge found an explanation, although not a justification, for this in the possibility that Indian Affairs personnel at the time took a rather paternalistic attitude towards the

Indian people whom they regarded as wards of the Crown.

The eventual lease was dated January 1958 and provided that the term was seventy-five years, unless terminated earlier (which the Club could do, but not the Band), that the rent for the first fifteen years was $29,000 per year, that for each succeeding fifteen-year period the rent was to be determined by agreement or by arbitration (except that the rent was to be the fair rent for the lands as if they were still in an uncleared and unimproved condition as at the date of each determination and restricted to use as a golf course, that the maximum increase for the second fifteen-year period was $4,350 per year and that the Club could terminate on six months' notice at the end of any fifteen-year period). The Club could remove any buildings and other structures, as well as any course improvements and facilities.

These terms bore little resemblance to what had been discussed and approved at the surrender meeting. The trial judge found that had the Band been aware of the terms that were, in fact, in the lease, they would never have surrendered the land. The Band was not given a copy of the lease and did not receive one until twelve years later, in 1970.

The Court concluded that the Crown had a fiduciary obligation to the Band to protect and preserve the Band's interests from destruction or invasion. That obligation is enforceable by the courts. The obligation was breached when the Crown leased the lands to the Club on terms much less favourable to the Band than had been agreed. It committed the Band to an unauthorized long-term lease that deprived it of the opportunity to use the land for any other purpose. That lost opportunity to develop the land for any other purpose for a period of up to seventy-five years was to be compensated as at the date of trial, notwithstanding that market values may have increased since the date of the breach of the fiduciary obligation (1958).

A similar approach was adopted by the other judges who came to the same conclusion by a slightly different route.

> In my view, the nature of Indian title and the framework of the statutory scheme established for disposing of Indian land places upon the Crown an equitable obligation, enforceable by the courts, to deal with the land for the benefit of the Indians. This obligation does not amount to a trust in the private

law sense. It is rather a fiduciary duty. If, however, the Crown breaches this fiduciary duty it will be liable to the Indians in the same way and to the same extent as if such a trust were in effect.

The trial judge had determined the damages—the amount lost by the Band due to the unfavourable and unauthorized lease—to be $10 million. He had considered all of the evidence and other possible uses to which the land might otherwise have been put and acknowledged that it was impossible to be certain of the outcomes or rates of development, but nevertheless was satisfied that, as a global assessment, even though it could not be mathematically demonstrated, it was clear that the enormous increases in the property values in the area made use of it as a golf course completely uneconomical. The final amount of damages was, he said, "a considered reaction based on the evidence, the opinions, the arguments and, in the end, my conclusions of fact." None of the judges of the Court was prepared to interfere with his findings regarding damages.

In the end, therefore, the Band received something much closer to the economic value of their land, the government had its fingers severely rapped for its cavalier and condescending treatment of the Band, and the golfers must have had the broadest of smiles on their faces, celebrating their deal of a lifetime. Your tax dollars at work.

Aboriginal Property Rights: What Do They Mean?

Delgamuukw v. British Columbia [1997] 3 S.C.R. 1010

Without a doubt, one of the most complex aspects of Canadian society today is the matter of Aboriginal claims, especially with respect to Aboriginal title. This sounds deceptively simple, but the concept of Aboriginal title itself, including what it really means, is difficult to grasp, and is further complicated by questions such as who can assert the claim, how is it established, what the practical implications may be, and whether there are superior claims that may trump any Aboriginal rights that might exist. Governments, Aboriginals, and the courts have been wrestling with these claims ever since Europeans landed on this continent and began to occupy lands over which Aboriginals claimed ownership. Theories of ownership by conquest or exploration collided with those of pre-existing ownership through use or connection with the same lands. The problems persist to this day and it is unlikely that our generation will witness their satisfactory resolution.

This case involved a claim for vast tracts of land in what is now the province of British Columbia. The plaintiff, suing on his own behalf as well as on behalf of all members of various Houses of Aboriginals, began by claiming both ownership and jurisdiction over the particular territories, although by the time it got to the Court, the claim morphed into one of Aboriginal title and self-government. British Columbia's position was that there was no such title—or, passing the buck—that the claim should properly have been one for compensation from the federal government. There were procedural issues and questions of what the Court could do in relation to factual findings by the trial judge, but the Court was able nevertheless to deal with the matter of Aboriginal title, how it is protected by the *Constitution Act, 1982*, and what is required to prove it.

How Aboriginal title arises:

> ... aboriginal title arises from the prior occupation of Canada by aboriginal peoples. That prior occupation is relevant in two different ways: first, because of the physical fact of occupation, and second, because aboriginal title originates in part from pre-existing systems of aboriginal law. However, the law of aboriginal title does not only seek to determine the historic rights of aboriginal peoples to land; it also seeks to afford legal protection to prior occupation in the present day. Implicit in the protection of historic patterns of occupation is a recognition of the importance of the continuity of the relationship of an aboriginal community to its land over time.

As to the use of Aboriginal lands:

> ... land subject to aboriginal title cannot be put to such uses as may be irreconcilable with the nature of the occupation of that land and the relationship that the particular group has had with the land which together have given rise to the aboriginal title in the first place. ... one of the critical elements in the determination of whether a particular aboriginal group has aboriginal title to certain lands is the matter of the occupancy of those lands. Occupancy is determined by reference to the activities that have taken place on the land and the uses to which the land has been put by the particular group. If lands are so occupied, there will exist a special bond between the group and the land in question such that the land will be part of the definition of the group's distinctive culture. It seems to me that these elements of aboriginal title create an inherent limitation on the uses to which the land, over which such title exists, may be put. For example, if occupation is established with reference to the use of the land as a hunting ground, then the group that successfully claims aboriginal title to that land may not use it in a fashion as to destroy its value (e.g., by strip mining it). Similarly, if a group claims a special bond with the land because of its ceremonial or cultural significance, it may not use the land in such a way as to destroy that relationship (e.g., by developing it in such

a way that the bond is destroyed, perhaps by turning it into a parking lot).

> It is for this reason also that lands held by virtue of aboriginal title may not be alienated. Alienation would bring to an end the entitlement of the aboriginal people to occupy the land and would terminate their relationship with it. I have suggested above that the inalienability of aboriginal lands is, at least in part, a function of the common law principle that settlers in colonies must derive their title from Crown grant and, therefore, cannot acquire title through purchase from aboriginal inhabitants. ... What the inalienability of lands held pursuant to aboriginal title suggests is that those lands are more than just a fungible commodity. The relationship between an aboriginal community and the lands over which it has aboriginal title has an important non-economic component. The land has an inherent and unique value in itself, which is enjoyed by the community with aboriginal title to it. The community cannot put the land to uses which would destroy that value.

This latter principle does not, however, mean that the community cannot surrender the land to the Crown for valuable consideration, simply that if they want to use the land in a way that Aboriginal title does not permit, they must surrender the land and convert it into non-title land.

In order to establish a claim for Aboriginal title, there are three criteria to be satisfied by the Aboriginal group: first, that it occupied the land at the time when the Crown asserted sovereignty over the land; second (if present occupation is relied upon as proof of pre-sovereignty occupation), that there is a continuity between present and pre-sovereignty occupation; and third, that occupation at sovereignty must have been exclusive. Courts must be careful with regard to the second criterion, since there may have been disputes regarding occupation and use of the land due to a refusal of European colonizers to recognize Aboriginal title, so the test is not so much an "unbroken chain of continuity" as a "substantial maintenance of the connection between the people and the land."

Much of the difficulty surrounding Aboriginal claims arises from the fact that the Aboriginal cultures were based almost exclusively on oral tradition, with little or no written records of even the most crucial matters, including title to Aboriginal lands. The oral traditions may be reflected in ceremony and communal memory and even in songs and dances. Today's judges have an enormous challenge in determining the degree of reliance that can be placed on such evidence, for example, as to occupation of lands claimed as Aboriginal or possibly competing claims to the same lands. Typical of the challenges is the discussion by the Court regarding proof of exclusive occupation of the particular lands.

As with the proof of occupation, proof of exclusivity must rely on both the perspective of the common law and the aboriginal perspective, placing equal weight on each. At common law, a premium is placed on the factual reality of occupation, as encountered by the Europeans. However, as the common law concept of possession must be sensitive to the realities of aboriginal society, so must the concept of exclusivity. Exclusivity is a common law principle derived from the notion of fee simple ownership and should be imported into the concept of aboriginal title with caution. As such, the test to establish exclusive occupation must take into account the context of the aboriginal society at the time of sovereignty. For example, it is important to note that exclusive occupation can be demonstrated even if other aboriginal groups were present, or frequented the claimed lands. Under those circumstances, exclusivity would be demonstrated by "the intention and capacity to retain exclusive control." ... Thus, an act of trespass, if isolated, would not undermine a finding of exclusivity, if aboriginal groups intended to and attempted to enforce their exclusive occupation. Moreover ... the presence of other aboriginal groups might actually reinforce a finding of exclusivity. For example, "[w]here others were allowed access upon request, the very fact that permission was asked for and given would be further evidence of the group's exclusive control."

A consideration of the aboriginal perspective may also lead to the conclusion that trespass by other aboriginal groups does not undermine, and that presence of those groups by permission may reinforce, the exclusive occupation of the aboriginal group asserting title. For example, the aboriginal group asserting the claim to aboriginal title may have trespass laws which are proof of exclusive occupation, such that the presence of trespassers does not count as evidence against exclusivity. As well, aboriginal laws under which permission may be granted to other aboriginal groups to use or reside even temporarily on land would reinforce the finding of exclusive occupation. Indeed, if that permission were the subject of treaties between the aboriginal nations in question, those treaties would also form part of the aboriginal perspective.

Because the trial judge had refused to consider some important Aboriginal perspectives that might have produced a different outcome, the Court ordered a new trial, but urged the parties to attempt to negotiate, reminding the Crown that it was under a moral, if not legal, duty to enter into and conduct those negotiations in good faith to achieve "the reconciliation of the pre-existence of Aboriginal societies with the sovereignty of the Crown."

It seems fairly clear that whatever consultations may be required will extend to the potential use of the lands to which there may be Aboriginal title issues attached, including the development (or non-development) of natural resources.

As Chief Justice Antonio Lamer concluded, in his final words at an appeal in New Brunswick, "Let us face it, we are all here to stay."

Aboriginal Land Claims: Where Ancient Rights Trump Current Might

Tsilhqot'in Nation v. British Columbia [2014] S.C.C. 44

In 1983, the British Columbia government awarded timber-cutting rights to land claimed by way of Aboriginal title by the Tsilhqot'in Nation. There were no previous consultations nor any benefit derived by the Tsilhqot'in Nation as a result of that award for the exploitation of the lands.

Litigation ensued and an exhausting trial eventually commenced in 2002, spread over a five-year period and consuming some 339 days of hearings, many of which took place in the remote area that was the subject of the claim for Aboriginal title. The trial judge concluded that the Tsilhqot'in were, in principle, entitled to a declaration of Aboriginal title regarding a portion of the area, but refrained, on procedural grounds (later abandoned by the province) from making a formal declaration of title. The British Columbia Court of Appeal took a much narrower view of the title claim and rejected it, setting the stage for an appeal to the Supreme Court of Canada, which was heard in November 2013. Judgment was rendered by a unanimous Court on June 26, 2014, in favour of the Tsilhqot'in, holding that Aboriginal title had been established, from which a number of conclusions followed.

Before considering the consequences of the decision, there are some interesting facets of it that are worth bearing in mind.

The first is the importance of the findings of fact made by the trial judge, whose responsibility is to hear and weigh the evidence brought by the parties, particularly those who claim Aboriginal title and, in particular, to choose between conflicting or inconsistent evidence. Absent any palpable (obvious) error, appellate courts are unlikely to interfere with factual conclusions reached by the judge who saw and heard the witnesses. The Supreme Court found no such errors and the conclusions of the trial judge were allowed to stand.

The second is that, if the judgment of the Court seems like something of a primer on Aboriginal title, what it means, and how to establish it, that is undoubtedly what the Court intended, since there remain hundreds of unresolved claims of Aboriginal title in British Columbia and other provinces. Claimants need to know what they are required to establish, government lawyers need to know the limitations of government actions and their consultation obligations when a claim of Aboriginal title is raised, trial judges need to know what will be expected of them, and appellate courts need to be reminded of the proper approach to consideration of such claims and the tests to be applied.

Although the media treated the decision as something of a bombshell, the outcome was entirely predictable, based on the direction in which the Supreme Court had been moving for several years. Indeed, it would have been far more surprising had the Court failed to conclude as it did. The speed with which the judgment was issued and the unanimity, together with the fact that the reasons were written by the Chief Justice, were indicators of the fact that not only was the decision important, but also that there had been no particular difficulty in reaching the decision. Perhaps the only real novelty was that the declaration of Aboriginal title in this case covered a specific and identifiable territory, based on the evidence presented to and accepted by the trial judge.

The principal jurisprudential foundation for the decision was another case arising in British Columbia, *Delgamuukw v. British Columbia*, decided in 1997 (see page 249), but other decisions of the Court had also pointed the way to proper consideration of such claims. These principles included the constitutional protection of unextinguished Aboriginal rights and declarations of a fiduciary responsibility on the Crown regarding those rights.

It was already clear from *Delgamuukw* that "not every passing traverse grounds title." The overall test was expressed in the Tsilhqot'in case as follows:

> In my view, the concepts of sufficiency, continuity and exclusivity provide useful lenses through which to view the question of Aboriginal title. This said, the court must be careful not to lose or distort the Aboriginal perspective by forcing ancestral practices into the square boxes of common law concepts, thus frustrating the goal of faithfully translating pre-sovereignty Aboriginal interests into equivalent modern legal rights. Sufficiency, continuity and exclusivity are not ends in themselves, but inquiries that shed light on whether Aboriginal title is established.

Sufficiency had to be approached from the perspectives of both Aboriginal (laws, practices, customs, and traditions, as well as the size of the group, manner of life, material resources, technological abilities, and character of the lands claimed) and the common law (possession and control of the lands, which extends beyond portions that are physically occupied, such as a house). It is very much a fact-specific inquiry.

> To sufficiently occupy the land for purposes of title, the Aboriginal group in question must show that it has historically acted in a way that would communicate to third parties that it held the land for its own purposes. This standard does not demand notorious or visible use akin to proving a claim for adverse possession, but neither can the occupation be purely subjective or internal. There must be evidence of a strong presence on or over the land claimed, manifesting itself in acts of occupation that could reasonably be interpreted as demonstrating that the land in question belonged to, was controlled by, or was under the exclusive stewardship of the claimant group. ... The notion of occupation must also reflect the way of life of the Aboriginal people, including those who were nomadic or semi-nomadic.

The common-law equivalent would have been that of a general occupant asserting possession of land where no one else had a present interest or where the title was uncertain. The Aboriginal template, however, needed to be applied.

> In summary, what is required is a culturally sensitive approach to sufficiency

of occupation based on the dual perspectives of the Aboriginal group in question – its laws, practices, size, technological ability and character of the land claimed – and the common law notion of possession as a basis for title. It is not possible to list every indicia of occupation that might apply in a particular case. The common law test for possession – which requires an intention to occupy or hold land for the purposes of the occupant – must be considered alongside the perspective of the Aboriginal group which, depending on its size and manner of living, might conceive of possession of land in a somewhat different manner than did the common law.

Key to all of this is that the matter of possession of the land is a question of fact and that the onus of establishing or proving that possession falls on the group claiming the Aboriginal title. The Court served notice that its decision, while a breakthrough for Aboriginal title, was not an opening of the proverbial "floodgates." The evidentiary hurdles still exist and it will be for the trial judges in the future, who are faced with particular claims, to determine whether the burden of proof will have been satisfied. The same will be true regarding the continuity of possession, which must be rooted in pre-sovereignty times (i.e., before the Crown asserted its ownership of the lands). Exclusivity of possession is also an important question of fact (again, to be determined by the trial judge) in establishing Aboriginal title.

Exclusivity should be understood in the sense of intention and capacity to control the land. The fact that other groups or individuals were on the land does not necessarily negate exclusivity of occupation. Whether a claimant group had the intention and capacity to control the land at the time of sovereignty is a question of fact for the trial judge and depends on various factors such as the characteristics of the claimant group, the nature of other groups in the area, and the characteristics of the land in question. Exclusivity can be established by proof that others were excluded from the land, or by proof that others were only allowed access to the land with the permission of the claimant group. The fact that permission was requested and granted or refused, or that treaties were made with other groups, may show intention and capacity to control the land. Even the lack of challenges to occupancy may support an inference of an established group's intention and capacity to control.

The trial judge's findings of facts, based on the evidence before him, that the Tsilhqot'in had repelled other people from the land and demanded that those who wished to pass over it request permission, led him to the conclusion that they had treated the land as exclusively theirs. The Supreme Court found no basis to disturb that finding.

Once the smoke cleared, the outcome was that the Tsilhqot'in had established their claim of Aboriginal title to the lands. That, of course, led to the question of what this really meant.

When it asserted European sovereignty, the Crown acquired underlying title to all lands in the province, but that title was burdened by an independent legal interest, based on the pre-existing legal rights of Aboriginal peoples who had used and occupied land prior to European arrival. The Eurocentric doctrine of *terra nullius* (a concept that no one owned the land prior to the assertion of European sovereignty) never applied in Canada. That underlying legal interest gave rise to a fiduciary duty on the part of the Crown when dealing with Aboriginal lands. In fact, even before Aboriginal title may have been legally established, the Crown must consult in good faith about the proposed use of the land and attempt to accommodate the interests of any claimant group. This will require some assessment of the strength of the claim and the seriousness of the possible adverse impact on those claims. Once Aboriginal title has been established, the duty hardens into seeking consent of the title-holding group to the proposed developments. If no consent is given, the Crown can only proceed after discharging its duty to consult and if it is then able to justify the intrusion under the *Constitution Act, 1982.*

> In summary, Aboriginal title confers on the group that holds it the exclusive right to decide how the land is used and the right to benefit from those uses, subject to one carve-out—that the uses must be consistent with the group nature of the interest and the enjoyment of the land by future generations. Government incursions not consented to by the title-holding group must be undertaken in accordance with the Crown's procedural duty to consult and must also be justified on the basis of a compelling and substantial public interest, and must be consistent with the Crown's fiduciary duty to the Aboriginal group.

In this case, the Crown had neither consulted with the Tsilhqot'in when planning for the removal of timber nor had made any effort to accommodate their interests. In addition, the Crown was unable to demonstrate any compelling public interest in granting the timber-cutting rights on the lands to a third party. A somewhat half-hearted assertion had been made at the trial level that there was an infestation that required removal of the timber, but that was later abandoned, presumably because the evidence did not support the argument.

The Court also considered the impact of Aboriginal title on general provincial laws dealing with forest management. This consideration was not necessary to dispose of the Tsilhqot'in appeal, but was nevertheless important not only to that group, but also to other Aboriginals in British Columbia and elsewhere, and had been argued extensively in the courts below.

In general, the *Constitution Act, 1982,* gives the provincial legislatures the power to regulate land use in the province, as matters of "property and civil rights in the province," although there are constitutional limitations on the power to legislate where the land is held under Aboriginal title.

> Provincial power to regulate land held under Aboriginal title is constitutionally limited in two ways. First, it is limited by s. 35 of the *Constitution Act, 1982.* Section 35 requires any abridgment of the rights flowing from Aboriginal title to be backed by a compelling and substantial governmental objective and to be consistent with the Crown's fiduciary relationship with the title holders. Second, a province's power to regulate lands under Aboriginal title may in some situations also be limited by the federal power over "Indians, and Lands reserved for the Indians" under s. 91(24) of the *Constitution Act, 1867.*

The British Columbia forestry legislation was clearly intended to apply to all forests, even those under potential claim by way of Aboriginal title, certainly so long as such title had not been established with respect to a particular portion. Once Aboriginal title was established, however, the beneficial interest in the lands became vested in the rights-holding group and the lands were no longer "Crown" lands.

This shift engaged the Court in consideration of where and when the Constitution might trump the provincial land-use legislation. The

Court, not having had to deal with this question in order to dispose of the appeal in front of it, was careful not to do more than outline general approaches and questions for consideration, many of which would necessarily depend on particular factual contexts to be considered by the courts as they arose. While lines of enquiry could be identified, definitive conclusions could not.

This is an important decision of the Court, expanding on the line of cases emphasizing the need for accommodation of Aboriginal rights, the existence of fiduciary obligations on the part of the governments and the need to continually bear in mind the honour of the Crown in its dealings with Aboriginal peoples. The guidelines established by the Court should prove beneficial to all those having a genuine interest in resolving claims to Aboriginal title. This does not mean that unsettled cases which are required to proceed before the courts will be any less complex, less expensive, nor less time-consuming, but there is now at least a clear map through the legal and factual maze.

Aboriginal Treaties: the "Word of the White Man"

Attorney General of Quebec v. Sioui [1990] 1 S.C.R. 1025

O n September 5, 1760, Brigadier General James Murray was the highest-ranking British officer in Canada. General Wolfe had been killed in the battle on the Plains of Abraham and Generals Townshend and Monckton had returned to Britain. General Jeffrey Amherst, the Commander-in-Chief of the British forces in the Americas, returned from what is now the United States, was assembling his troops for the attack on Montreal, the last remaining stronghold of the French in Canada. An attack proved to be unnecessary and Montreal capitulated only three days later.

Murray, appointed Governor of the Quebec region, was almost at Montreal, preparing to assist Amherst. He was called upon that same day by leaders of the Huron and other nations. Following the meeting he signed and delivered a document to the Huron which read:

> THESE are to certify that the CHIEF of the HURON tribe of Natives, having come to me in the name of His Nation, to submit to His BRITANNICK MAJES-TY, and make Peace, has been received under my Protection, with his whole Tribe; and henceforth no English Officer or party is to molest, or interrupt them in returning to their Settlement at LORETTE; and they are received upon the same terms with the Canadians, being allowed the free Exercise of their Religion, their Customs, and Liberty of trading with the English:—recommending it to the Officers commanding the Posts, to treat them kindly.

Given under my hand at Longueuil, this 5th day of September, 1760.

By the Genl's Command,

JOHN COSNAN,   Ja. MURRAY

Adjut. Genl.

Two hundred and thirty years later, the Supreme Court of Canada would be called upon to interpret that document, to decide whether it amounted to a treaty and, generally, to determine the worth of the "white man's word."

The background to the litigation was the creation of Jacques Cartier Park by the Quebec government, in a part of Quebec that the Huron tribe had used regularly since about 1650. The Quebec legislation prohibited users of the park from destroying, mutilating, removing, or introducing any kind of plant, and from camping and lighting fires other than in places designated and arranged for those purposes. The Huron involved in the case had been convicted and fined for cutting down trees, camping, and making fires in places not designated. An appeal from the Court of Sessions to the Quebec Superior Court was unsuccessful, but the Court of Appeal (in a split decision) allowed the Natives' appeal and acquitted them. Quebec then appealed to the Supreme Court of Canada.

There were several fascinating issues involved in the appeal, but none more important than setting the right framework for approaching the interpretation of a document written solely by the British, in the context of dealing with Natives completely unfamiliar with written communications, and which could easily bear different interpretations. This, as it related to whether or not a treaty had been created, was particularly important, since the key provision of the *Indian Act*, which might exempt the Natives from compliance with the statute relating to Jacques Cartier Park, was section 88:

> Subject to the terms of any treaty and any other Act of Parliament, all laws of
> general application from time to time in force in any province are applicable
> to and in respect of Indians in the province, except to the extent that those
> laws are inconsistent with the Act or any order, rule regulation or by-law made
> thereunder, and except to the extent that those laws make provision for any
> matter for which provision is made by or under this Act. [emphasis added.]

If, therefore, the document signed by General Murray was a treaty, as opposed to some other form of agreement, then (depending on a proper interpretation of the treaty), the Huron might well be exempted from the application of the Quebec statute.

Reading the Court's reasons for judgment may give the impression that Quebec threw everything but the kitchen sink at the Huron in this appeal. Every possible argument that could have been raised was put before the Court. This, in a litigious context, is quite proper, and even desirable. It is important that there be a complete consideration of the entire spectrum of possible outcomes, since what is sought in a case of this nature is the greatest possible certainty attached to the outcome, combined with an explanation of the proper judicial approach to future cases of a similar nature.

First and foremost is the principle that treaties and statutes in relation to Native Peoples are to be liberally construed and that uncertainties are to be resolved in favour of the Natives. All the advantages in relation to written documents and treaties at the time rested with the white man. He was familiar with written language and the applicable legal concepts. The content of any document would be explained by the white man's interpreter to Natives who had no experience in negotiations with public authorities. All this called for a generous and liberal approach to the interpretation of any documents so generated.

One of the arguments advanced by Quebec was that Murray had no capacity to enter into a treaty, both because the British Crown could not enter into a treaty with the Huron, since it was not "sovereign" in Canada in 1760, and because Murray himself had insufficient authority to make a treaty on behalf of Britain. It was, however, clear that the British controlled the portion of Quebec in which the Huron were located. Murray, as Governor of the Quebec District, was the highest-ranking British officer with whom the Huron could have dealt and it was reasonable for them to believe that Murray possessed the power to enter into a treaty with them. The Court concluded that both the Huron and Murray had the capacity to enter into a treaty.

This led to consideration of what is meant by a treaty, especially one with the Natives. It is an agreement *sui generis* (lawyers love expressions like this—it is their special code to exclude the laity—all it means is that such an agreement has its own special character), and one neither created nor terminated according to the rules of international law. What characterizes a treaty is the intention of the parties to create mutually binding obligations and a certain measure of solemnity. The word "treaty" is not a term of art, but merely identifies agreements by which the "word of the white man is given" and by which the white man made certain of the Natives' cooperation. The Court quoted from another case to provide flavour to the approach:

> In view of the argument before us, it is necessary to point out that on numerous occasions in modern days, rights under what were entered into with Indians as solemn engagements, although completed with what would now be considered informality, have been whittled away on the excuse that they do not comply with present day formal requirements and with rules of interpretation applicable to transactions between people who must be taken in the light of advanced civilization to be of equal status. Reliance on instances where this has been done is merely to compound injustice without real justification. The transaction in question here was a transaction between, on the one hand, the strong representative of a proprietary company under the Crown and representing the Crown, who had gained the respect of the Indians by his integrity and the strength of his personality and was thus able to bring about the completion of the agreement, and, on the other hand, uneducated savages. The nature of the transaction itself was consistent with the informality of frontier days in this Province and such as the necessities of the occasion and the customs and the illiteracy of the Indians demanded. ... The unusual (by the standards of legal draftsmen) nature and form of the document considered in the light of the circumstances ... does not detract from it as being a "Treaty."

Applying those concepts to the current case, the Court noted that the historical context was important, including the applicable interpersonal relationships at the time, and that formalities were of secondary importance when deciding on the nature of a document which contains an agreement with the Natives. The Court then considered the elements in the document that suggested that it might not be a treaty, such as language consistent with an act of surrender, language personal to General Murray ("having come to me," "has been received under my Protection," and "By the Genl's Command"), orders to English officers, reference to the single event of return to Lorette, and the lack of formality usually found in treaties. All of those indicators might tend to a conclusion that the agreement fell short of something as important as a treaty.

But the Court must read the document in its entirety and, as such, it could not ignore the presence of a clause guaranteeing the free exercise of religion, customs, and trade with the English. Such a guarantee would not have been necessary if the agreement was one of a few days' duration (i.e., until the Huron returned to Lorette), but would have been more natural in a treaty where the "word of the white man" had been given. On the other hand, the same language was used in documents provided to the French who had surrendered, and there was no issue of any "treaty" with them. There was, obviously, some ambiguity arising from the language used, which required looking to extrinsic evidence (i.e., evidence from outside the document itself), including a study of historical documents, whether provided by the parties or found by the Court on the basis of its own research.

Without including the details of the research, the direction of the Court's approach can be seen from the following extracts, which provide, in effect, a high-speed, abridged history of the situation in Quebec at the time:

> On September 5, 1760, France and England were engaged in a war begun four years earlier, which ended with the Treaty of Paris signed on February 10, 1763. About a year earlier, the battle of the Plains of Abraham had allowed the British to take control of Québec City and surrounding area. During the year following this victory, British troops had worked to consolidate their military position in Canada and to solve the supply and other practical problems engendered by the very harsh winter of 1759.
>
> ...
>
> As the advantageous position and strength of the British troops became more and more apparent, several groups did surrender and it appears that this movement accelerated in the days preceding that on which the document at issue was signed.
>
> ...
>
> In fact, the total defeat of France in Canada was very near: the Act of Capitulation of Montreal, by which the French troops stationed in Canada laid

down their arms, was signed on September 8, 1760, and signalled the end of France's *de facto* control in Canada.

...

I consider that ... we can conclude from the historical documents that both Great Britain and France felt that the Indian nations had sufficient independence and played a large enough role in North America for it to be good policy to maintain relations with them very close to those maintained between sovereign nations.

...

The mother countries did everything in their power to secure the alliance of each Indian nation and to encourage nations allied with the enemy to change sides. When these efforts met with success, they were incorporated in treaties of alliance or neutrality. This clearly indicates that the Indian nations were regarded in their relations with the European nations which occupied North America as independent nations.

...

Further, both the French and the English recognized the critical importance of alliances with the Indians, or at least their neutrality, in determining the outcome of the war between them and the security of the North American colonies.

...

England also wished to secure the friendship of the Indian nations by treating them with generosity and respect for fear that the safety and development of the colonies and their inhabitants would be compromised by Indians with feelings of hostility.

Additional evidence was also presented to demonstrate that other tribes, including enemies of the Huron, considered that there had been a treaty entered into by the Huron and other Native nations. There was a differentiation between the level of the arrangements with the French and the Natives, and shortly after the capitulation of Montreal, a more solemn occasion was held, with the presentation of a belt, a traditional method of solemnizing the content of undertakings that had been made, amounting to a ratification of the peace agreement made earlier.

Quebec then argued that the treaty had been extinguished and that, if not extinguished, then was not effective to render the Jacques Cartier Park regulations inoperable. The extinguishment argument referred to the *Act of Capitulation* of September 8, 1760, the *Treaty of Paris* of February 10, 1763, the *Royal Proclamation* of October 7, 1763, the legislative and administrative history of the Huron lands, and the effect of time and non-reliance on the treaty. The onus is on the party arguing in favour of termination to provide convincing proof that the treaty was extinguished, which Quebec was unable to do. For example, the agreements between Britain and France had no impact on agreements or treaties between Britain and the Natives, especially those who had already disassociated themselves from the French.

The final matter to be dealt with was where the Huron could exercise their treaty rights. As the Court noted, "for a freedom to have real value and meaning, it must be possible to exercise it somewhere." It also called for the Court to adopt a realistic approach that would reflect the intention of both parties to the treaty, not just that of the Huron. This ended up somewhere between the entire territory used by the Huron and the lands at Lorette: one was obviously more than General Murray had intended and the other had merely been the destination of the safe conduct given, since exercise of the rights granted would require territory extending beyond Lorette.

> I readily accept that the Huron were probably not aware of the legal consequences, and in particular of the right to occupy to the exclusion of others, which the main European legal systems attached to the concept of private ownership. Nonetheless, I cannot believe that the Huron ever believed that the treaty gave them the right to cut down trees in the garden of a house as part of their right to carry on their customs.

That said, what then of the park set aside for public use by Quebec?

> For the exercise of rites and customs to be incompatible with the occupancy of the park by the Crown, it must not only be contrary to the purpose underlying that occupancy, it must prevent the realization of that purpose. First, we are dealing with Crown lands, lands which are held for the benefit of the community. Exclusive use is not an essential aspect of public ownership. Second, I do not think that the activities described seriously compromise the Crown's objectives in occupying the park. Neither the representative nature of the natural region where the park is located nor the exceptional nature of this natural

site are threatened by the collecting of a few plants, the setting up of a tent using a few branches picked up in the area or the making of a fire according to the rules dictated by the caution to avoid fires. These activities also present no obstacle to cross-country recreation. I therefore conclude that it has not been established that the occupancy of the territory of Jacques-Cartier park is incompatible with the exercise of Huron rites and customs with which the respondents are charged.

Canada has had a dubious record in its treatment of Aboriginal peoples, as well as in its interpretation of agreements and treaties with them. It is encouraging to see that the courts are far more willing, in recent years, than the Executive branch of government, to take into account the context, purpose, and probable intended meanings of documents created entirely by the white man, familiar with the concepts, and communicated to the Aboriginals entirely on his own terms.

Unconstitutional Restriction on Band Voting Rights

Corbière v. Canada (Minister of Indian and Northern Affairs) [1999] 2
S.C.R. 203

The matter arising in this appeal was whether section 77(1) of the *Indian Act*, which defines voter eligibility in Native bands, requiring band members to be at least eighteen years old and "ordinarily resident on the reserve," violated s. 15(1) of the *Charter*, which provides:

> Every individual is equal before and under the law and has the right to the equal protection and equal benefit of the law without discrimination and, in particular, without discrimination based on race, national or ethnic origin, colour, religion, sex, age or mental physical disability.

While, in relation to the particular band involved in the appeal, the residency requirement had not been enforced from 1902 to 1962, since the latter date, only band members living on one of the three reserves owned by the band had been allowed to vote. The voting problem had been exacerbated in recent years due to expansion of numbers, especially of those living off the reserve, by restoration of Native status to many who had lost it (e.g., women who may have married someone who did not have Native status) because of certain provisions of the *Indian Act*, as well as to their descendants.

These were not the only people who lost their status. The enfranchisement provisions of the *Indian Act* were designed to encourage Aboriginal people to renounce their heritage and identity and to force them to do so if they wished to take a full part in Canadian society. In order to vote or hold Canadian citizenship, status Indians had to "voluntarily" enfranchise. They were then given a portion of the former reserve land in fee simple, and they lost their Indian status. At various times in history, status Indians who received higher education, or became doctors, lawyers, or ministers were automatically enfranchised. Those who wanted to be soldiers in the military during the two World Wars were required to enfranchise themselves and their whole families, and those who left the country for more than five years without permission also lost Indian status. ...

This history shows that Aboriginal policy, in the past, often led to denial of status and the severing of connections between band members and the band. It helps show why the interest in feeling and maintaining a sense of belonging to the band free from barriers imposed by Parliament is an important one for all band members, and especially for those who constitute a significant portion of the group affected, who have been directly affected by these policies and are now living away from the reserves, in part, because of them.

By 1991, less than a third of the registered members of the band lived on the reserve.

Both the Federal Court – Trial Division (now the Federal Court of Canada) and the Federal Court of Appeal found that there was a *Charter* violation. The trial judge declared that the violation did not extend to voting in elections, but did insofar as it prevented the off-reserve band members from exercising rights in relation to dispositions of land and band expenditures. The Federal Court of Appeal concluded that the restriction was discriminatory, that a stereotype had been attached to those living off the reserve, since many had been characterized as being unworthy of trust in using their electoral power for the benefit of the band. Unlike the trial judge, the appellate court found the distinction was discriminatory in relation to all powers of the band, not just those related to the governance of the reserve territory. The Federal Court of Appeal thought that the appropriate remedy was a constitutional exemption applicable to the band.

In two sets of reasons, the full bench of the Supreme Court of Canada agreed with the conclusions of the courts below. Its approach was, not unusually, somewhat different. The first consideration was the constitutionality of the legislation generally. There was no doubt that there was differential treatment of the off-reserve members, since they were excluded as electors. Now, did that treatment fall within the identified criteria in s. 15(1), or an analogous distinction that had the potential to violate human dignity, self-respect, and self-worth? Quoting from an earlier case, the Court noted:

> It [human dignity] is concerned with physical and psychological empowerment and integrity. Human dignity is harmed by unfair treatment premised on personal traits or circumstances which do not relate to individual needs, capacities, or merits. It is enhanced by laws which are sensitive to the needs, capacities and merits of different individuals, taking into account the context underlying their differences. Human dignity is harmed when individuals and groups are marginalized, ignored, or devalued, and is enhanced when laws recognize the full place of all individuals and groups within Canadian society. Human dignity within the meaning of the equality guarantee does not relate to the status or position of an individual in society *per se*, but rather concerns the manner in which a person legitimately feels when confronted with a particular law.

The nature of decisions made by band members as to whether to live on or off the reserve are quite different from those made by other Canadians in relation to their place of residence. They are, for example, important as to their identity and personhood, whether to live with other members of the band to which they belong or apart from them. They relate to a community and a land that have particular social and cultural significance to many or most members of the band. Many are unable to live on the reserve due to lack of land, often scarce job opportunities on reserves and the need to go far from the community for schooling. In addition, members living off-reserve have generally experienced disadvantage, stereotyping, and prejudice. They formed a "discrete and insular minority" defined by race and place of residence. This satisfied the "analogous" aspect of the distinction. Five of the judges expressed the thought in this manner:

What then are the criteria by which we identify a ground of distinction as analogous? The obvious answer is that we look for grounds of distinction that are analogous or like the grounds enumerated in s. 15—race, national or ethnic origin, colour, religion, sex, age, or mental or physical disability. It seems to us that what these grounds have in common is the fact that they often serve as the basis for stereotypical decisions made not on the basis of merit but on the basis of a personal characteristic that is immutable or changeable only at unacceptable cost to personal identity. This suggests that the thrust of the identification of analogous grounds at the second stage of the ... analysis is to reveal grounds based on characteristics that we cannot change or that the government has no legitimate interest in expecting us to change to receive equal treatment under the law. To put it another way, s. 15 targets the denial of equal treatment on grounds that are actually immutable, like race, or constructively immutable, like religion. Other factors identified in the cases as associated with the enumerated and analogous grounds, like the fact that the decision adversely impacts on a discrete and insular minority or a group that has been historically discriminated against, may be seen to flow from the central concept of immutable or constructively immutable personal characteristics, which too often have served as illegitimate and demeaning proxies for merit-based decision making.

The next question was whether a reasonable person would find that the legislation would impose a disadvantage or withhold a benefit. All the judges agreed that it would. The impugned distinction perpetuated the historic disadvantage experienced by off-reserve band members by denying them the right to vote and participate in the governance of their band. The denial of full participation was based on a personal characteristic, affecting the cultural identity of off-reserve Aboriginals in a stereotypical way.

It presumes that Aboriginals living off-reserve are not interested in maintaining meaningful participation in the band or in preserving their cultural identity, and are therefore less deserving members of the band. The effect is clear, as is the message: off-reserve band members are not as deserving as those band members who live on reserves. This engages the dignity aspect of the s. 15 analysis and results in the denial of substantive equality.

The effect of the legislation was that band members were forced to choose between living on the reserve and exercising their political rights, or living off the reserve and renouncing such exercise. The legislation was connected with the legislative policy being pursued (to give a voice only to those band members most affected by the bulk of the decisions of the band council, namely those living on the reserve), but the restriction of the s. 15 rights did not satisfy the second branch of the test, namely a minimal impairment of those rights. The legislation provided for a complete denial of the off-reserve band members' rights to participate in band affairs. There was no evidence of the difficulties of maintaining an electoral list of off-reserve band members, no evidence of efforts or schemes considered and costed, and no argument or judicial authority in support of the conclusion that costs and administrative convenience could justify a complete denial of the constitutional right.

The constitutional exemption proposed by the Federal Court of Appeal, as opposed to declaring s. 77(1) of the *Indian Act* unconstitutional, was unattractive. There was evidence before that Court that there were off-reserve members of most, if not all, Native bands in Canada affected by the provision. Where there is inconsistency between the *Charter* and a legislative provision, the *Constitution Act, 1982*, provides that the provision shall be rendered void to the extent of the inconsistency. This led to the conclusion that the words *and is ordinarily resident on the reserve* in the provision should be struck. The implementation of the declaration of invalidity was to be suspended for eighteen months, a technique sparingly used (since the impugned rights might continue to be violated during such period) to provide enough time for the legislature to engage in the necessary consultations and to make amendments to the particular provision, if it wished to do so. It is also a way to ensure that any policy questions that may not have been raised in the legal proceedings can be taken into account by the legislature, since the Court and the parties appearing in the appeal may well not be in possession of all of the relevant considerations, nor be aware of the full range of consequences that might flow from the decision. If no amendments were to be made, at the end of the eighteen-month period of suspension, the off-reserve members of the band would, as a result of the Court's decision, obtain their voting rights within the existing legislative scheme.

This decision is important as a demonstration that even legislation of long standing is not immune from *Charter* challenges. It also shows the extent to which the list of factors in s. 15 of the *Charter* is far from complete and the means by which the Court can expand such a list in the face of particular circumstances. In addition, several of the "classic" approaches to *Charter* cases can evolve to deal with cases that might not have been in the contemplation of the Court when rendering judgments in particular cases on other occasions. When dealing with *Charter* appeals, the Court has made it clear—and properly so—that it will adopt whatever approaches may be required to give purposive effect to the *Charter* as a fundamental plank in the Constitution of Canada.

Aboriginal Treaties: the "Honour of the Crown"

Regina v. Marshall [1999] 3 S.C.R. 456

In 1993, John Marshall, a Mi'kmaq Indian in Nova Scotia, was arrested and prosecuted for fishing for eels without a license during the closed season, and for using a net that did not conform to applicable regulations. Marshall and his fishing companion landed 463 pounds of eels, which they sold for $787.10. He was prosecuted in the provincial court of Nova Scotia in a trial that required forty days of court hearing time. He admitted the essential facts underlying the charges and his only defence was that he had a treaty right to catch and to sell fish under treaties entered into between the British and the Mi'kmaq in 1760–1761. He was convicted on all three counts and the provincial Court of Appeal upheld the convictions. On further appeal to the Supreme Court of Canada, by a five to two decision, he was acquitted on all counts.

The trial judge ... accepted as applicable the terms of a Treaty of Peace and Friendship signed on March 10, 1760 at Halifax. The parties disagree about the existence of alleged oral terms, as well as the implications of the "trade clause" written into that document. From this distance, across more than two centuries, events are necessarily seen as "through a glass darkly." The parties were negotiating in March 1760 in the shadow of the great military and political turmoil following the fall of the French fortresses at Louisbourg, Cape Breton (June 1758) and Quebec (September 1759). The Mi'kmaq signatories had been allies of the French king, and Montreal would continue to be part of

New France until it subsequently fell in June 1760. [In *Sioui*, see page 261, the date of the capitulation of Montreal was given as September 8, 1760.] The British had almost completed the process of expelling the Acadians from southern Nova Scotia. Both the Treaty of Paris, ending hostilities, and the Royal Proclamation of 1763 were still three years in the future. Only six years prior to the signing of the treaties, the British Governor of Nova Scotia had issued a Proclamation (May 14, 1756) offering rewards for the killing and capturing of Mi'kmaq throughout Nova Scotia, which then included New Brunswick. The treaties were entered into in a period where the British were attempting to expand and secure their control over their northern possessions. The subtext of the Mi'kmaq treaties was reconciliation and mutual advantage.

Central to the issue before the court was the meaning of the "trade clause" in the treaty. Read in isolation, it was doubtful that Marshall could make out his defense: "And I [the Mi'kmaq Chief in 1760] do further engage that we will not traffick, barter or Exchange any Commodities in any manner but with such persons or the managers of such Truck houses [trading posts] as shall be appointed or Established by His Majesty's Governor at Lunenbourg or Elsewhere in Nova Scotia or Accadia." It was interpreted by the lower courts as a negative covenant, not as a right conferred on the Mi'kmaq, but rather a mechanism imposed by the British to ensure that the peace would be a lasting one.

The question became whether the Court could consider extrinsic evidence (evidence from sources outside the document itself) where the plain meaning of the words in the treaty were not ambiguous. The lower courts had taken a strict approach, which the Supreme Court rejected on three counts. First, because even in modern commercial matters, evidence could be presented to show that a document did not include all of the terms of an agreement. Second, even where a treaty document purports to contain all of the terms, extrinsic evidence of the historical and cultural context may be received even in the absence of ambiguity. And third, where a treaty was concluded verbally and was later written up by representatives of the Crown, it would be unconscionable for the Crown to ignore the oral terms while relying on the written terms.

When all was said and done, in 1760, the British had a major interest in coming to terms with the Mi'kmaq. Notwithstanding their recent military victories, the British could not feel completely secure in Nova

Scotia and wanted peace and a safe environment for their current and future settlers. Very shortly after the fall of Louisbourg in June 1758, the British sent emissaries to the Mi'kmaq, holding out an offer of the enjoyment of peace, liberty, property, possessions, and religion.

> ... the Mi'kmaq were a considerable fighting force in the 18th century. Not only were their raiding parties effective on land, Mi'kmaq were accomplished sailors. ...

> The Mi'kmaq, according to the evidence, had seized in the order of 100 European sailing vessels in the years prior to 1760. There are recorded Mi'kmaq sailings in the 18th century between Nova Scotia, St. Pierre and Miquelon and Newfoundland. They were not a people to be trifled with. However, by 1760, the British and the Mi'kmaq had a mutual self-interest in terminating hostilities and establishing the basis for a stable peace.

The trade issue was viewed in terms of peace, on the theory that people who trade together do not fight. Peace, therefore, was inseparable from the ability of the Mi'kmaq to sustain themselves economically. Starvation breeds discontent and the British would not have wanted the Mi'kmaq to become a financial drain on either the colony or the Empire itself, so it became necessary to protect the traditional Mi'kmaq economy, largely hunting, gathering, and fishing.

An additional factor was that the British Crown had entered into a series of negotiations with communities of first nations spread across what is now New Brunswick and Nova Scotia, in identical terms, with the intention of later having a single comprehensive treaty, although that anticipated single treaty did not happen. The request by the Mi'kmaq for the trading posts carried with it the requirement to trade with the British government; it was not a condition imposed on them by the British. The trading posts, with their advantageous terms, were part of the British peace strategy—indeed the Governor described the greatest advantage derived from the trade article (of the treaty) as the friendship of the Mi'kmaq, a true investment in peace and the promotion of ongoing colonial settlement. The flip side of that coin was that the Mi'kmaq were assured, whether implicitly or explicitly, at the same time, of continuing access to the hunting and fishing needed for them to trade with the British. That was all they could have had to trade, so the British, knowing how they lived, were effectively creating a treaty right to live in Nova Scotia in their traditional ways, which was by hunting, and they had a right to trade in the produce of their hunting (and gathering and fishing).

The Crown had raised the "floodgate" argument, to the effect that the treaty right, if recognized, could lead to uncontrollable exploitation of the natural resources. Instead of the small fishing boat used by Marshall, he might reappear with a big trawler and gather up a huge catch forbidden to non-Aboriginal fishermen. The answer to this was that the treaty provided that there might be a truck house established for the furnishing of the Mi'kmaq with "necessairies." This has been interpreted as the modern equivalent of "moderate livelihood," which includes food, clothing, and housing, supplemented by a few amenities, but not the accumulation of wealth. What was contemplated in the treaty was a right to trade for "necessairies," not to trade generally for economic gain. The latter aspect could be contained by regulation.

Determining and dealing with historical facts carries some risks. The Court took note of some criticisms and gave an unrepentant response:

> The courts have attracted a certain amount of criticism from professional historians for what these historians see as an occasional tendency on the part of judges to assemble a "cut and paste" version of history. ...

> While the tone of some of this criticism strikes the non-professional historian as intemperate, the basic objection, as I understand it, is that the judicial selection of facts and quotations is not always up to the standard demanded of the professional historian, which is said to be more nuanced. Experts, it is argued, are trained to read the various historical records together with the benefit of a protracted study of the period, and an appreciation of the frailties of the various sources. The law sees a finality of interpretation of historical events where finality, according to the professional historian, is not possible. The reality, of course, is that the courts are handed disputes that require for their resolution the finding of certain historical facts. The litigating parties cannot await the possibility of a stable academic consensus. The judicial process must do as best it can.

Fortunately, in this particular case, there had been an "unusual level of agreement" among the historians who had testified regarding the underlying expectations of the participants regarding the treaty obligations resulting from the negotiations between the Crown and the Mi'kmaq.

> In my view, the Nova Scotia judgments erred in concluding that the only enforceable treaty obligations were those set out in the written document of March 10, 1760, whether construed flexibly (as did the trial judge) or narrowly (as did the Nova Scotia Court of Appeal). The findings of fact made by the trial judge taken as a whole demonstrate that the concept of a disappearing treaty right does justice neither to the honour of the Crown nor to the reasonable expectations of the Mi'kmaq people. It is their common intention in 1760, "not just the terms of the March 10, 1760 document" to which effect must be given.

One of the principles that applies when there are dealings with Aboriginal peoples is the "honour of the Crown," a concept which holds that there is a basic assumption that the Crown intends to fulfill its promises and that there must be no appearance of "sharp dealing."

> The principle that the Crown's honour is at stake when the Crown enters into treaties with first nations dates back at least to this Court's decision in 1895, *Province of Ontario v. Dominion of Canada and Province of Quebec; in re Indian Claims.* ... In that decision, Gwynne J. (dissenting) stated...:

> ... what is contended for and must not be lost sight of, is that the British sovereigns, ever since the acquisition of Canada, have been pleased to adopt the rule of practice of entering into agreements with the Indian nations or tribes in their province of Canada, for the cession or surrender by them of what such sovereigns have been pleased to designate the Indian title, by instruments similar to those now under consideration to which they have been pleased to give the designation of "treaties" with the Indians in possession of and claiming title to the lands expressed to be surrendered by the instruments, and further that the terms and conditions expressed in those instruments as to be performed by or on behalf of the Crown, have always been regarded as involving a trust graciously assumed by the Crown to the fulfilment of which with the Indians the faith and honour of the Crown is pledged, and which trust

has always been most faithfully fulfilled as a treaty obligation of the Crown. [Emphasis added.]

This has been a central theme in Canadian jurisprudence and the Canadian courts have often been called upon as a last resort where Aboriginal rights are involved. This is not to say, however, that every claim advanced on the part of Aboriginal peoples has been well-founded.

Métis: Not Part-Time Indians

Blais v. The Queen [2003] 2 S.C.R. 236

The federal government decided to transfer certain rights to the western provinces by means of quasi-constitutional agreements, designed to put them in the same position as the other provinces with respect to jurisdiction over and ownership of their natural resources. The Manitoba version of the Natural Resources Transfer Agreement (NRTA) included a provision that provincial legislation relating to game applied to Natives, subject to the continuing right of Natives to hunt, trap, and fish on unoccupied Crown lands.

> 13. In order to secure to the Indians of the Province the continuance of the supply of game and fish for their support and subsistence, Canada agrees that the laws respecting game in force in the Province from time to time shall apply to the Indians within the boundaries thereof, provided, however, that the said Indians shall have the right, which the Province hereby assures to them, of hunting, trapping and fishing game and fish for food at all seasons of the year on all unoccupied Crown lands and on any other lands to which said Indians may have a right of access.

Blais was a Métis. He was charged with hunting deer out of season. His sole defence was that he was an "Indian" for purposes of the NRTA and therefore exempt under the hunting provisions of the NRTA. It was agreed that he was a Métis, that he was hunting food for himself and members of his immediate family and that he was hunting on unoccupied Crown land. He had no success with this defence in the Manitoba courts and the matter found its way to the Supreme Court of Canada, where it was heard by the full Court, which issued a unanimous decision of the Court dismissing his appeal.

The key to interpretation of the NRTA was the use of the word *Indian* and whether that expression applied to the Métis. The term *Métis*

> ... does not designate all individuals with mixed heritage, "rather, it refers to distinctive peoples who, in addition to their mixed ancestry, developed their own customs, way of life, and recognizable group identity separate from their Indian or Inuit and European forebears." Members of Métis communities in the prairie provinces collectively refer to themselves as the "Métis Nation," and trace their roots to the western fur trade. ... Other Métis communities emerged in eastern Canada. ... The sole question before us is whether the appellant, being a Métis, is entitled to benefit from the protection accorded to "Indians" in the NRTA. He can claim this benefit only if the term "Indians" encompasses the Métis.

Blais had been arrested and charged for hunting out of season because he was not a member of an Indian band, but a member of the Manitoba Métis community. Manitoba said that s. 13 of the NRTA did not exempt the Métis from the obligation to comply with the deer-hunting regulations; Blais said that it did.

The starting point was:

> The NRTA is a constitutional document. It must therefore be read generously within these contextual and historical confines. A court interpreting a constitutionally guaranteed right must apply an interpretation that will fulfill the broad purpose of the guarantee and thus secure "for individuals the full benefit of the [constitutional] protection." ... "At the same time it is important not to overshoot the actual purpose of the right or freedom in question, but to recall that the [constitutional provision] was not enacted in a vacuum, and must therefore ... be placed in its proper linguistic, philosophic and historical contexts." ...

> Applied to this case, this means that we must fulfill—but not "overshoot"—

the purpose of para. 13 of the NRTA. We must approach the task of determining whether Métis are included in "Indians" under para. 13 by looking at the historical context, the ordinary meaning of the language used, and the philosophy or objectives lying behind it.

The record showed that the Métis were treated differently from Natives. They were, for example, not considered as wards of the Crown, both from the Crown's perspective as well as the Métis' own perspective. The evidence demonstrated that the Métis were independent and proud of their identity separate and apart from the Natives.

> The difference between Indians and Métis appears to have been widely recognized and understood by the mid-19th century. In 1870, Manitoba had a settled population of 12,228 inhabitants, almost 10,000 of whom were either English Métis or French Métis. Government actors and the Métis themselves viewed the Indians as a separate group with different historical entitlements; in fact, many if not most of the members of the Manitoba government at the time of its entry into Confederation were themselves Métis.

Several examples of the separate identities were noted by the Court, including the differentiations made by government officials between "Indians" and "half-breeds," who enjoyed the full franchise and property rights of British subjects, not "labouring under the Indian state of pupilage." These clear differentiations made for fundamental differences in government relations and obligations toward each group. In a census prepared by the Hudson's Bay Company in 1856–57, "whites and half-breeds" were a separate identifiable group from the Indians. Red River Métis also distinguished themselves from the Indians, excluding the latter from voting. There was an emphasis on the importance of concluding treaties between Canada and the different Native tribes of the province, with the cooperation of the Local Legislature, then a Métis-dominated body. While *half-breed* sounds derogatory today, in the mid-nineteenth century it was the most frequently used term to refer to all persons of mixed ancestry. Two interesting points emerged in the discussion. The first was that the appellant's expert was unable to draw to the courts' attention any source in which the Canadian government had used the term *Indian* to refer to all Aboriginal peoples, including the Métis. The second was that counsel for the Métis National Council had told the Manitoba Court of Appeal—perhaps too candidly—that "the Métis want to be 'Indian' under the NRTA, but for no other purpose."

> The protection accorded by para. 13 was based on the special relationship between Indians and the Crown. Underlying this was the view that Indians required special protection and assistance. Rightly or wrongly, this view did not extend to the Métis. The Métis were considered more independent and less in need of Crown protection than their Indian neighbours. ... Shared ancestry between the Métis and the colonizing population, and the Métis' own claims to a different political status than the Indians in their List of Rights, contributed to this perception. The stark historic fact is that the Crown viewed its obligations to Indians, whom it considered as its wards, as different from its obligations to the Métis, who were its negotiating partners in the entry of Manitoba into Confederation.

> This perceived difference between the Crown's obligations to Indians and its relationship with the Métis was reflected in separate arrangements for the distribution of land. Different legal and political regimes governed the conclusion of treaties and the allocation of Métis scrip. Indian treaties were concluded on a collective basis and entailed collective rights, whereas scrip entitled recipients to individual grants of land. While the history of scrip speculation and devaluation is a sorry chapter in our nation's history, this does not change the fact that scrip was based on fundamentally different assumptions about the nature and origins of the government's relationship with scrip recipients than the assumptions underlying treaties with Indians.

One of the appellant's arguments was that the Court should expand the historical purpose of para. 13 on the basis of the "living tree" analogy adopted by the Privy Council in the "*Persons*" case (see page 215). The argument was that, given the constitutional nature of para. 13, its provisions should be read broadly, providing solutions to future problems, and that whatever its original meaning, "contemporary values, including the Crown's fiduciary duty towards Aboriginal people and general principles of restitutive justice, required reading 'Indians' as including the Métis." The Court declined to do so.

This Court has consistently endorsed the living tree principle as a funda-mental tenet of constitutional interpretation. Constitutional provisions are intended to provide "a continuing framework for the legitimate exercise of governmental power. ... But at the same time, this Court is not free to invent new obligations foreign to the original purpose of the provision at issue. The analysis must be anchored in the historical context of the provision. As em-phasized above, we must heed Dickson J.'s admonition "not to overshoot the actual purpose of the right or freedom in question, but to recall that the *Char-ter* was not enacted in a vacuum, and must therefore ... be placed in its proper linguistic, philosophic and historical contexts." ... Dickson J. was speaking of the *Charter*, but his words apply equally to the task of interpreting the NRTA. Similarly, Binnie J. emphasized the need for attentiveness to context when he noted in *R v. Marshall* (see page 275) ... that "[g]enerous rules of interpre-tation should not be confused with a vague sense of after-the-fact largesse." Again the statement, made with respect to the interpretation of a treaty, ap-plies here.

Thus, the term *Indian* in para. 13 of the NRTA did not include the Mé-tis and there was no reason to modify its intended meaning. The Court was also clear that its ruling did not preclude the Métis from arguing for site-specific hunting rights under the *Constitution Act, 1982*, which had not been raised as a separate issue in this case.

This seems to have been something of an overreach by the appellant, taken out of a long-standing context and status sought for by the Métis as a whole. A loss put nothing of this at risk. A win might have had un-foreseen implications.

A Bargaining Chip for Aboriginal Negotiations

Manitoba Métis Federation Inc. v. Canada (Attorney General) [2013] S.C.C. 14

There can be little doubt that, in general, Canada's treatment of Aboriginal peoples has been less than admirable in many respects over the years, nor that in recent years, it has been the courts that have pushed the issues in a far more generous fashion to attempt to redress some of the shortcomings of their treatment at the hands of various governments. This case is an example of the Supreme Court of Canada going perhaps a step too far and without sufficient consideration of the possible consequences of the decision.

The case originated in Manitoba and arose from decisions and actions taken well over a century ago, around the time that Manitoba was considering entry into Confederation, an event that occurred on July 15, 1870. At the time, English-speaking descendants of unions between Native people and European settlers and fur traders were known as half-breeds and the French and Catholic descendants were known as Métis. The term *Métis* is now used for both. The Métis, who, along with the First Nations, were the dominant population, were concerned that the anticipated deluge of European settlers would overwhelm them. As one of the conditions of entry into Confederation, they negotiated with the Canadian government to have some 1.4 million acres of land allotted to the Métis children, to give them something of a head start. It was anticipated, on the basis of a preliminary survey, that this would amount to some 240 acres of land for each person.

It took much longer than had been anticipated by the government or expected by the Métis to identify the lands, to survey them, to process applications for the land grants and to effect many of the necessary steps involved in such a massive undertaking. The Canadian government of the day was far less sophisticated and omnipresent than it is today, the distances were huge, the complications not fully appreciated and the competing demands on government equally pressing. It was important for the new Confederation to continue moving toward a coast-to-coast Dominion and particularly important that there be peace in the northwest, where the Métis were dominant, militarily strong, very much involved in the government and business affairs of the territory, and not altogether convinced that joining Confederation was in their best interests. This "land deal" was an important plank in the overall arrangements.

Despite the delays and difficulties encountered, the arrangements were eventually completed to the general satisfaction of most of the Métis. There were some abuses and issues of valuation and location, speculation at the possible expense of some Métis, and the arrival of many new settlers before the land settlements were completed, which, in some cases, meant that the anticipated head start was less attractive than had been anticipated. There were many individual cases of litigation brought by Métis in the interim and many expressions of discontent with the original implementation of the agreement regarding the 1.4 million acres contemplated in 1870. No legal proceedings were, however, instituted until more than one hundred years after the events.

The Métis sought a declaration that: the Crown had breached a fiduciary obligation owed to the Métis in implementing the legislation, that the federal Crown had failed to implement the legislation in a manner consistent with the honour of the Crown, and that certain legislation passed by Manitoba affecting the implementation of the legislation was *ultra vires* the Manitoba legislature. The latter point was held to be moot, since the statutes had long since lapsed.

The most interesting strategic aspect of the whole matter was not that the Métis wanted a specific redress, but simply a declaration that could be used as leverage in ongoing discussions and negotiations with the federal government. The Supreme Court was not being asked to do anything but provide a bargaining chip for the Métis.

In a case of this nature, brought so long after the events giving rise to it, there are several challenging issues. The first, of course, is whether the claimants had waited too long to bring the action. All jurisdictions have limitation periods beyond which, even if the claim might have merit, it is just too late to bring it. Certainty of legal responsibility is a desirable feature of all societies. The maximum period in Manitoba was thirty years and most claims are required to be brought within six years of either the event or of the time at which the claimant first had knowledge of the existence of a claim. Another challenge is that, after such a long period, access to historical documents, direct evidence, and an understanding of the specific circumstances of the delays are necessarily limited. A third is that there is a risk of determining responsibilities and imposing obligations today that are far different from those applicable at the time.

The Manitoba courts had ruled that the claim was time-barred. The trial judge had made findings of fact concerning the conduct of the Crown and concluded that there was no breach of any fiduciary duty. The Court of Appeal, given those findings of fact, did not need to determine whether there was a fiduciary duty and rejected the claim of honour of the Crown as subsidiary to a fiduciary claim, and held that it did not itself give rise to an independent duty in the circumstances of the claim.

Enter the Supreme Court of Canada: it agreed that there was no fiduciary duty involved, but reached a different conclusion regarding the honour of the Crown—the principle that servants of the Crown must conduct themselves with honour when acting on behalf of the Sovereign. The ultimate purpose of the principle is said to be the reconciliation of pre-existing Aboriginal societies with the assertion of Crown sovereignty, arising from the impact of superimposing European laws and customs on the Aboriginal societies. Where the issue is the implementation of a constitutional obligation to an Aboriginal people (i.e., the legislation granting the 1.4 million acres of land), the principle requires that the Crown take a broad purposive approach to the interpretation of the promise, and that it act diligently to fulfill it.

The Court concluded that the federal government did not act diligently to fulfill the specific obligation to the Métis as required by the honour of the Crown. It also concluded that the law of limitations did not preclude a declaration to that effect.

> ... this Court has found that limitations of actions statutes cannot prevent the courts, as guardians of the Constitution, from issuing declarations on the constitutionality of legislation. By extension, limitations acts cannot prevent the courts from issuing a declaration on the constitutionality of the Crown's conduct.
>
> ...
>
> Furthermore, the Métis seek no personal relief and make no claim for damages for land. Nor do they seek restoration of the title their descendants might have inherited had the Crown acted honourably. Rather, they seek a declaration that a specific obligation set out in the Constitution was not fulfilled in the manner demanded by the Crown's honour. They seek this declaratory relief to assist them in extra-judicial negotiations with the Crown in pursuit of the overarching constitutional goal that is reflected in s. 35 of the Constitution.

The principle of reconciliation demanded that such declarations not be barred. They are, in any event, narrow remedies and may be made even if consequential relief is not available. Thus, a claim for a declaration that the Crown failed to act in accordance with the honour of the Crown is not barred by the Métis' failure to have acted for such a long period of time. The Court concluded that the appellants were entitled to the following declaration: "That the federal Crown failed to implement the grant provision ... in accordance with the honour of the Crown."

It remains to be seen what the Métis will attempt to do with this declaration. Its usefulness, however, will likely be severely tempered by the sharply critical statements made by the two dissenting judges. To the extent that their comments pour cold water on the opinion of the majority, any negotiations relying on the declaration will be met by compelling observations of the minority. It is likely that future cases purporting to rely on the majority's reasoning will lead to considerable reading-down of the decision.

The interpretive war began with this volley:

> In this case, the majority has created a new common law constitutional obli-

gation on the part of the Crown, one that, they say, is unaffected by the common law defence of laches [failure to prosecute a claim without undue delay] and immune from the legislature's undisputed authority to create limitation periods. They go this far notwithstanding that the courts below did not consider the issue, and that the parties did not argue the issue before this Court. As a result of proceeding in this manner, the majority has fashioned a vague rule that is unconstrained by laches or limitation periods and immune from legislative redress, making the extent and consequences of the Crown's new obligations impossible to predict.

Apart from the view that the claim was barred, it was the expansion of the duties derived from the honour of the Crown that was the real problem, since it had the potential to expand Crown liability in unpredictable ways. As to delay, the minority noted that there was some irony in the majority having crafted its approach around governmental delay, while excusing the Métis' delay in bringing their action for more than one hundred years.

The minority also criticized the majority of playing somewhat loose with the facts and the inferences and conclusions drawn by it from the record.

> As in all appellate reviews, the trial judge's factual findings should not be interfered with absent palpable and overriding error. ... While the majority does not do so explicitly, aspects of their review and use of the facts depart from the findings of fact made by the trial judge. However, at no point do they show that the trial judge made any palpable or overriding error in reaching his conclusions. Nor did the Métis claim that the findings ... were based on palpable and overriding error.

The two main areas in which this occurred, absent a finding of palpable and overriding error were the extent of the delay in distributing the land and the effect of that delay on the Métis. These departures from the appropriate standard of appellate review put the majority's analysis into question.

> Historical evidence was presented at trial and the bulk of it was accepted by the trial judge. Based on that evidence and on the reasons of the trial judge,

I have summarized the process of how the land grants were distributed below. Though I accept the finding of the trial judge that there was a lengthy delay in the distribution of the land grants, this history reveals a steady and persistent effort to distribute the land grants in the face of significant administrative challenges and an unstable political environment. While a faster process would most certainly have been better, I cannot accept the majority's conclusion that this evidence reveals a pattern of inattention, a finding that is nowhere to be found in the reasons of the trial judge.

There follows an extensive review of the relevant evidence. As to the effect of the delay on the Métis:

The majority attributes a number of negative consequences to the length of time that it took for the land grants to be made. In my respectful view, in so doing they have departed from the factual findings made by the trial judge and drawn inferences that are not supported by the evidence. While the length of time that it took for the land to be distributed may have been frustrating for some of the Métis, it was not the cause of every negative experience that followed for them.

Finally, the minority was concerned with the impact of imposing an unargued duty on a party to litigation.

Moreover, it is particularly unsatisfactory to impose a new duty upon a litigant without giving that party an opportunity to make submissions as to the validity or scope of the duty. This inroad on due process is no less concerning when the party to the proceedings is the government. As a result of the majority's reasons, the government's liability to Aboriginal peoples has the potential to be expanded in unforeseen ways. The Crown has not had the opportunity to address what impact this new duty might have on its ability to enter into treaties or make commitments to Aboriginal peoples. It is inappropriate to impose duties on any party, including the government, without giving that party an opportunity to make arguments about the impact that such liability might have. In the case of government where the new duty is constitutionally derived and therefore cannot be refined or modified through ongoing dialogue with Parliament is of very serious concern.

This may well end up being one of those cases which everyone will quietly ignore, but that may be too much to hope for, especially in marginal cases in which claimants may have not acted within limitation periods or their cases may otherwise be weak on the merits. More serious, perhaps, is the indirect insertion of the Court into ongoing negotiations between the Métis and the government.

Provincial Involvement in Federal Treaties

Reference re Minimum Wages Act [1936] S.C.R. 461; [1937] A.C. 326 (decided 28 January 1937)

This case arose in connection with treaties entered into by Canada as it gradually acquired an increasingly autonomous position in the international arena. It is probably fair to say that, in 1867, little if any attention was paid to the question of whether a Dominion within the British Empire would ever have an independent treaty-making capacity, except under the United Kingdom's sponsorship. By the time this case arose, the issue was not the ability of Canada to enter into such international commitments, but rather where the legislative competence rested regarding enactment or alteration of any domestic laws in order to perform the treaty obligations assumed by Canada.

The federal government had adopted certain statutes in 1934 and 1935. These included *The Weekly Rest in Industrial Undertakings Act*, *The Minimum Wages Act* and *The Limitation of Hours of Work Act*. The background to such legislation was to conform with conventions adopted by the International Labour Organization of the League of Nations, in accordance with the Labour Part of the Treaty of Versailles dated June 28, 1919, in which Canada had been represented. This portion of the Treaty was in pursuance of the object of the League of universal peace, which was felt to be achievable only if based on social justice, which in turn required the improvement of labour conditions throughout the world. Conventions were adopted for this purpose, which were eventually ratified by Canada in 1935, followed shortly thereafter by federal legislation on the subject matter.

Treaties can be neat or messy, especially in federal states. There is a difference between entering into a treaty and ratifying it, on the one hand, and the performance of the obligations arising from the treaty, on the other hand. Generally, the British system regards entering into a treaty as an executive act. If the obligations created by the treaty require any alteration to the existing law, such alterations require legislative action. So, even though the executive branch of government may decide to incur the obligations of the treaty, it still has to obtain the approval of Parliament in respect of any legislative changes, and Parliament is free to give or to refuse to give such approval, even if that leaves the government in default of the treaty obligations. The problem is made more complex where a federal state exists and legislative authority may be defined or limited by a constitutional document—in Canada at that time, the *British North America Act, 1867*.

The federal government referred a question to the Supreme Court of Canada. There was no dispute that the statutes in question affected property and civil rights within each province and that the onus was on the federal government to establish that the statutes had been validly enacted under the legislative powers given to it. The first argument, that the legislation could be justified under section 132 of the *BNA Act* as "necessary or proper for performing the obligations of Canada or any Province thereof as part of the British Empire towards foreign countries arising under treaties between the Empire and such foreign countries," was disposed of very easily. The treaties were entered into by Canada alone, as a country with international status and a founding member of the League of Nations. They did not arise under a treaty between the British Empire and foreign countries.

That left the federal government with only one other basis on which to argue in support of its power to enact the legislation, namely the division of powers in sections 91 and 92 of the *BNA Act*. The Supreme Court of Canada had decided in 1925 that provincial legislatures were the competent authorities to deal with the subject matter of another treaty, and that Canada's obligation was to bring the convention before the provincial legislatures, with only the provisions bearing on federal servants and parts of Canada not within a province (e.g., the Territories) being put before Parliament. This position had seemingly been accepted as a statement of the law. The federal venture to adopt the legislation now before the courts had obviously prompted some concern as to its legislative power to do so, and thus to the reference case.

On this point, the six judges in the current reference were equally divided. Three of them, including the Chief Justice, seemed to be of the view that subsequent decisions of the Privy Council (the *Aeronautics* and *Radio* cases, decided in 1932) now required them to conclude that legislative jurisdiction in respect of treaty obligations rested entirely with the federal government. The other three were of the view that the legislation was *ultra vires* (beyond the power) of the federal Parliament, along much the same lines as the 1925 decision. In the result, there was no operative decision of the Court, but merely the decisions of each set of judges. Not surprisingly, the matter was submitted to the Privy Council.

The Privy Council first agreed that the Supreme Court had been correct in rejecting the section 132 argument. Regarding the section 91 and 92 issue, it noted that there was no dispute that the legislation affected what would be normally within the "property and civil rights" class of subject matter and was, therefore, within the provincial legislative competence.

It then proceeded to disagree with the judges who considered that the Privy Council decisions in the *Aeronautics* and *Radio* cases had the effect that the judges should feel bound by them in the current case. [I like my wording better.] The *Aeronautics* case dealt with a treaty between the Empire and foreign countries, which meant that section 132 clearly applied, thus giving the Dominion Parliament the exclusive legislative authority to implement the treaty. Examining the *Radio* case, it noted that the true ground of that decision had been that the convention there in issue dealt with classes of matters that did not fall within those identified in section 92, reserved to the provinces, nor even within the enumerated classes in section 91. This had led to the conclusion that the legislation required to perform Canada's treaty obligations in those circumstances was solely within the powers of the Dominion. But, this did not mean that any general principle had been adopted to the effect that all Canadian treaty obligations (to the extent that they required new or amended legislation) were entirely Dominion matters.

On the contrary:

> For the purposes of sections 91 and 92, i.e., the distribution of legislative pow-
> ers between the Dominion and the Provinces, there is no such thing as treaty
> legislation as such. The distribution is based on classes of subjects: and as a
> treaty deals with a particular class of subjects so will the legislative power of
> performing it be ascertained. No one can doubt that this distribution is one
> of the most essential conditions, probably the most essential condition, in the
> inter-provincial compact to which the B.N.A. Act gives effect. If the position of
> Lower Canada, now Quebec, alone were considered, the existence of her sep-
> arate jurisprudence as to both property and civil rights might be said to de-
> pend upon loyal adherence to her constitutional right to the exclusive com-
> petence of her own legislature in these matters. Nor is it of less importance for
> the other Provinces, to preserve their own right to legislate for themselves in
> respect of local conditions which may vary by as great a distance as separates
> the Atlantic from the Pacific. It would be remarkable that while the Dominion
> could not initiate legislation however desirable which affected civil rights in
> the Provinces, yet its Government not responsible to the Provinces nor con-
> trolled by Provincial Parliaments need only agree with a foreign country to
> enact such legislation; and its Parliament would be forthwith clothed with
> authority to affect Provincial rights to the full effect of such agreement. Such a
> result would appear to undermine the constitutional safeguards of Provincial
> constitutional autonomy.

If this were not clear enough, the Privy Council drove the point home by
going on to state that the federal government "cannot merely by making promises to foreign countries clothe itself with legislative authority
inconsistent with the constitution which gave it birth."

Finally, as to treaties generally, the Privy Council made concluding
observations:

> It must not be thought that the result of this decision is that Canada is incom-
> petent to legislate in performance of treaty obligations. In totality of legislative
> powers, Dominion and Provincial together, she is fully equipped. But the leg-
> islative powers remain distributed and if in the exercise of her new functions
> derived from her new international status she incurs obligations they must,
> so far as legislation be concerned when they deal with provincial classes of

subjects, be dealt with by the totality of powers, in other words, by co-operation between the Dominion and the Provinces. While the ship of state now sails on larger ventures and into foreign waters she still retains the watertight compartments which are an essential part of her original structure.

The last sentence, and particularly the "watertight compartments" was to become a hallmark of Canadian constitutional law, emphasizing the importance of respecting the legislative competence of each of the federal and provincial governments.

Regulation of Firearms: Federal or Provincial Responsibility?

Reference re Firearms Act [2000] 1 S.C.R. 783

In 1995, the federal Parliament amended the *Criminal Code* by enacting the *Firearms Act*, which required all holders of firearms to obtain license and to register their guns. Alberta initiated a reference case to its Court of Appeal to determine whether the provisions, as they related to ordinary firearms, were within the power of the federal Parliament to enact, and a majority of that court decided that it was a valid exercise of the criminal-law power of the federal Parliament. The matter was then referred to the Supreme Court of Canada.

While Canada runs well behind the obsessive preoccupation of the United States regarding firearms, the degree of interest in this reference case from a broad range of interveners was quite remarkable and the case required two days of hearing, even with stringent time limits imposed on the additional parties. The Attorneys General of Ontario, Nova Scotia, New Brunswick, Manitoba and Saskatchewan, the Government of the Northwest Territories, the Minister of Justice for the Government of the Yukon Territory, the Federation of Saskatchewan Indian Nations, the Coalition of Responsible Firearm Owners and Sportsmen, the Law-Abiding Unregistered Firearms Association, the Shooting Federation of Canada, *l'Association pour la santé publique du Québec inc.*, the Alberta Council of Women's Shelters, CAVEAT, *la Fondation des victims du 6 décembre contre la violence,* The Canadian Association for Adolescent Health, the Canadian Pediatric Society, the Coalition for Gun Control, the Canadian Association of Chiefs of Police, the Corporation of the City of Toronto, and the cities of Montreal and Winnipeg all appeared and filed briefs with the Court.

The Court began by making it clear that it was not deciding whether gun control was good or bad, whether it was fair or unfair to gun owners, nor whether it would be effective in the reduction of harm due to the misuse of firearms. This is an all-but-routine disclaimer with respect to anything which may smack of policy reflected in legislation. The only question the Court had to decide was whether the federal Parliament had the constitutional authority to enact the law.

> The answer to this question lies in the Canadian Constitution. The Constitution assigns some matters to Parliament and others to the provincial legislatures: *Constitution Act, 1867.* The federal government asserts that the gun control law falls under its criminal law power, s. 19(27), and under its general power to legislate for the "Peace, Order and good Government" of Canada. Alberta, on the other hand, says the law falls under its power over property and civil rights, s. 92(13). All agree that to resolve this dispute, the Court must first determine what the gun control law is really about—its "pith and substance"—and then ask which head or heads of power it most naturally falls within.

> We conclude that the gun control law comes within Parliament's jurisdiction over criminal law. The law in "pith and substance" is directed to enhancing public safety by controlling access to firearms through prohibitions and penalties. This brings it under the federal criminal law power. While the law has regulatory aspects, they are secondary to its primary criminal law purpose. The intrusion of the law into the provincial jurisdiction over property and civil rights is not so excessive as to upset the balance of federalism.

This was a familiar constitutional positioning, with the provinces relying on the property and civil-rights jurisdiction to justify their litigious position, while the federal government took the position that it had legislated validly on the basis of its criminal-law jurisdiction. Also, the "pith and substance" test referred to by the Court had a lengthy history as the means of searching for the core of the subject matter of a statute, since almost any federal legislation would likely have some impact on property and/or civil rights.

The *Criminal Code* had, for many years, restricted access to automatic weapons (prohibited firearms) and handguns (restricted firearms). The amendments under attack extended this to a third category (generally, rifles and shotguns), referred to as "ordinary firearms." The legislation required a license in order to possess a firearm. Eligibility for a license reflected safety interests—an applicant with a criminal record involving drug offences or violence, or a history of mental illness, might be denied a license. An applicant must first pass a safety course requiring a basic understanding of firearm safety and legal responsibilities of firearm ownership. The issuer of licenses (chief firearms officer) would be entitled to conduct a background check on an applicant to determine eligibility and could attach conditions to any license. A license, once issued, would be valid for five years, but it could be revoked for certain criminal convictions or for a breach of any conditions. An appeal to a court was provided for any refusal or revocation of a license. Registration provisions applied to each firearm, which could only occur if the applicant was licensed to possess it and was valid as long as the holder owned the firearm (normally identified by serial number). On a transfer of ownership, the new owner was required to register the firearm and any possession of an unregistered firearm was an offence.

The first responsibility of the Court was to determine the "pith and substance" of the legislation, namely what is its true meaning, its essential character, its core. To do that, the purpose of the enacting body and the legal effect of the law must be examined. The purpose of a law is often stated in the legislation itself, but the courts are now willing to consider extrinsic material, such as the recorded parliamentary debates reported in Hansard and other government publications. Care must be exercised to make sure, in the context of party politics, that the evidence is relevant and reliable, and is not given undue weight. Another manner of determining the purpose of the legislation is to look at the "mischief," namely the problem that Parliament was attempting to solve. Determination of the legal effect is a matter of considering how the law will operate and how it will affect Canadians.

The question of whether the law will be effective is not a relevant consideration for the Court. Alberta said that criminals will not register their guns and that rural farmers would be burdened with pointless red tape. The Court said that those concerns had been properly directed to and considered by Parliament, and that, within its constitutional sphere, Parliament is the judge of whether a measure is likely to achieve its intended purpose.

Legislation may be classified as criminal law "if it possesses three prerequisites: a valid criminal law purpose backed by a prohibition and a penalty. Because guns are dangerous, regulation of them as dangerous products is a valid purpose within the criminal law power. The law clearly met the other two conditions of prohibition and penalty.

The principal other objections raised included that the law was essentially regulatory rather than criminal because of its complexity and the discretion granted to the chief firearms officer. Complexity was a red herring: many other pieces of legislation under the criminal power were complex (e.g., the *Food and Drugs Act* and the *Canadian Environmental Protection Act*). The exercise of discretion was provided in the legislation, which specified the limits of that discretion and provided a recourse to the courts, which would determine whether there was a "good and sufficient reason" for the exercise of the discretion. Nor were the prohibitions and penalties regulatory in nature. Instead, they stood on their own, "independently serving the purpose of public safety." The intention of Parliament was "not to regulate property, but to ensure that only those who prove themselves qualified to hold a license are permitted to possess firearms of any sort."

A more subtle argument was that if the purpose of the law was to reduce misuse of firearms, it should deal with misuse directly. The Court dealt with this suggestion quite easily.

> On this view, Parliament could prohibit the careless or intentional misuse of guns ... but could not prohibit people from owning guns if they present risks to public safety or regulate how people store their guns. Again, the answer is that Parliament may use indirect means to further the end of public safety. The risks associated with ordinary firearms are not confined to the intentional or reckless conduct that might be deterred by a prohibition on misuse. The Attorney General of Canada argued, for example, that the suicide rate is increased by the availability of guns. A person contemplating suicide may be

more likely to actually commit suicide if a gun is available, it was argued; therefore Parliament has a right to prevent people at risk, for example due to mental illness, from owning a gun. A prohibition on misuse is unlikely to deter a potential suicide; a prohibition on gun ownership may do so. Other examples where a prohibition on misuse falls short are not hard to envisage. A prohibition on misuse is unlikely to prevent the death of a child who plays with a gun; a prohibition on irresponsible ownership or careless storage may do so. Again, reducing availability may have a greater impact on whether a robber uses a gun than a law forbidding him to use it. Whether the 1995 gun law actually achieves these ends is not at issue before us; what is at issue is whether Parliament, in targeting these dangers, strayed outside its criminal law power. In our view, it did not.

Alberta persisted, arguing that the gun-control scheme was indistinguishable from existing provincial property-regulation schemes such as automobile and land-title registries.

The argument that the federal gun control scheme is no different from the provincial regulation of motor vehicles ignores the fact that there are significant distinctions between the roles of guns and cars in Canadian society. Both firearms and automobiles can be used for socially approved purposes. Likewise, both may cause death and injury. Yet their primary purposes are fundamentally different. Cars are used mainly as means of transportation. Danger to the public is ordinarily unintended and incidental to that use. Guns, by contrast, pose a pressing safety risk in many if not all of their functions. Firearms are often used as weapons in violent crime, including domestic violence; cars generally are not. Thus Parliament views guns as particularly dangerous and has sought to combat that danger by extending its licensing and registration scheme to all classes of firearms. Parliament did not enact the Firearms Act to regulate guns as items of property. The Act does not address insurance or permissible locations of use. Rather, the Act addresses those aspects of gun control which relate to the dangerous nature of firearms and the need to reduce misuse.

None of the other subsidiary arguments carried any weight with the Court, including that the law upsets the balance of Canada's federal system. The provinces' rights to regulate the property and civil rights aspects of guns, such as hunting, discharge within municipal bound-aries, and a host of other legitimate subjects of provincial jurisdiction, were not affected.

> We recognize the concerns of northern, rural and aboriginal Canadians who fear that this law does not address their particular needs. They argue that it discriminates against them and violates treaty rights, and express concerns about their ability to access the scheme, which may be administered from a great distance. These apprehensions are genuine, but they do not go to the question before us—Parliament's jurisdiction to enact this law. Whether a law could have been designed better or whether the federal government should have engaged in more consultation before enacting the law has no bearing on the division of powers analysis applied by this Court. If the law violates a trea-ty or a provision of the Charter, those affected can bring their claims to Parlia-ment or the courts in a separate case. The reference questions, and hence this judgment, are restricted to the issue of the division of powers.

Changing from Denominational to Linguistic Basis of School Organization

Reference re Education Act (Quebec) [1993] 2 S.C.R. 511

Some of the issues of today's society can only be solved if you know your history. The 1993 Reference case on educational reform in Quebec is a good example.

The pre-Confederation educational system in the Canadas was organized on religious or denominational lines, primarily Roman Catholic and Protestant, although the Privy Council had since held out the possibility that other branches of religion and even other religions might avail themselves of the protections contained in the *British North America Act, 1867* (now imported into Canada and re-enacted as the *Constitution Act*). Even this sentence contains a large amount of historical "backswing," since in the Canadian context, it grew out of the existence of a large Roman Catholic population in what is now Quebec (mainly but not entirely French-speaking) with a Protestant minority, the reverse of the situation in what is now Ontario.

The general governmental policy on education was to provide for common schools, funded by government, but to permit religious minorities to exercise a right of dissent, to opt for their own denominational schools. In the event of such dissent, the government was required to fund the dissentient schools on a fair and equitable basis.

The process leading to Confederation required the resolution of many issues, one of which was the protection of religious rights in the new

Dominion, including such rights within the educational system. Religion played a much more active role in society than it does today and church authorities were far more influential. Disagreements between communities were based more on religion than on language. Education was to be a provincial matter. Some academics have expressed the view that the provincial jurisdiction over education had been critical to obtain the support of Lower Canada in the negotiations leading to Confederation. Part of that Confederation bargain was that protection of existing religious rights was to be absolute.

The principles were easily and clearly expressed in section 93 of the *BNA Act*:

> 93. In and for each Province the Legislature may exclusively make Laws in relation to Education, subject and according to the following provisions:
>
> ...
>
> (1) Nothing in any such Law shall prejudicially affect any Right or Privilege with respect to Denominational Schools which any class of Persons have by Law in the Province at the Union:
>
> (2) All the Powers, Privileges, and Duties at the Union by Law conferred and imposed in Upper Canada on the Separate Schools and School Trustees of the Queen's Roman Catholic Subjects shall be and the same are hereby extended to the Dissentient Schools of the Queen's Protestant and Roman Catholic Subjects in Quebec:

Any constitutional examination of subsequent legislation on education requires an examination of what was or was not protected in 1867. This, of course, varies between the different provinces, not all of which even existed in 1867. From a broad perspective, the Court observed:

> Section 93 of the Constitution crystallizes the rights and privileges pertaining to denominational schools under the law in effect at the time of Confederation: it is in a sense a snapshot of the legislative situation in 1867. The picture it provides indicates that in the rural areas of Quebec religious minorities alone were entitled to denominational schools, by means of dissenting rights, and

> that in the two major cities [i.e., Quebec and Montreal], Catholics and Protestants were also entitled to denominational schools, regardless of their respective numbers. In the "rural" areas, the religious majority was not entitled to any constitutional protection. The framers of the Constitution preserved the characteristics which the schools had in 1867 by providing protection based on the legal status of the institutions.

Little, if any, significant legislation in the educational field had occurred in Quebec for almost a century following Confederation. It was only with the advent of the Lesage government in 1960 that movement toward increasing secularization of education began to occur, leading to legislation in 1964 to enact two statutes, the *Department of Education Act* and the *Superior Council of Education Act*. The latter created a Catholic and a Protestant committee, each responsible for supervising the denominational aspects of schools. Further legislation was aimed at ensuring that the whole of Quebec would be served by school boards.

The big move leading to the Reference case occurred in 1988, when Quebec moved to abolish the entire denominational basis of education and, instead, to create linguistic school boards that were to be denominationally neutral, to delineate their respective territories and to assign the property of the old denominational boards to the new language-based boards. The right to dissent was maintained, but now on the basis of language rather than religion.

It came as no surprise that such a radical change raised a number of questions and added the increasingly touchy question of language rights to the embedded denominational protection. Quebec had already moved aggressively in matters of language and had, at the time of patriation of the Constitution in 1982, made certain that it had the right (by way of the famous "notwithstanding clause") to override the *Charter of Rights and Freedoms* in matters of provincial jurisdiction. It had not hesitated to exercise that right in relation to language and the mandatory use of French. Both Catholic and Protestant and French and English groups took part in the Reference case, which was first launched in the Quebec Court of Appeal and then moved on by way of appeal to the Supreme Court of Canada.

The Court concluded that the provisions of the legislation were constitutional and that the Quebec government was pursuing a legitimate purpose within its constitutional jurisdiction. Despite the fundamental upheaval affecting longstanding institutions, the legislature's power to create some other kind of school system had long been recognized. The key aspect to staying within the constitutional parameters was to maintain the right of dissent outside the areas of Quebec and Montreal (where the right to denominational schools had been maintained), rather than to focus on the particular administrative structures and processes that might be adopted. While the means of exercising the right of dissent under the new legislation were different, the rights were nevertheless retained and the embedded constitutional protection was not breached by the new system. There had been concerns expressed that verification of membership in a denominational minority by a linguistic school board might lead to potential abuse, but the Court held that did not limit the right to dissent and, in any event, the linguistic school board had no discretionary authority—its only function was to recognize a situation of fact, namely the existence of a religious minority.

The following series of observations addressed some of the concerns expressed by the parties to the litigation, who were obviously worried that the right to dissent could effectively be thwarted, even on an interim basis, depending on how the Quebec authorities might choose to respond to such dissent. The Court sent a far-from-subtle message to the Quebec government that it could not manoeuvre around the constitutional protections by the manner in which it might administer the new law.

> It must be noted that the Constitution provides no guarantee that existing institutions or vested rights will be maintained. Consequently, reform of the educational system is possible, with the transitional inconvenience involved in any major institutional reorganization. However, such inconvenience must not make the effective exercise of the right to dissent impracticable or have a serious adverse effect on it. In this regard, a distinction must be made between difficulties which are inevitable because they are due to the Act itself and those which arise in its implementation. I agree that the periods specified by *Bill 107* [the new law] may lead to problems, but I am not persuaded that they are a necessary consequence. If they occur, they are more likely to be attributable to those responsible for implementing the Act. Other remedies

would then be available to ensure that the right to dissent can be exercised on an equal basis.

Quebeckers living outside Quebec or Montreal are entitled to denominational schools, if they are a religious minority; if living in Quebec or Montreal, if they are Catholics and Protestants. A subsidiary issue had arisen regarding the definition of appropriate territories of the cities of Quebec and Montreal, one view being that they should be limited to their geographic limits at the time of Confederation, the other that they should be whatever their present limits might be. The Court concluded, sensibly, that the right interpretation was not so much territorial in nature (since both cities had grown considerably), but rather by the appropriate administrative and legal institutions.

The proof of the organizational pudding can be tied to the duty to provide the necessary governmental resources, especially to a minority-language school board.

> Doubts have been expressed concerning an intervention by the Minister of Education in the event of a dispute ... at the time of the allocation of property and rights, as it is argued that there is always a risk of bad faith. The latter should not be presumed, however. Further, as counsel for the respondent [the Attorney General of Quebec] pointed out, the Minister's intervention and the fairness of the decision go more to the implementation of *Bill 107* than to the constitutionality of the provisions. Of course, if a statute is drafted so that it cannot be applied, its quality may be doubted: but that is not the case here.

> The same [sections] contain a criterion which is particularly noteworthy, since the legislature speaks of "property necessary" for the operation of the dissentient school boards and denominational boards. This necessity test is objective: the level of available services is the yardstick. It means that the means for exercising the right to dissent must be made available without discrimination, with no prejudicial effects, and the dissentient boards must be on the same footing in this respect as the linguistic boards from which they separate. This includes equality of access to public funds, to means of taxation and, in the event of a reorganization, to the distribution of immovable property, physical facilities and existing personnel.

War-Time Reality: Acting in the Interests of the Nation

Reference re Validity of Regulations in Relation to Chemicals [1943]
S.C.R. 1

This case is an example of how the courts deal somewhat differently with legislation (and legislation-like situations) during periods of war or other emergencies.

When a country is at war, it does not have the luxury of normal rhythms of the legislative process, with the preparation of discussion papers, public consultation, parliamentary debate, and approval of both Houses of Parliament. Urgent measures are required to deal with situations that are fluid and with the necessity of ensuring that the resources available to the nation are applied quickly and efficiently. The technique used by Canada for that purpose was developed during the First World War, in the form of the *War Measures Act*, which was still on the statute books, although not then in force, when the Second World War broke out in 1939. The *Act* was reactivated during the new conflict. The obvious intention of Parliament was to provide the Executive with the widest, indeed almost with limitless, powers in times of danger.

For readers who have not experienced life during a war, the concentration of powers under that *Act* are extraordinary and, on their face, potentially quite alarming to those accustomed to the checks and balances, legal protections and recourses ordinarily available to citizens. Some readers may recall the invocation of the *Act* in October 1971 in Quebec, during the FLQ crisis, at the request of the public authorities in Quebec and the City of Montreal. Quite apart from the immediate circumstances that led to the application of the *Act*, many, if not most, observers were horrified with the extent of the powers immediately available to the authorities and the suspension of civil rights and liberties permitted in the ordinary course. In wartime, however, there is generally public acceptance of the need for such measures, as can be seen from Parliament's decision to adopt or invoke the *Act* and the Court's decision in this Reference case.

To give some idea of the extent of the powers concentrated in the Cabinet under the *Act*, the following extract will illustrate what is involved:

> 3. (1) The Governor in Council [i.e., the Cabinet] may do and authorize such acts and things, and make from time to time such orders and regulations, as he may by reason of the existence of real or apprehended war, invasion or insurrection deem necessary or advisable for the security, defence, peace, order and welfare of Canada; and for greater certainty, but not so as to restrict the generality of the foregoing terms, it is hereby declared that the powers of the Governor in Council shall extend to all matters coming within the classes of subjects hereinafter enumerated, that is to say:
>
> (a) Censorship and the control and suppression of publications, writings, maps, plans, photographs, communications and means of communication;
>
> (b) Arrest,, detention, exclusion and deportation;
>
> (c) Control of the harbours, ports and territorial waters of Canada and the movements of vessels;
>
> (d) Transportation by land, air, or water and the control of the transport of persons and things;
>
> (e) Trading, exportation, importation. Production and manufacture;
>
> (f) Appropriation, control, forfeiture and disposition of property and of the use thereof.
>
> (2) All orders and regulations made under this section shall have the force of law, and shall be enforced in such manner and by such courts, officers and authorities as the Governor in Council may prescribe. And may be varied, extended or revoked by any subsequent order or regulation; but if any order or regulation is varied, extended or revoked, neither the previous operation thereof nor anything duly done thereunder, shall be affected thereby, nor

> shall any right, privilege, obligation or liability acquired, accrued, accruing or
> incurred thereunder be affected by such variation, extension or revocation.

As can easily be seen, not only is this a remarkable concentration of special, even arbitrary, powers in the federal Cabinet, but also the subject matter cuts across the normal division of constitutional powers allocated to the federal and provincial legislatures. None of the provinces intervened in the Reference, since the proper enactment of and the constitutionality of the *Act* had been definitively settled by the Privy Council in 1923 and there were no additional arguments to be offered on their account.

Relying on the legislation, orders were issued in relation to chemicals required for the purposes of munitions and a Controller of Chemicals was appointed with broad powers to administer the collection and control of such materials. This included a very wide control of crude, refined, or dynamite glycerine, as to its sale, dealing in, consumption, import, or export, the general scheme of which was that none of these things could be done except by way of a permit by the Controller or a license issued by one of two identified federal ministers.

What led to the Reference was that an Ontario County Court judge had recently dismissed a charge of an offence laid by the Controller, on the basis that the order conferring power on the Controller was invalid, since it constituted delegation of the authority of the Governor in Council under the *Act*, and other magistrates had similarly dismissed complaints or were withholding decisions for the time being. In the direction giving rise to the Reference, it was noted that the method or system of control of the essential supplies was in principle identical to that adopted in other fields in connection with the conduct of the war. An urgent opinion of the Court was required on the extent of the powers of the Governor in Council under the *Act*.

The Court took both elements to heart. The Reference was heard in mid-December 1942 and judgment was rendered on January 5, 1943. Each of the six judges wrote reasons for the unanimous decision, so obviously they worked over the year-end holidays!

A number of points of principle emerged from the various judgments.

(1) An order-in-council issued in conformity with the conditions

prescribed by and the provisions of, the *Act* may have the effect of an Act of Parliament.

> The powers conferred upon the Governor in Council by the *War Measures Act* constitute a law-making authority, an authority to pass legislative enactments such as should be deemed necessary and advisable by reason of war; and, when acting within those limits, the Governor in Council is vested with plenary powers of legislation as large and of the same nature as those of Parliament itself. ... Within the ambit of the Act by which his authority is measured, the Governor in Council is given the same authority as is vested in Parliament itself. He has been given a law-making power.

> The conditions for the exercise of that power are: The existence of a state of war, or of apprehended war, and that the orders or regulations are deemed advisable or necessary by the Governor in Council by reason of such state of war, or apprehended war.

> Parliament retains its power intact and can, whenever it pleases, take the matter directly into its own hands. How far it shall seek the aid of subordinate agencies and how long it shall continue them in existence, are matters for Parliament and not for courts of law to decide. Parliament has not abdicated its general legislative powers. It has not effaced itself, as has been suggested. It has indicated no intention of abandoning control and has made no abandonment of control, in fact. The subordinate instrumentality, which it has created for exercising the powers, remains responsible directly to Parliament for the continuance of its official existence.

(2) Enactments under the *Act* in relation to subject matters otherwise falling within the legislative capacity may nevertheless be paramount

> ... in an emergency such as war, the authority of the Dominion in respect of legislation relating to the peace, order and good government of Canada may, in view of the necessities arising from the emergency, displace or overbear the authority of the provinces in relation to a vast field in which the provinces would otherwise have exclusive jurisdiction. It must not, however be taken for granted that every matter within the jurisdiction of the Parliament of Can-

ada, even in ordinary times, could be validly committed by Parliament to the Executive for legislation in the case of an emergency.

(3) There is nothing in the language so narrow as to preclude the Governor in Council from acting through subordinate agencies having a delegated authority to make orders and rules. The power of delegation is absolutely essential. The Governor in Council can legislate as Parliament itself could, which means it can delegate its powers, whether legislative or administrative.

(4) There is always some risk of abuse when wide powers are committed in general terms to any body of men, but under the *Act*, the final responsibility for the acts of the Executive rests upon Parliament, which abandons none of its powers and none of its control over the Executive, legal or constitutional.

(5) Subordinate agencies appointed by the Governor in Council are not, by the *Act*, outside the settled rule that all statutory powers must be employed in good faith for the purposes for which they are given, although the Court noted that, for purposes of the present Reference, that rule was of theoretical interest only.

(6) Orders-in-council derive their validity from the statute itself, not from the executive body by which it is made. They must be read as subject to an implied proviso that nothing in them allows them to depart from the limitations (of time or otherwise) fixed by the statute itself.

(7) The Court noted, with respect to personal liberties, that even though such matters could never be swept aside, nevertheless, times of war may have some impact on the difference between normal times and times of emergency, by incorporating language taken from a British case decided only a month or two before the Reference case:

> In the first place, it is important to have in mind that the regulation in question is a war measure. This is not to say that the courts ought to adopt in war canons of construction different from those which they follow in peace time. The fact that the nation is at war is no justification for any relaxation of the vigilance of the courts in seeing that the law is duly observed, especially in a matter so fundamental as the liberty of the subject, rather the contrary. But in a time of emergency when the life of the whole nation is at stake it may well be that a regulation for the defence of the realm may quite properly have a

meaning which because of its drastic invasion of the liberty of the subject the courts would be slow to attribute to a peace time measure. The purpose of the regulation is to ensure public safety, and it is right to interpret emergency legislation so as to promote rather than to defeat its efficacy for the defence of the realm. That is in accordance with a general rule applicable to the interpretation of all statutes or statutory regulations in peace time as well as in war time.

The most important thing to understand about such legislation is that there had been no improper or unauthorized usurpation of powers by the Executive, but a deliberate delegation of those powers by Parliament itself, in recognition of the particular exigencies forced upon the country by the emergency and the need to be able to respond to the emergency in the best interests of the country as a whole. If Parliament is not satisfied with the manner in which those delegated powers are exercised, it retains its own power to withdraw them.

All that said, in an ideal world, one hopes that the circumstances leading to invocation of such legislation will never be required.

Fooling with the Senate: Law as Opposed to Politics

Reference re Authority of Parliament in Relation to the Upper House
[1980] S.C.R. 54

One of the recurrent Canadian political footballs is the existence, function, and membership of the Senate. It is perceived by many as a matter of partisan patronage, having no legitimacy derived from election of its members and possessing no effective powers. There are periodic calls for its abolition, or at least substantial reform, and recent years have brought to light several scandals that attract far more media attention than similar scandals among elected members of Parliament.

In November 1978, the federal government initiated a reference case to the Supreme Court of Canada, in which it posed two sets of revealing questions. The first was to ask whether it was within the legislative authority of the Parliament of Canada (i.e., would it be legal) to repeal sections 21 to 36 of the *British North America Act, 1867*, and to amend other sections of that *Act* to delete any reference to an Upper House or the Senate. If not, in what particular or particulars and to what extent? The second had a number of subsets. Was it within the legislative authority of the Parliament of Canada to enact legislation altering, or providing a replacement for, the Upper House of Parliament, so as to effect any or all of the following:

(a) to change the name of the Upper House;

(b) to change the numbers and proportions of members by whom provinces and territories are represented in that House;

(c) to change the qualifications of members of that House;

(d) to change the tenure of members of that House;

(e) to change the method by which members of that House are chosen by

    i. conferring authority on provincial legislative assemblies to select ... some members of the Upper House ... and

    ii. conferring authority on the House of Commons to select ... some members of the Upper House from each province ...

    iii. conferring authority on the Lieutenant Governors in Council of the provinces [i.e., the provincial Cabinets] or on some other body or bodies to select some or all of the members of the Upper House, or

    iv. providing for the direct election of some or all of the members of the Upper House by the public; or

(f) to provide that Bills approved by the House of Commons could be given assent and the force of law after the passage of a certain period of time notwithstanding that the Upper House has not approved them

If not, in what particular or particulars and to what extent?

Anyone familiar with the "debate" about the Senate will recognize the usual "hot buttons" contained in the reference questions. Implicit in the first question (although not stated outright) is the power of Parliament to abolish the Senate. Sections 2(a) to (d) are straightforward, but contain some important constitutional issues. Section 2(e) canvasses the different means by which many have suggested that members of the Senate might be selected, including by decision of the provincial legislature, the House of Commons, provincial Cabinets and by direct election. Section 2(f) sought advice on being able to ignore the Senate entirely if it had not approved Bills approved by the House of Commons within a certain period of time. High-powered lawyers from the federal government and the governments of Ontario, Nova Scotia, New Brunswick, Prince Edward Island, Saskatchewan, Alberta, and Newfoundland made submissions to the Court. British Columbia did not participate and Quebec, no doubt hoping for a constitutional miscue that would fuel the inevitable referendum, remained watchfully aloof.

The federal government argued that it had the legislative authority to abolish the Senate. The provincial representatives argued that it did not. The argument in favour was based on a 1949 amendment to the *BNA Act* giving the federal Parliament the authority to amend the "Constitution of Canada" subject to certain listed exceptions. Because the *BNA Act* was a British statute, there was no possibility of the Canadian Parliament amending that statute on its own account.

The previous constitutional practice had always been to submit a joint address of both Houses of Parliament (in some instances following consultation with one or more provinces). In response to such address, the British Parliament would invariably enact the requested amendment. The corollary was that the British Parliament would not make any amendments without such an address and that it would not make any amendment on the basis of a request from a provincial government. The position of the British government on the latter point was that it should not intervene into the affairs of Canada except at the request of the federal government representing all of Canada. Interestingly, the first attempt by a province to obtain such an amendment was made in 1868, by a province then dissatisfied with the terms of Confederation.

The issue, then, was whether the 1949 amendment gave the federal government the power to do anything except for the specific limitations. It clearly allowed the federal government to deal with "housekeeping" matters, especially those which did not affect federal-provincial relationships in any substantial way. But the question obviously went far beyond mere housekeeping, even if it did not directly affect federal–provincial relationships by changing their respective legislative powers. It contemplated the elimination of one of the two Houses of Parliament, thus altering the structure of the federal Parliament, to which legislative power was given.

The Court then examined the role of the Senate in the legislative process. The preamble to the *BNA Act* contemplated a constitution similar in principle to that of the United Kingdom, in which the Upper House (the House of Lords) was and is not an elected body, and the Lower House (the House of Commons) was and is an elected body. This prompted a review of the historical background leading to the creation of the Senate as part of the legislative process, mainly the debates at the Quebec Conference in 1864, where there had been considerable discussion regarding the Senate. Two speeches were identified, one by John A. Macdonald and the other by George Brown. Macdonald said:

In order to protect local interests and to prevent sectional jealousies, it was found requisite that the three great divisions into which British North America is separated, should be represented in the Upper House on the principle of equality. There are three great sections, having different interests, in this proposed Confederation. ... To the Upper House is to be confided the protection of sectional interests: therefore is it that the three great divisions are there equally represented for the purpose of defending such interests against the combinations of majorities in the Assembly.

And Brown stated:

But the very essence of our compact is that the union shall be federal and not legislative. Our Lower Canada friends have agreed to give us representation by population in the Lower House, on the express condition that they shall have equality in the Upper House. On no other condition could we have advanced a step; and, for my part, I am quite willing they should have it. In maintaining the sectional boundaries and handing over the control of local matters to local bodies, we recognize, to a certain extent, a diversity of interests; and it is quite natural that the protection of those interests, by equality in the Upper Chamber, should be demanded by the less numerous provinces.

Thus, the Court was able to conclude that a primary purpose of the Senate was to afford protection to the various sectional interests in Canada in relation to the enactment of federal legislation. The original three divisions (Ontario, Quebec, and the Maritime provinces) was later amended to four, with the Western provinces added.

The legislative "place" of the Senate came from section 17 of the *BNA Act*: "There shall be One Parliament for Canada, consisting of the Queen, an Upper House styled the Senate, and the House of Commons." The federal power was conferred (by the British Parliament) in section 91 upon "the Queen, by and with the Advice and Consent of the Senate and the House of Commons." The body which had been created for the purpose of protecting sectional and provincial interests was therefore made a participant in the legislative process.

The Court then considered what was meant by the words *Constitution of Canada*, a phrase which does not otherwise appear in the *Act*. It concluded that it did not mean Canada as a geographical unit, but instead to the juristic federal unit; not the entire *BNA Act,* but the constitution of the federal government, distinct from provincial governments. The power in section 91 given to the federal government related to matters of interest only to that government. The Court drew from a Privy Council decision in another case to drive home the historical background once again.

> Inasmuch as the Act embodies a compromise under which the original Provinces agreed to federate, it is important to keep in mind that the preservation of the rights of minorities was a condition on which such minorities entered into the federation, and the foundation upon which the whole structure was subsequently erected. The process of interpretation as the years go on ought not to be allowed to dim or to whittle down the provisions of the original contract upon which the federation was founded, nor is it legitimate that any judicial construction of the provisions of ss. 91 and 92 should impose a new and different contract upon the federating bodies.

The general power of legislation could only be exercised by the Queen, by and with the advice and consent of the Senate and House of Commons, and the provisions of section 91(1) could not be construed to confer power to supplant the whole rest of the section or to allow the transfer of the legislative powers to some body other than those specifically designated in it. For that matter, neither Parliament nor any legislature could delegate to nor receive from the other any legislative powers. The elimination of the Senate would go much further, involving a transfer by Parliament of all its legislative powers to a new body, of which the Senate would not be a member. The provision confers a power of amendment which contemplates the continued existence of both the Senate and House of Commons.

The Court decided that question 2(f) should be answered in the negative, since Parliament cannot impair the role of the Senate in the legislative process. The proposal would have allowed Parliament to legislate without the consent of the Senate.

As to the other questions, the Court, quite understandably, ducked. There was insufficient factual context to provide a satisfactory answer. Wrapping up its comments on the second question, the Court concluded:

Dealing generally with Question 2, it is our opinion that while s. 91(1) would permit some changes to be made by Parliament in respect of the Senate as now constituted, it is not open to Parliament to make alterations which would affect the fundamental features, or essential characteristics, given to the Senate as a means of ensuring regional and provincial representation in the federal legislative process. The character of the Senate was determined by the British Parliament in response to the proposals submitted by the three provinces in order to meet the requirement of the proposed federal system. It was that Senate, created by the Act, to which a legislative role was given by s. 91. In our opinion, its fundamental character cannot be altered by unilateral action by the Parliament of Canada and s. 91(1) does not give that power.

The Constitution was patriated subsequent to this decision and the matter of the relevance of the Senate has continued to fester, at least as a matter of politics. It is not surprising, therefore, that yet another reference case was put forward to the Court, in which the current political agenda of the federal government could be easily deduced from the nature of the questions asked. In a 2014 decision that was widely regarded as a stinging defeat of that government, the Court answered each of the proposed questions in the negative on constitutional grounds. It held that the changes proposed could not be implemented by the federal government acting alone and without the concurrence of the provinces. The decision was yet another example demonstrating that the Constitution trumps Parliament and that the courts often provide the only protection of important rights in the face of a parliamentary majority.

Patriation of Constitution: No Need to Consult the Provinces

Reference re Resolution to Amend the Constitution [1981] 1 S.C.R. 753

O n October 2, 1980, the federal government published a proposed Resolution containing an address to be presented to Her Majesty the Queen in right of the United Kingdom, and attached a statute providing for the repatriation of the *British North America Act* (with an amending procedure) and a *Charter of Rights and Freedoms*. Only two provinces, Ontario and New Brunswick, approved the proposed Resolution. All but one of the others argued that the consent of all the provinces was required in order for the address to be forwarded to Her Majesty along with the appended statutes. Several instituted proceedings regarding the proposed Resolution, which was nevertheless adopted by the House of Commons and by the Senate on April 23 and 24, 1981. The Reference case was argued in the Supreme Court of Canada starting on April 28, 1981, and its decision was rendered on September 28 the same year. The whole matter was fraught with political difficulties and tensions, with some provinces fearing they might lose a portion of their powers pursuant to the *BNA Act* and subsequent judicial decisions, others seeing an opportunity to enter a political *souk* to see what additional powers and concessions they might wrest from the federal government, and Quebec, having no particular desire to cooperate with anything having to do with the rest of Canada. The Court was also deeply divided on several of the questions.

A substantial majority of the Court (seven to two) concluded that the proposed Resolution requesting the amendment was within the legislative competence of the Canadian Parliament notwithstanding that it affected provincial legislative powers. Proceeding without the concurrence of the provinces did not offend any legal principles of federalism and no requirement of any particular level of provincial consent had crystallized into law. The Canadian Parliament had authority to adopt its own procedures, including the Resolution, and, in any event, whatever process was followed had no bearing on the competence of the Parliament at Westminster to give effect to the Resolution. A slightly narrower majority (six to three) decided that a substantial degree of provincial consent (to be determined by the politicians and not by the courts) was conventionally required for amendment of the Canadian constitution. The convention was said to exist because the federal principle could not be reconciled with a state of affairs in which the federal authorities could unilaterally modify provincial legislative powers. The proposed amendments could not be separated despite the fact that the *Charter* offended the federal principle and the proposed amending formula did not. The principal area of encroachment on provincial (and, indeed, federal) legislative powers resulted from the new *Charter*, which was a clear suppression of certain provincial legislative powers, as well as a limitation on future federal legislation.

Putting the overall problem in perspective, the Court framed it in the following manner:

> Two observations are pertinent here. First, we have the anomaly that although Canada has international recognition as an independent, autonomous and self-governing state, as, for example, a founding member of the United Nations, and through membership in other international associations of sovereign states, yet it suffers from an internal deficiency in the absence of legal power to alter or amend the essential distributive arrangements under which legal authority is exercised in the country, whether at the federal or provincial level. When a country has been in existence as an operating federal state for more than a century, the task of introducing a mechanism that will thereafter remove the anomaly undoubtedly raises a profound problem. Secondly, the authority of the British Parliament or its practices and conventions are not matters upon which this Court would presume to pronounce.

It was obvious that there were no existing laws in Canada regarding either patriation of the constitution or amendment of it. The lack of legislation on the latter point was obvious, since the Canadian constitution was not even a Canadian statute. An argument was raised regarding the process, namely that even though there may have been no law, there had developed a "convention," an unwritten political practice that, over time, had effectively assumed the force of law.

> The proposition was advanced ... that a convention may crystallize into law and that the requirement of provincial consent to the kind of resolution that we have here, although in origin political, has become a rule of law. (No firm position was taken on whether the consent must be that of the governments or that of the legislatures.)

> In our view, this is not so. No instance of an explicit recognition of a convention as having matured into a rule of law was produced. The very nature of a convention, as political in inception and as depending on a consistent course of political recognition by those for whose benefit and to whose detriment (if any) the convention developed over a considerable period of time is inconsistent with its legal enforcement.

The factual crux of the matter is that there was no legal mechanism for what was being undertaken by way of the Resolution.

> We are involved here with a finishing operation, with fitting a piece into the constitutional edifice; it is idle to expect to find anything in the *British North America Act* that regulates the process that has been initiated in this case. Were it otherwise, there would be no need to resort to the Resolution procedure invoked here, a procedure which takes account of the intergovernmental and international link between Canada and Great Britain. There is no comparable link that engages the provinces with Great Britain. It is to confuse the issue of process, which is the basic question here, with the legal competence of the British Parliament when resort is had to the direct-indirect argument. The legal competence of that Parliament, for the reasons already given, remains unimpaired, and it is for it alone to determine if and how it will act.

Some of the provinces tried to invoke the prospect of a complete collapse of the federal system if the proposed Resolution were to proceed, and that Canada would become, instead, a unitary state. The Court had little patience with any such argument.

> It was argued that the federal authorities were assuming a power to act without restraint in disregard of provincial wishes which could go so far as to convert Canada into a unitary state by means of a majority vote in the Houses of Parliament. A few words will suffice to lay that argument at rest. What is before the Court is the task of answering questions posed in three References. As has been pointed out, the Court can do no more than that. The questions all deal with the constitutionality of precise proposals for constitutional amendment and they form the complete subject-matter of the Court's inquiry and our comments must be made with reference to them. It is not for the Court to express views on the wisdom or lack of wisdom of these proposals. We are concerned solely with their constitutionality. In view of the fact that the unitary argument has been raised, however, it should be noted, in our view, that the federal constitutional proposals, which preserve a federal state without disturbing the distribution or balance of power, would create an amending formula which would enshrine provincial rights on the question of amendments on a secure, legal and constitutional footing, and would extinguish, as well, any presently existing power on the part of the federal Parliament to act unilaterally in constitutional matters. In so doing, it may be said that the parliamentary resolution here under examination does not, save for the enactment of the *Charter of Rights*, which circumscribes the legislative powers of both federal and provincial legislatures, truly amend the Canadian Constitution. Its effect is to complete the formation of an incomplete constitution by supplying its present deficiency, i.e., an amending formula, which will enable the Constitution to be amended in Canada as befits a sovereign state. We are not here faced with an action which in any way has the effect of transforming this federal union into a unitary state. The *in terrorem* argument raising the spectre of a unitary state has no validity.

There will always be major difficulty in effecting constitutional change, especially in a federal state, and especially where zero-sum calculations or arguments are made—one party can only gain at the expense of some other party. The Court recognized the practical implications of this and the politicians did the same, mainly by agreeing to water down the Charter provisions to enable invocation of a "notwith-standing clause" that would permit legislation clearly in conflict with the Charter to trump supposedly inviolable rights and freedoms.

Finally, although the longstanding legal umbilical connection with the United Kingdom has finally been severed, the fact remains that the Canadian Constitution, including the *Charter of Rights and Freedoms*, remain British statutes, merely reenacted in Canada for purposes of self-esteem and possible subsequent amendment.

Judges Cannot Negotiate their Salaries

Reference re Remuneration of Judges; Reference re Independence and Impartiality of Judges [1997] 3 S.C.R. 3

If ever there is a topic about which judges obsess, it is the question of judicial independence—what it means, how it is expressed, how it may be affected and how it can be protected. The constitutional importance of the concept is at the very centre of the separation of powers between the legislative, the executive, and the judiciary. The judiciary stand as the protector of society against unlawful action by the legislature (if it enacts legislation that violates a constitutional principle), and by unlawful or arbitrary action by the executive branch. The characteristics of the independence necessary to act in such circumstances have been identified as security of tenure, financial security, and administrative independence. Independence applies to individual judges as well as to the collective independence of the courts on which they sit.

This was not the first occasion on which the Supreme Court of Canada has had to consider the importance and characteristics of judicial independence. The basic subject matter has been examined on many occasions. Two factors, however, that had not previously been considered in detail, called for further elaboration of the principle. The first was a unilateral reduction of the salaries of provincial court justices in Prince Edward Island and Manitoba, and the second a challenge to the independence of the judges by persons charged with offences in Alberta, relying on section 11(d) of the *Charter of Rights and Freedoms*, which guarantees that:

> Any person charged with an offence has the right
>
> ...
>
> (d) to be presumed innocent until proven guilty according to law in a fair and public hearing by an independent and impartial tribunal;

The crux of the Alberta challenges was that the provincial court judges, whose salaries are paid by the provinces, could not be independent and impartial, since they were paid by the same provincial government that was charging them with the particular offences.

The reported decision in the reference case was an environmentally unfriendly 211 pages.

One of the principal matters in issue was that of judges' remuneration and the court was at pains to note that the question was not simply how much the judges might earn, but the importance of the underlying premise of financial security and how a lack of such security might affect the perception of the independence of the judiciary.

> Financial security must be understood as merely an aspect of judicial independence, which in turn is not an end in itself. Judicial independence is valued because it serves important societal goals—it is a means to secure those goals.
>
> One of these goals is the maintenance of public confidence in the impartiality of the judiciary, which is essential to the effectiveness of the court system. Independence contributes to the perception that justice will be done in individual cases. Another social goal served by judicial independence is the maintenance of the rule of law, one aspect of which is the constitutional principle that the exercise of all public power must find its ultimate source in a legal rule. It is with these broader objectives in mind that these reasons, and the dispositions of these appeals, must be understood.

One of the challenges for the Court in this case was that there is nothing in the written constitution of Canada that deals with provincial court judges, so it expanded on some previous thinking to the effect that there is a deeper set of unwritten understandings that are not found in the constitution itself. The constitution was held to have emerged from "a constitutional order whose fundamental rules are not authoritatively set down in a single document, or a set of documents." Key to the approach of the court on this occasion was reference to the preamble to the *Constitution Act, 1867*. While the preamble is not a source of positive law, it nevertheless has important legal effects and "is not only a key to construing the express provisions of the *Constitution Act, 1867*, but also invites the use of those organizing principles to fill out gaps in the express terms of the constitutional scheme. It is the means by which the underlying logic of the Act can be given force of law." It is not the purpose of this work to go through the full legal analysis used by the Court. Suffice it to say that if the Court is determined to find a way to justify its ability to achieve a particular solution or to render an important decision, it will find a way. Thus, in this case, the Court emerges from the difficult issue by stating: "The preamble identifies the organizing principles of the Constitution Act, 1867, and invites the courts to turn those principles into the premises of a constitutional argument that culminates in the filling of gaps in the express terms of the constitutional text."

From this flexible platform, the Court went on to say that the concept of judicial independence had grown into a principle that extends to all courts, not just the superior courts that were identified in the constitution, and to no matter what types of cases they might be called upon to decide. It finished the discussion on the point as follows:

> In conclusion, the express provisions of the *Constitution Act, 1867* and the *Charter* are not an exhaustive written code for the protection of judicial independence in Canada. Judicial independence is an unwritten norm, recognized and affirmed by the preamble to the *Constitution Act, 1867*. In fact, it is in that preamble, which serves as the grand entrance hall to the castle of the Constitution, that the true source of our commitment to this foundational principle is located.

There is little doubt that government bodies can attempt to influence judges. One way is through financial pressures. In that respect, judges have their hands tied behind their backs—there is no way in which they can be seen to be negotiating their salaries with either the executive or legislative branches of government, without fundamentally compromising judicial independence, since the negotiations would be fundamentally political in nature and involve the give-and-take of negotiations in general. Judges may be able to express concern or representations on the adequacy of judicial remuneration, but they cannot negotiate, either individually or collectively.

> With respect to the judiciary, the determination of the level of remuneration from the public purse is political in another sense, because it raises the spectre of political interference through economic manipulation. An unscrupulous government could utilize its authority to set judges' salaries as a vehicle to influence the course and outcome of adjudication. Admittedly, this would be very different from the kind of political interference with the judiciary by the Stuart Monarchs in England which is the historical source of the constitutional concern for judicial independence in the Anglo-American tradition. However, the threat to judicial independence would be as significant.

The solution to this (at least in theory) is to interpose an independent body—a judicial compensation commission, an "institutional sieve"— between the judiciary and the political organs of government. In the final analysis, the salaries of judges will be paid from public funds, but the purpose of having such commissions is to depoliticize the process of increasing, decreasing or freezing those salaries. Such commissions must meet three criteria: independence, objectivity, and effectiveness.

The Court raised the existence and operation of such commissions to a constitutional requirement. Changes or freezes to judicial remuneration that did not go through the commission process were declared to be unconstitutional. Faced with government inaction, commissions should meet for further consideration of the adequacy of judicial remuneration. The Court left open the frequency of such meetings, as well as the manner in which governments were to deal with the commission reports (e.g., the reports would be binding, and would be adopted unless the legislature votes to reject or change them, or an affirmative resolution procedure, by which the report is laid before, but need not be adopted by the legislature). The Court also indicated that an unjustified decision by government could lead to a finding of unconstitutionality.

The need for public justification, to my mind, emerges from one of the purposes of s. 11(d)'s guarantee of judicial independence—to ensure public confidence in the justice system. A decision by the executive or the legislature, to change or freeze judges' salaries, and then to disagree with a recommendation not to act on that decision made by a constitutionally mandated body whose existence is premised on the need to preserve the independence of the judiciary, will only be legitimate and not be viewed as being indifferent or hostile to judicial independence, if it is supported by reasons.

Applying the expanded constitutional principles to the particular situations, the Court found the Prince Edward Island reductions unconstitutional because no recourse had been had to an independent, objective, and effective process. The Manitoba reduction was unconstitutional for the same reason—the absence of such a process, which is what s. 11(d) of the Charter requires to ensure judicial independence. Manitoba had created a judicial compensation commission, but in reducing the judges' salaries, had completely ignored that process and, indeed, put unacceptable pressure on the judges' association to prevent any constitutional challenge to the legality of the salary reductions. The court had harsh words regarding the actions of the Manitoba government.

The facts of this appeal vividly illustrate why salary negotiations between the judiciary and the other branches of government are unconstitutional. Negotiations force the organs of government to engage in conduct which is inconsistent with the character of the relationship between them. For example, the Manitoba government relied on pressure tactics of the sort which are characteristic of salary negotiations. Those tactics created an atmosphere of acrimony and discord, and were intended to induce a concession from the judiciary. Alternatively, the judiciary may have responded with a pressure tactic of its own. The expectations of give and take, and of threat and counter-threat, are fundamentally at odds with judicial independence. They raise the prospect that the courts will be perceived as having altered the manner in which they adjudicate cases, and the extent to which they will protect and enforce the Constitution, as part of the process of securing the level of remuneration they consider appropriate. In the light, the conduct of the Manitoba government was unacceptable.

The willingness of the Court to look to fundamental constitutional principles that are not expressed in the constitution itself enabled it to declare unilateral salary freezes and reductions of judicial remuneration to be unconstitutional as essential attacks on the independence of the judiciary. An independent judiciary is a bedrock principle of Canadian democracy: who but the judiciary is in a position to tell governments when they have overstepped? Absent a strong and independent judiciary, who stands between citizens and the untrammeled power of the state? If we embrace a system of the rule of law, then an independent judiciary must be in a position to decide whether legislation or conduct conforms with the law.

Quebec Secession: Legal Treatment of a Political Issue

Secession of Quebec [1998] 2 S.C.R. 217

Picture yourself as one of nine judges of the Supreme Court of Canada. You cannot be unaware of the political tensions arising from the desire of some elements in Quebec to become a separate country and of threats of a unilateral declaration to that effect. The federal government has now initiated a Reference case, calling for the Court's advisory opinion on the following three questions:

1. Under the Constitution of Canada, can the National Assembly, legislature, or government of Quebec effect the secession of Quebec from Canada unilaterally?

2. Does international law give the National Assembly, legislature, or government of Quebec the right to effect the secession of Quebec from Canada unilaterally? In this regard, is there a right to self-determination under international law that would give the National Assembly, legislature or government of Quebec the right to effect the secession of Quebec from Canada unilaterally?

3. In the event of a conflict between domestic and international law on the right of the National Assembly, legislature, or government of Quebec to effect the secession of Quebec from Canada unilaterally, which would take precedence?

Aside, perhaps, from an initial "Why me?" you realize that you and your colleagues are going to have to deal with one of the most important and highly politically charged issues that perhaps has ever faced the country.

Although there would undoubtedly be challenges to the jurisdiction of the Court to decide such a case, it is pretty clear that, should it wish to grapple with the matter, it can. There have been occasions in the past when the Court has ducked reference cases, when the question has been too vague or ambiguous to permit a complete or accurate answer, or where the parties have not provided sufficient information to allow the court to provide a complete or accurate answer. Neither of those situations can be said to apply to the questions posed, so your Court is going to have to deal with them. There is one other unstated challenge, namely that on such an important Reference, the opinion must be one rendered by the full Court. There cannot be dissenting or even separate opinions on this one—it would send a terrible message.

One thing that becomes clear very quickly is the level of careful thought given to the wording and extent of the questions posed. The federal government has tried to be sure that it has left Quebec no wiggle room to say that an option it may exercise had not been dealt with by the Court. This is a high-stakes political initiative, which the government cannot afford to mismanage. Even the deliberate reference to the "National Assembly, legislature, or government of Quebec" has been designed to leave no argument available to dispute which authority or body may have acted. The first question focuses on the constitution of Canada, the country whose future is at stake. The second preempts an undealt-with appeal to some possible source of international law that might have application if a unilateral Quebec action purports to be based on an asserted right of self-determination. And the third asks, in the event of a conflict between domestic and international law, which would trump?

The Court has its own challenge in managing the process as well. It is all but certain that Quebec will not participate in the case, since its position would be weakened if it appeared and made submissions, perhaps even to the point of being legally bound by the decision. On the other hand, the Court might then end up in the position of deciding an important matter involving Quebec without the benefit of submissions on its behalf. It decided, therefore, to appoint an *amicus curiae* (friend of the court) to represent the interests of Quebec. As anticipated, there were several Intervenants, including the provinces of Manitoba and Saskatchewan, the Northwest and Yukon territories, Aboriginal groups, individuals, and organizations that the court allowed to make submissions. The Big Hitters, however, were the Attorney General of Canada and the *amicus curiae*.

Just as Quebec might have argued, the *amicus curiae* first challenged the right of the Court even to hear the Reference. It claimed that the constitution did not give Parliament the authority to grant the jurisdiction to hear such a case and, even if it did, the kinds of questions asked in the Reference should be excluded. The reference to international law was asserted to be beyond the jurisdiction of the Court. Finally, even if the jurisdiction existed, the questions referred to the Court were speculative, of a political nature, and were not "ripe" for judicial decision and, therefore, not justiciable. While a jurisdictional challenge was likely anticipated, the manner in which this was put forward no doubt caused the federal government a certain amount of heartburn, especially the international argument and the political nature of the questions. It was certainly worried enough to make a number of formal objections to the right of the *amicus curiae* even to raise the questions. The Court decided that the *amicus curiae* was within his rights to raise the preliminary objections, although it decided against all of them. So the stage was finally set to deal with the questions themselves.

The Constitution of Canada

This was the primary focus of the Canadian government.

One of the fundamentals of the Canadian constitution is federalism, a principle that recognizes the diversity of the component parts of Confederation and the autonomy of provincial governments to develop their societies within their respective spheres of jurisdiction. As this applies to Quebec, the Court said:

> The principle of federalism facilitates the pursuit of collective goals by cultural and linguistic minorities which form the majority within a particular province. This is the case in Quebec, where the majority of the population is

French-speaking, and which possesses a distinct culture. This is not merely the result of chance. The social and demographic reality of Quebec explains the existence for the Canadian union in 1867, of the province of Quebec as a political unit and indeed, was one of the essential reasons for establishing a federal structure.

It then moved on to the democratic aspects of federalism and noted that the *Constitution Act, 1982*, confers

> ... a right to initiate constitutional change on each participant in Confederation. In our view, the existence of this right imposes a corresponding duty on the participants in Confederation to engage in constitutional discussions in order to acknowledge and address democratic expressions of a desire for change in other provinces. This duty is inherent in the democratic principle which is a fundamental predicate of our system of governance.

The court also addressed the importance of the rule of law, which is supreme over the acts of both governments and private persons.

> An understanding of the scope and importance of the principle of the rule of law and constitutionalism is aided by acknowledging explicitly why a constitution is entrenched beyond the reach of simple majority rule. There are three overlapping reasons.

> First, a constitution may provide an added safeguard for fundamental human rights and individual freedoms which might otherwise be susceptible to government interference. Although democratic government is generally solicitous of those rights, there are occasions when the majority will be tempted to ignore fundamental rights in order to accomplish collective goals more easily or effectively. Constitutional entrenchment ensures that those rights will be given due regard and protection. Second, a constitution may seek to ensure that vulnerable minority groups are endowed with the institutions and rights necessary to maintain and promote their identities against the assimilative pressures of the majority. And third, a constitution may provide for a division of political power that allocates political power amongst different levels of government. That purpose would be defeated if one of those democratically elected levels of government could usurp the powers of the other simply by

exercising its legislative power to allocate additional political power to itself unilaterally.

The next question to be addressed was the matter of how a will to secede could be determined. A mere referendum would not be sufficient.

> The federalism principle, in conjunction with the democratic principle, dictates that the clear repudiation of the existing constitutional order and the clear expression of the desire to pursue secession by the population of a province would give rise to a reciprocal obligation on all parties to Confederation to negotiate constitutional changes to respond to that desire.

This led to consideration of the nature of any such negotiations, in respect of which the Court rejected any suggestion that there was a legal obligation on the other provinces and the federal government to accede to the secession of a province subject only to negotiation of the related logistics. But, it also said that the other provinces and the federal government could not take the view that there was no obligation on their part to negotiate. The Court also recognized that there would be no absolute legal entitlement to secession and no assumption that an agreement reconciling all relevant rights and obligations would actually be reached. In other words, even negotiations carried out in accordance with the underlying constitutional principles could reach an impasse. The Court was very careful to distance itself (quite properly) from the political aspects of any such negotiations, other than to note that a failure by one party to negotiate based on constitutional principles might undermine that party's claim to legitimacy (especially on the international scene).

The court closed off its discussion of the Canadian constitution by warning that a mere assertion of the right to unilateral secession as a matter of law simply amounts to the contention that the law may be broken as long as it can be broken successfully, which is contrary to the rule of law and must be rejected.

International Law
Here the Court focussed essentially on the internationally recog-

nized principle that "peoples" have a right to self-determination. While recognizing that the definition of *people* remains uncertain, the court concluded that it was not necessary to explore the matter for purposes of answering the second question, nor whether, if a Quebec people exists, such a people encompasses the entire population of the province or just a portion of it. It rejected any notion of the Quebec people being in some way oppressed to the point of justifying unilateral secession under international law. Even the *amicus curiae* made that point quite forcefully. The Court went on to consider the impact of secession being successful "in the streets" and the potential difficulties of achieving international recognition where the legitimacy of the process whereby the secession occurred could be challenged.

> It may be that a unilateral secession by Quebec would eventually be accorded legal status by Canada and other states, and thus give rise to legal consequences; but this does not support the more radical contention that subsequent recognition of a state of affairs brought about by a unilateral declaration of independence could be taken to mean that secession was achieved under colour of a legal right.

It was not necessary for the Court to answer the third question, since it had found no conflict between domestic and international law on the matters to be addressed.

The Court was fully aware that it was tiptoeing through a political minefield and that there were limits to what it might say in the course of the Reference without accelerating any potential polarization of constitutional matters or provoking a crisis. It even added a summary of its conclusions, underlining that the constitution was more than a written text, that it was not a straitjacket and that there is a reciprocal duty on all participants to engage in discussions to address any legitimate initiative to change the constitutional order. Quebec could not, despite a clear referendum result, purport to invoke a right of self-determination to dictate the terms of a proposed secession to the other parties to the federation.

> The negotiations that followed such a vote would address the potential act of secession as well as its possible terms should in fact secession proceed.

There would be no conclusions predetermined by law on any issue. Negotiations would need to address the interests of the other provinces, the federal government, Quebec and indeed the rights of all Canadians both within and outside Quebec, and specifically the rights of minorities. No one suggests that it would be an easy set of negotiations.

Even though this is an advisory opinion of the Court, it may have profound effects on how Canada evolves. The desire for secession remains a critical concern on the part of (to date) a minority of those who live in Quebec. Until the Quebec elections in 2014, the minority government then in power in Quebec was committed to secession. The issue will undoubtedly continue to fester, regardless of the particular political party that may control the National Assembly from time to time. Whether the warnings contained in the advisory opinion (as well as the provisions of the *Clarity* Act adopted by Parliament following the Reference decision) will be heeded can only be a matter of speculation, but the obstacles to any precipitate unilateral action have been clearly stated and the eventual outcome, regardless of what Quebec might want, is far from certain—assuming, of course, that Quebec continues to adhere to the rule of law.

Prostitution: A Dangerous Profession Made More Dangerous

Attorney General of Canada v. Bedford, Lebovitch and Scott [2013] S.C.R. 72

Three active or formerly active prostitutes challenged the constitutionality of certain provisions of the *Criminal Code* on the basis that the provisions infringed their *Charter* rights of security of the person, because they prevented prostitutes from implementing certain safety measures (such as hiring security guards or drivers, screening potential clients, having access to controlled environments) that might protect them from violent clients.

The provisions attacked were the "common bawdy-house" (a place kept, occupied, or used for purposes of prostitution) restriction, the living on "the avails of prostitution" provision, and the restriction on stopping or communicating with anyone for the purposes of engaging in prostitution. All three provisions have been part of the criminal law of Canada for many years.

The applicants were almost entirely successful at the trial level, somewhat less so before the Ontario Court of Appeal (which had a five-judge panel to hear the appeal—most appeals are heard by only three judges) and were completely vindicated by a unanimous Supreme Court of Canada.

It did not take the Court long to make clear where it was headed.

The first paragraphs of the reasons for judgment set the stage and gave the outcome.

> It is not a crime in Canada to sell sex for money. However, it is a crime to keep a bawdy-house, to live on the avails of prostitution or to communicate in public with respect to a proposed act of prostitution. It is argued that these restrictions on prostitution put the safety and lives of prostitutes at risk, and are therefore unconstitutional.
>
> These appeals ... are not about whether prostitution should be legal or not. They are about whether the laws Parliament has enacted on how prostitution may be carried out pass constitutional muster. I conclude that they do not. I would therefore make a suspended declaration of invalidity, returning the question of how to deal with prostitution to Parliament.

Many people were probably under the impression that prostitution as such is illegal, but it is not. Legal prostitution is confined by Parliament to street prostitution and "out-calls" where the prostitute goes to meet the client at a designated location.

Against the background of cases like Morgentaler (see page 54), it would not have been difficult to predict the outcome in the present appeal. The *Charter* has assumed a greater and greater role in Canadian society and the interpretation of it has evolved considerably as the courts have had more and more exposure to appeals relying on *Charter* rights and protections, much of which has occurred in the past couple of decades. In addition, the availability of richer and more definitive evidence and the intervention of special interest groups have made *Charter* litigation increasingly sophisticated. Here, the evidence before the trial court came to some 25,000 pages.

Common sense, in addition to the evidence, would confirm that prostitution is a risky business, not only with respect to health, but especially the risk of physical violence to and even death of the prostitutes. The Court referred several times to Robert Pickton's serial murders of prostitutes in the Vancouver area, many of which may well have been made easier by the restrictions under attack in this appeal. The trial judge had weighed the mass of evidence before her and concluded that the restrictions in the *Criminal Code* did, in fact, increase the risks incurred by prostitutes and, therefore, ruled that the legislation was unconstitutional. Those findings were the foundation for the Supreme Court's own decision and the judgment could have been much shorter, but for two collateral matters.

The first was the impact of a 1990 Supreme Court Reference case on prostitution in which the Court had upheld the validity of the common bawdy-house and communication provisions. In the present proceedings, the trial judge had decided that she was not prevented from considering their constitutionality because the *Charter* jurisprudence had evolved considerably since then, she had better evidence based on research not available in 1990, the social assumptions underlying the Reference case may no longer be applicable, and the type of expression in this case was different from that considered in the Reference. The Ontario Court of Appeal, however, said she was not entitled to disregard the Reference and that all she could do was assemble the evidence so that the higher courts (particularly the Supreme Court) could consider it and decide whether it might wish to change its previous opinion.

Dealing with that issue, the Court raised the question of whether reference opinions are legally binding, leaving the question unanswered, but noting that they have been followed in practice. As to what the trial judge had done, the Court disagreed with the Court of Appeal, stating that a trial judge may decide on arguments not raised in the Reference case, or if new legal issues are raised "as a consequence of significant developments in the law, or if there is a change in the circumstances or evidence that fundamentally shifts the parameters of the debate." In addition, the Court agreed with the argument that the common law of *stare decisis* (following precedents) is subordinate to the Constitution. A court, therefore, cannot be required to uphold a law which is unconstitutional, even if precedent might have indicated otherwise. It is a matter of balancing the need for finality and stability with recognition that even lower courts must be able to perform their full role in appropriate cases where precedent ought to be revisited.

The Ontario Court of Appeal had also determined that the trial judge's findings on social and legislative facts were not entitled to deference on the part of appellate courts. The Supreme Court disagreed.

When social and legislative evidence is put before a judge of first instance, the judge's duty is to evaluate and weigh that evidence in order to arrive at the conclusions of fact necessary to decide the case. The trial judge is charged with the responsibility of establishing the record on which subsequent appeals are founded. Absent reviewable error in the trial judge's appreciation of the evidence, a court of appeal should not interfere with the trial judge's conclusions on social and legislative facts. This division of labour is basic to our court system. The first instance judge determines the facts; appeal courts review the decision for correctness in law or palpable and overriding error in fact. This applies to social and legislative facts as much as to findings of fact as to what happened in a particular case.

Apart from the duplication of effort, there would be an increase in costs as well as delays in the court proceedings if appellate courts had to be led through the entire body of evidence put before the trial judge. Social science evidence introduced by experts reflected both a preference expressed by the Court and the fact of greater use of such evidence in *Charter* cases, which meant that trial judges have to deal with the credibility of the expert witnesses as part of their overall appreciation of the evidence. No gradation of deference was justified between adjudicative and legislative facts. The standard of review of all findings of fact is palpable and overriding error.

Having dealt with these matters, the Court then turned to considering whether the *Criminal Code* provisions imposed limits on security of the person.

> Section 7 [of the *Charter*] provides that the state cannot deny a person's right to life, liberty or security of the person, except in accordance with the principles of fundamental justice. At this stage, the question is whether the impugned laws negatively impact or limit the applicants' security of the person, thus bringing them within the ambit of, or engaging, s. 7 of the *Charter*.

> Here, the applicants argue that the prohibitions on bawdy-houses, living on the avails of prostitution, and communicating in public for the purposes of prostitution, heighten the risks they face in prostitution—itself a legal activity. The application judge found that the evidence supported this proposition and the Court of Appeal agreed.

... I am of the same view. The prohibitions at issue do not merely impose conditions on how prostitutes operate. They go a critical step further, by imposing *dangerous* conditions on prostitution; they prevent people engaged in a risky—but legal—activity from taking steps to protect themselves from the risks.

....

The practical effect of [the bawdy-house prohibition] is to confine lawful prostitution to two categories: street prostitution and out-calls. ... In-calls, where the john comes to the prostitute's residence, are prohibited. Out-calls, where the prostitute goes out and meets the client at a designated location, such as the client's home, are allowed. Working on the street is also permitted, though the practice of street prostitution is significantly limited by the prohibition on communicating in public.

The trial judge had found that the safest form of prostitution is working independently from a fixed location, a far less dangerous circumstance than street prostitution. Out-call work is not as safe as in-call work, especially because prostitutes are prohibited from hiring a driver or security guard. Bawdy-house prohibition materially increases the risks faced by prostitutes under the current system. Similarly, hiring drivers, receptionists, and bodyguards could increase their safety, but the law prevents them from doing so. The same was true regarding communication, where the trial judge had found that face-to-face communication (which the law prohibits) was an essential tool in enhancing the safety of street prostitutes, allowing them to screen potential clients for intoxication or likely violence, to reduce the risks they face. The Court agreed with those findings.

The government argument was that the prostitutes choose to engage in an inherently risky activity. The prostitutes could avoid both the inherent risks and any increased risks as a result of the legal impositions simply by choosing not to engage in the activity. That choice, it argued, not the law, is the real cause of their injury. (The argument seems vaguely reminiscent of that of the NRA in the United States—Guns don't kill people—people kill people.) Parliament, it continued, is empowered to regulate prostitution as it sees fit and anyone who sells sex for money must accept the conditions, even if they prejudice their security. Not surprisingly, the Court did not accept such an argument. Choice itself is often unclear and many prostitutes, especially street prostitutes, often have little choice in resorting to selling their bodies for money. The real question was whether the laws made a legal activity more dangerous.

The next consideration was whether the deprivation was in accordance with fundamental justice, the basic underpinning of the constitutional order.

> The s. 7 analysis is concerned with capturing inherently bad laws: that is laws that take away life, liberty, or security of the person in a way that runs afoul of our basic values. The principles of fundamental justice are an attempt to capture those values. Over the years, the jurisprudence has given shape to the content of these basic values. In this case, we are concerned with the basic values against arbitrariness, overbreadth, and gross disproportionality.

> The concepts of arbitrariness, overbreadth, and gross disproportionality evolved organically as courts were faced with novel *Charter* claims.

> ....

> All three principles—arbitrariness, overbreadth, and gross disproportionality—compare the rights infringement caused by the law with the objective of the law, not with the law's effectiveness. That is, they do not look to how well the law achieves its object, or to how much of the population the law benefits. They do not consider ancillary benefits to the general population. Furthermore, none of the principles measure the percentage of the population that is negatively impacted. The analysis is qualitative, not quantitative. The question under s. 7 is whether *anyone's* life, liberty or security of the person has been denied by a law that is inherently bad; a grossly disproportionate, overbroad, or arbitrary effect on one person is sufficient to establish a breach of s. 7.

The Court's final conclusion was that none of the provisions were saved by section 1 of the *Charter* and all were declared void, as inconsistent with the *Charter*.

Having done so, the Court then punted (as it should) to Parliament.

I have concluded that each of the challenged provisions, considered independently, suffers from constitutional infirmities that violate the *Charter*. That does not mean that Parliament is precluded from imposing limits on where and how prostitution may be conducted. Prohibitions on keeping a bawdy-house, living on the avails of prostitution and communications related to prostitution are intertwined. They impact on each other. Greater latitude in one measure—for example, permitting prostitutes to obtain the assistance of security personnel—might impact on the constitutionality of another measure—for example, forbidding the nuisances associated with keeping a bawdy-house. The regulation of prostitution is a complex and delicate matter. It will be for Parliament, should it choose to do so, to devise a new approach, reflecting different elements of the existing regime.

The declaration of invalidity was suspended for a year to allow Parliament to consider what action it might wish to take in the circumstances and not to leave the country with no regulation at all regarding prostitution.

Index

A

Aboriginal property rights, 249–53
and land claims, 254–60
Aboriginal treaties, 261–68, 275–76
Aboriginal voting rights, 269–74
abortion, decriminalizing, 54–59
abuse of contractual rights, 232–37
abuse of power, 149–53
administrative vs. constitutional law, 71
amicus curiae (friend of the court), 334
Amselem, Moase, 60–66
analogous distinction, 271–72
assisted suicide, 78–83
Attorney General of Canada v. Bedford, Lebovitch and Scott, 339–45
Attorney General of Quebec v. Blaikie et al., 124–28
Attorney General of Quebec v. Sioui, 261–68

B

Baker, Mavis, 96–101
Baker v. Canada (Minister of Citizenship and Immigration), 96–101
battered-wife defence, 171–75
Becker, Rosa, 224–25
bias, 99–100
Big M Drug Mart Ltd., 44–49
Bill of Rights (1960), 48
Blaikie, Peter, 124–28
Blais v. The Queen, 281–85
bodily samples, taking of, 195–96
"born-alive" principle, 132–34
Boucher, Ovila, 154–58
Boucher v. The Queen, 154–58
British North America Act 1867 (BNA Act), 16, 125
and education rights, 304–8

federal vs. provincial responsibility, 199–203, 211–12

patriation of, 321–25

on the Senate (Upper House), 315–20

and women as "Persons," 215–19

Brody, Dansky, Rubin v. The Queen, 159–64

burden of proof, 154

Burns, Glen Sebastian, 182–86

C

Canada v. PHS Community Services Society, 119–23

Canadian Industrial Gas & Oil Ltd. v. Saskatchewan, 204–0

Canadian Union of Public Employees (CUPE), 90–95

CEPU v. Irving Pulp & Paper, Limited, 135–40

Chaoulli v. Quebec (Attorney General) and Canada (Attorney General), 108–13

Chaput, Esymier, 39–43

Chaput v. Romain, 39–43

Charkaoui, IRPA case, 24

Charter of Rights and Freedoms (1982), 44–45

and Aboriginal voting rights, 269–74

and abortion debate, 54–55

and equality of individuals, 238–39

on fundamental freedoms, 177

justifiable limits on, 50–53

and Supreme Court of Canada, 16–20

on unreasonable search or seizure, 194

chemicals, validity of regulations in relation to, 309–14

Chinese, rights of, 29–33

Christie, Fred, 34–38

Christie v. The York Corporation, 34–38

circumstantial evidence, 154

Citizens' and The Queen Insurance Cos. v. Parsons, 199–203

Civil Code of Québec, 226–31

claims to Aboriginal land, 254–60

co-ownership of property, 60–66

coercion, 47–48

Combines Investigation Act, 209–14

commissions, 329, 330

common-law spouses, 238–43

consent in rape cases, 165–70

Constitution Act (1867), 328

Constitution Act (1982), 335

Constitution of Canada, 334–36

constitutionality of legislation, 46–47, 68, 86–87

contractual rights, 232–37

Controlled Drugs and Substances Act (CDSA), 119–23

convention, 323
Corbière v. Canada (Minister of Indian and Northern Affairs), 269–74
corporations, rights of, 45
correctness, 117–18
Criminal Code, 74, 191–92, 193–94
and abortion, 54–56
and assisted suicide, 79, 80–81
and the clergy, 40–41
and gun control, 298, 300
obscenity, definition of, 159
on promoting hatred, 176–77, 179–80
on prostitution, 339–45
on self-defence, 172
Crown attorney *see* prosecuting attorney, role of
cruel and unusual punishment, 192
C.U.P.E. v. N.B. Liquor Corporation, 90–95
Cuthbertson v. Rasouli, 83

D

damages, liability and recovery of, 232–37
damages, responsibility for, 144–48
de facto spouses (Quebec), 226–31
death penalty and extradition, 182–86
deference, 116–17
Delgamuukw v. British Columbia, 249–53
deportation issue, 96–101
disclosure, full, 24–27
discretionary decision-making, 100–101
discrimination, 34–38
against *de facto* spouses, 228
and equality of individuals, 238–43
and sexual orientation, 84–89
dissenting opinions, 22, 220–223–224, 289–91
DNA, search and seizure of, 193–98
domestic violence issue, 171–75
Doucet-Boudreau v. Nova Scotia (Minister of Education), 102–7
Doucet, Jean, 145–48
drug injection sites (Insite), 119–23
Drysdale v. Dugas [1896], 141–44
Duff, Mr. Justice, 216–17
Dunsmuir v. New Brunswick, 114–18
Duplessis, Maurice, 43, 149–53
Durand, Roland, 124–28

E

Education Act (Quebec), 304–8
emergency measures in wartime, 309–14
employment statute, Saskatchewan, 29–30
enforcement of judgment, 102–7
expert evidence, role of, 173–75
expression, freedom of, 176–81
extradition with death penalty, 182–86

F

fair trial, 76, 189–90
the "Famous Five," 215–219
federal paramountcy, 121
federal vs. provincial responsibility, 199–203, 204–8
and *Combines Investigation Act*, 209–14
and *Firearms Act* (2000), 298–303
and patriation of the Constitution, 321–25
Firearms Act (2000), 298–303
foetal rights, 56–58, 129–34
free and democratic society, 47, 51–53
freedom, 47–49
French-language schooling, 102–7
full disclosure, 24–27
functional value of legislation, 242

G

General Motors of Canada Ltd. v. City National Leasing, 209–14
Goldstein, Yoine, 124–28
good faith, 152
Guerin v. The Queen, 244–48
gun control law *see Firearms Act* (2000)

H

Harkat, Mohamed, 23–28
hate crimes, 176–81
health care issues, 108–13
Henrietta Edwards et al. v. Attorney General of Canada, 215–19
honour of the Crown, 287–90
hospital waiting times, 108–13
Houle v. National Bank of Canada, 232–37
human dignity, 271

I

Immigration and Refugee Protection Act (IRPA), 23–28
independence and impartiality of judges, 326–31
Indian Act, enfranchisement provisions, 269–70
Indian Act, section 88, 262
Indian Affairs Branch (Vancouver), 244–48
Individual's Rights Protection Act (Alberta), 84
Insite (safe-injection facility), 119–23
insurance liability issue, 199–203
international law and self-determination, 336–38
intravenous drug users, 119–23
Irving Pulp & Paper Limited, 135–40

J

Jacques Cartier Park (Quebec), 261–68
Jehovah's Witnesses, 39–43, 149–53
judges, Supreme Court of Canada, 12–14
independence and impartiality of, 326–31
judicial independence, 326–31
judicial review, 114–18
jury nullification, 190–91

K

Keegstra, James, 176–81
Kindler, Joseph John, 183
King's College (Edmonton), 84–85
kirpan issue, 67–71

L

labour relations boards, 90–95
Lady Chatterley's Lover, 159–64
Lamer, Chief Justice Antonio, 253
language-based school boards (Quebec), 306–8
language rights, 124–28
Laskin, Bora, 220
Latimer, Robert, 187–92
Latimer, Tracy, 187–92
Lavallée, Angelique Lyn, 171–75
law of limitations, 286–92
legislation, constitutionality of, 46–47
legislation, "pith and substance" of, 300–302
liability and recovery of damages, 232–37

limitations, law of, 286–92
Lord's Day Act, 44–49
Lou Gehrig's disease, 78

M

McLachlin, Chief Justice Beverley, 231
mandatory alcohol testing, 135–40
mandatory sentences, 190–91
Manitoba Métis Federation Inc. v. Canada (Attorney General), 286–92
marital breakdown, 220–25
Marshall, John, 275
mercy, royal prerogative of, 191–92
Métis issues (Manitoba), 281–85
land deal, 286–92
Mi'kmaq fishing rights, 275–80
Minimum Wages Act, 293–97
Minister of Citizenship and Immigration v. Mohamed Harkat, 23–28
Miron, John, 238–43
Miron v. Trudel, 238–43
mistake of fact defence, 165–70
Morgentaler, Dr. Henry, 54–59
Multani v. Commission Scolaire Marguerite-Bourgeoys, 67–71
Murdoch v. Murdoch, 220–25
Murray, Brigadier General James, 261–64
Musqueam Indian Band, 244–48

N

narcotics, possession of, 50–53
National Bank of Canada, 232–37
national security, 24–28
Native status, 269–70
Natural Resources Transfer Agreement (NRTA), 281–85
Naturalization Act, 32
necessity defence, 187–92
New Brunswick Liquor Corporation (NBLC), 90–95
Ng, Charles Chitat, 183
niqab issue, 72–77
"notwithstanding clause," 325
nuisance issue, 141–44

O

Oakes, David Edwin, 50–53

obscenity, 159–64
oil rights (Saskatchewan), 204–8
Organization of Petroleum Exporting Countries (OPEC), 204
Orthodox Jews, 60–66

P

Pappajohn v. The Queen, 165–70
Parliamentary authority in relation to the Senate, 315–20
patriation of the Constitution, 321–25
possession of Aboriginal lands, 254–60
pregnancy and medical treatment, 129–34
presumption of innocence, 50–53
Privy Council, 12, 202–3, 209–14
    on direct and indirect taxes, 204–8
    on international treaties, 295–97
    termination of appeals, 14–16
    and women as "Persons," 217–19
procedural fairness, 96–101, 118
promoting hatred, 176–81
property rights of married women, 220–25
proportionality test, 52–53, 75, 180–81, 242
prosecuting attorney, role of, 155–58
prostitution issue, 339–45
provincial involvement in federal treaties, 293–97
Public Service Labour Relations Act, 90–95

Q

Quebec, and *de facto* spouses, 226–31
Quebec, and language-based school boards, 306–8
Quebec secession, 332–38
Quong-Wing, 29–33
Quong-Wing v. The King, 29–33

R

R. v. Big M Drug Mart Ltd., 44–49
R. v. Latimer, 187–92
R. v. Lavallée, 171–75
R. v. Morgentaler, 54–59
R. v. N.S., 72–77
R. v. Oakes, 50–53
R. v. S.A.B., 193–98
racist judgment, 29–33

Rafay, Atif Ahmad, 182–86
rape, 169–70
reading in, 88–89
reasonableness, 116, 118
References re
Authority of Parliament in Relation to the Upper House, 315–20
Education Act (Quebec), 304–8
Firearms Act, 293–303
Independence and Impartiality of Judges, 326–31
Minimum Wages Act, 293–97
Remuneration of Judges, 326–31
Resolution to Amend the Constitution, 321–25
Validity of Regulations in Relation to Chemicals, 309–14
Regina v. Keegstra, 176–81
Regina v. Marshall, 275–80
religion, freedom of, 39–43, 44–49
and education system, 304–8
and kirpan, wearing of, 67–71
and niqab, wearing of, 72–77
and Orthodox Jews, 60–66
remuneration of judges, 326–31
Report of the Special Committee on Hate Propaganda in Canada (1966), 178–79
responsibility for damages, 144–48
retention of jurisdiction, 102–7
reverse onus, 50–53
rights, abuse of, 232–37
rights and freedoms, 52–53
Rodriguez, Sue, 78–83
Rodriguez v. British Columbia, 78–83
Romain, Edmond, 39–43
Roncarelli, Frank, 149–53
Roncarelli v. Duplessis, 149–53
Rust, Kevin, 171–75

S

safe-injection facility *see* Insite
Saskatchewan employment statute, 29–30
secession of Quebec, 332–38
self-defence, 172
self-determination, 336–38
Senate appointment of women, 215–19
Senate, debate about, 315–20
sexual orientation, 84–89
shareholders' rights, 232–37
Shawinigan Carbide Co. v. Doucet, 145–48

Shawinigan Carbide Company, 145–48
Sikh religion, 67–71
Singh, Gurbaj, 67–71
special advocates, 24–26
spousal rights, 226–31
common-law spouses, 238–43
property rights of married women, 220–25
succahs and Succot, 60–66
suicide, assisted, 78–83
suicide vs. assisted suicide, 80–82
Sunday shopping, 44–49
Superior Council of Education Act (Quebec), 306
Supreme Court of Canada, 12–14
and *Charter of Rights and Freedoms*, 16–20
Syndicat Northcrest, 60–66
Syndicat Northcrest v. Amselem, 60–66

T

tax, direct vs. indirect, 206–7
terra nullius, doctrine of, 258
terrorism, threat of, 23–28
title to Aboriginal lands, 249–53, 254–60
treaties, 263–65, 275–76
international, 293–97
trusts, 223–24
Tsilhqot'in Nation v. British Columbia, 254–60

U

United States v. Burns, 182–86

V

Vallicre, Jocelyne, 238–43
voting rights, Aboriginal, 269–74
Vriend, Delwin, 84–89
Vriend v. Alberta, 17–20, 84–89

W

War Measures Act, 309–14
"watertight compartments" statement, 296–97
Winnipeg Child and Family Services (Northwest Area) v. D.F.G., 129–34
women and appointment to Senate, 215–19

women as "qualified persons," 215–19
women as Supreme Court judges, 13
workplace safety, 135–40

Y

York Corporation, 34–38